# Sects, Cults, and Spiritual Communities

**Recent Titles in**
**Religion in the Age of Transformation**

# Sects, Cults, and Spiritual Communities

## A SOCIOLOGICAL ANALYSIS

**Edited by
William W. Zellner
and Marc Petrowsky**

Religion in the Age of Transformation

*Anson Shupe, Series Adviser*

Westport, Connecticut
London

**Library of Congress Cataloging-in-Publication Data**

Sects, cults, and spiritual communities : a sociological analysis /
edited by William W. Zellner and Marc Petrowsky.
    p.  cm.—(Religion in the age of transformation, ISSN
1087–2388)
    Includes bibliographical references and index.
    ISBN 0–275–95860–4 (alk. paper).—ISBN 0–275–96335–7 (pbk.)
    1. Cults—United States—History—20th century.  2. Religion and
sociology—Case studies.  3. United States—Religion—1960–
I. Zellner, W. W.  II. Petrowsky, Marc, 1948–  .  III. Series.
BL2525.S58  1998
306.6'0973—DC21       97–32995

British Library Cataloguing in Publication Data is available.

Library of Congress Catalog Card Number: 97–32995
ISBN: 0–275–95860–4
    0–275–96335–7 (pbk.)
ISSN: 1087–2388

First published in 1998

Praeger Publishers, 88 Post Road West, Westport, CT 06881
An imprint of Greenwood Publishing Group, Inc.

Printed in the United States of America

The paper used in this book complies with the
Permanent Paper Standard issued by the National
Information Standards Organization (Z39.48–1984).

10 9 8 7 6 5 4 3 2 1

# Contents

# Introduction

Editors Bill Zellner and Marc Petrowsky found the editing of *Sects, Cults, and Spiritual Communities: A Sociological Analysis* a most gratifying experience. Our intent, as sociologists, was to illustrate concepts used by social scientists in the fields of their endeavor. The book is not, however, applicable just to the field of sociology, but is appropriate for use in other social science courses, including religion, history, anthropology, and psychology. By choosing authors with varying backgrounds and experiences, the editors have made the book an interdisciplinary experience.

Another reason for the book's appeal is that it is descriptive and explanatory rather than analytical. True, the description is interwoven with basic sociological concepts, but systematic analysis and inductive reasoning have been left to the reader.

There is probably as much cultural diversity in the United States as in any country of the world. Dozens of ethnic groups form interesting subcultures, some attractive to the dominant culture, some less so. Myriad religious denominations, sects, cults, and self-help groups vie for members. This tremendous range of associational groups sets the United States apart from all other nations in the world.

Of all the nontraditional groups that have been part of the American scene, nine have been chosen for inclusion in the present volume:

1. Total Overcomers Anonymous/Heaven's Gate
2. Jesus People USA

3. The Farm
4. Love Family
5. El Niño Fidencio
6. Santería
7. Amish women
8. Scientology
9. Freedom Park.

With the great diversity of groups to choose from, why were those listed above selected? First and foremost, to make readers aware of a variety of non-normative groups and their behaviors from a scientific perspective. All of the above accounts were written by social scientists with expertise in social movements. Each author applies the scientific method as an aid to understanding the selected group.

## SCIENTIFIC ILLUSTRATION

Each chapter is amenable to scientific illustration. For example, sociologist Tony Zavaleta notes that charisma, by nature, is unstable. It can exist in its pure form only as long as the charismatic leader is alive. The challenge for followers with vested interests in a charismatic's organization is to create a situation in which his or her charisma in some adulterated form persists after the leader's death. In other words, charisma must be routinized, institutionalized in a bureaucratic form. This is exactly what happened in Mexico after the death of the charismatic faith healer El Niño Fidencio.

Sociologist Rob Balch writes that most utopian societies in American history have struggled with the same dilemma. A conflict exists between two antithetical forms of social organization called *gemeinschaft* and *gesellschaft*. The terms were first used by the German sociologist Ferdinand Tönnies, in the late nineteenth century, to describe changes caused by the industrial revolution. *Gemeinschaft* refers to a community whose members are bound together by common values and intimate relationships. Commitment to tradition takes precedence over individuality, and social relationships are valued for their own sake. In *gesellschaft* societies, social relationships are organized around specific tasks, and tradition and intimacy take a backseat to getting a particular job done. Relationships tend to be impersonal, and individualism is valued more than group solidarity.

Signs of the transition from *gemeinschaft* to *gesellschaft* could be seen throughout the Love Family after 1980. As ties loosened, there was an increase in personal autonomy. Members could walk to work alone or visit friends on the way back without getting permission from the elders.

Thanks to a new policy that allowed them to have their own spending money, workers enjoyed the freedom to treat themselves to a cup of coffee or stop off for a beer after work. All this and more broke down the "communal spirit" of the Love Family.

Anson Shupe explores the concepts of *contract* and *covenant* in his study of Jesus People USA. The impression most people have when they hear the word "commune" is of a small, self-sufficient, inwardly focused group, physically isolated from the "real" world. Members have abandoned ordinary privacy, personal possession, and individual autonomy.

Images of promiscuous sex (once termed "free love") and rampant drug use or alternatively, strict celibacy and abstinence from worldly pleasures, may also be envisioned. Such stereotypes resemble some of the communitarian "hippie" experiments during the late 1960s and early 1970s. But like most stereotypes, they can be found misleading when confronted by actual examples.

So it is with one successful evangelical Christian communal group in downtown Chicago, the diverse, energetic, and outward-looking Jesus People USA. This commune, organized around a *covenantal* understanding of biblical precepts, overcame the demands of the blatantly *contractual* culture of one of America's largest cities.

Let us look at one more example of sociological illustration. David Bromley and Mitchell L. Bracey, Jr., study Scientology in terms of a quasi-religious therapy, a social-psychological perspective. Scientology is popular because it addresses feelings of alienation from government and business life. It also meets expectations for personal fulfillment.

## INTEREST

Another reason the nine groups were chosen is simply that they are interesting. Three of the chapters are devoted to countercultures developed in the 1960s (Love Family, Jesus People, The Farm). They were established on college campuses across the nation, and the youngsters who joined them rejected central aspects of American culture, such as financial success, achievement, authority, hard work, efficiency, premarital chastity, and the nuclear family.

Alternative living arrangements were developed, altered work styles replaced the eight-hour day, and there was a definitive sexual revolution. Drugs of every kind became part of the lifestyle.

The three countercultures discussed were begun by charismatic leaders, but no individual is a repeat of the other two. Although each of these groups reached a zenith and then declined, each has taken a different path and adapted. All, to a varying degree, are successful in today's world.

Much interest has been developed in the rural Amish. We know about their horse-and-buggy lifestyle and their rejection of modernity. We know that most Amish believe automobiles would contaminate their lifestyle to such an extent that they would imperil their cultural identity. We understand their economic system, the farming procedures, their relationships with the outside world. But until the study by Dachang Cong, published in this book, we knew very little of the gender roles of Amish women.

The fate of a cult usually hinges on the caprice of a charismatic leader. Clarence Klug, charismatic founder of Self-Initiation, developed a program that revealed how one could achieve union with God by following a strict regimen of spiritual exercises. In the beginning his classes had about 80 members, but near the end the number had dwindled to about 20 devoted students.

Klug, for whatever reason—perhaps advancing age, perhaps declining health—in 1976 led his followers to a pair of charismatics then called Guinea and Pig. Klug told them that his new friends, founders of a New Age flying saucer cult, Total Overcomers Anonymous, had the answers. Guinea and Pig were Marshall Herff Applewhite and Bonnie Lu Nettles. Everyone now knows Total Overcomers Anonymous by the name they used on their Web site, Heaven's Gate.

Sociologist Rob Balch, who observed Klug's students during the mid-1970s, the period when they were introduced to Total Overcomers Anonymous, believes that had it not been for Clarence and his students, Marshall Applewhite and Bonnie Lu Nettles might never have become cult leaders. Balch says he was shocked to learn that two of Klug's former students remained with Applewhite and died with him as members of the Heaven's Gate cult in March 1997.

Certainly interesting is the diversity of religions crossing the borders into the United States from Latin America. Not only is Tony Zavaleta's chapter on El Niño Fidencio rife with sociological illustration, it is extremely interesting. Contemporary followers of the Mexican faith healer El Niño Fidencio, who died in 1938, are bringing his practices, a brand of folk Catholicism, into the United States.

Interesting, too, is the chapter written by Mary Clark on Santería, a polytheistic religion with roots buried deep in Africa. Issues related to its practices have already reached the U.S. Supreme Court. Much to the chagrin of many in Hialeah, Florida, the Santerians won.

Finally, the editors, Bill Zellner and Marc Petrowsky, have included a chapter on the Freedom Park movement. The purpose of the chapter is to illustrate, through description, the social science definition of a cult. We hope the chapter is as interesting as the other eight.

## ABOUT THE AUTHORS

Who are these social scientists so interested in the affairs of others, and how did their interests develop? Preceding each chapter is a brief account of each author's response to the question "How did you get interested in the group you studied?" Students should find this facet of the book interesting. For example, how did Dachang Cong, born in the People's Republic of China and a Yale graduate, get interested in the gender roles of Amish women? Read our work, find out about us, and maybe you will become one of us.

# Chapter 1

# The Evolution of a New Age Cult: From Total Overcomers Anonymous to Death at Heaven's Gate

### Robert W. Balch

Rob Balch teaches sociology at the University of Montana, Missoula, where he became interested in alternative religions. His first research on a religious cult was a field study of the UFO cult now known as Heaven's Gate. His interest in the group began when he read a newspaper article describing how 20 people in Oregon had mysteriously disappeared after attending a meeting about UFOs. He later attended a lecture on UFOs, and discovered that the speakers were members of the cult he had been reading about. Because of the media hype surrounding the group, including charges of brainwashing, he decided to infiltrate the group to find out what was really going on. With David Taylor, a graduate student in sociology, he traveled and camped with members, took part in recruitment meetings, and kept a detailed record of everyday life "behind the scenes." Balch and Taylor spent another summer interviewing former members to find out why they had joined and why they had dropped out. During those interviews they discovered that nearly all of the original followers had previously belonged to an equally intriguing cult called Self-Initiation. "Never did we imagine that 22 years after beginning our research, the group would be on the front pages again, this time as Heaven's Gate, whose remaining 39 members committed mass suicide in 1997," said Balch, who is currently on leave, collecting additional data for a book on Heaven's Gate.

On April 9, 1975, about 50 people crowded into Laura Sutton's living room in Hollywood, California. Seated before them were a man and a woman in their mid-forties. Although the two people had ordinary human bodies, it was rumored that they had come from a distant galaxy to deliver a message of unparalleled cosmic importance. Nobody, except possibly an elderly gentleman named Clarence Klug, had any idea what to expect, but some members of the audience sensed that what they were about to hear would change the course of their lives.

The room fell silent as the man began to speak. "You might say she's Guinea and I'm Pig," he said. "We are guinea pigs in the sense that we are here to show how man, the caterpillar, can become a butterfly in the next kingdom." The man explained that eons ago our planet was planted with the seeds of consciousness by members of "our Father's kingdom." After millions of years of physical and spiritual evolution, a man called Jesus was sent from the "Next Level" to conduct Earth's first harvest, but his mission failed. When Jesus ascended by being "beamed up" to a spaceship, he left without his apostles because they could not understand the true meaning of his message. The speaker claimed that now mankind was being given another opportunity.

This time two individuals had been sent to conduct the harvest. The man claimed their mission was prophesied in Revelation (the final book of the New Testament), which describes "two witnesses" who will "ascend up to heaven in a cloud" after being assassinated. The cloud, he explained, refers to a UFO. Moments after their ascension, their disciples will be taken aboard spaceships destined for the Next Level. To prepare for the journey, members of the audience would have to leave their friends, families, jobs, possessions, and every other attachment to the human level. The speaker claimed the process of cutting ties to the past would initiate physiological changes that would transform spiritual seekers into immortal, androgynous beings.

Three weeks later, almost half the people who had been in Laura's house that night suddenly disappeared. They were to form the nucleus of a new religious movement that later became one of the most sensational religious cults in the United States. Their families and friends were stunned, not only by how quickly it happened but also by the apparent absurdity of it all. Two people calling themselves Guinea and Pig somehow had convinced 24 seemingly intelligent people to abandon their earthly lives in hope of going to heaven in spaceships.

Yet, alarmed as they were, nobody imagined that 22 years later the cult, then known as Heaven's Gate, would shock the nation with the biggest mass suicide in American history. What follows is the story of how Heaven's Gate began.

I learned about the Hollywood meeting when I was interviewing former Heaven's Gate members in Los Angeles. As I listened to their stories, I realized I could not understand how Heaven's Gate originated without digging into the bizarre events that led up to the meeting at Laura's house. Among the nine people I interviewed who had attended the meeting, seven had decided to follow Guinea and Pig. What emerged from their accounts was a fascinating tale of two religious cults so intertwined that one could not be understood without the other. When put into sociological perspective, the story of these groups helps answer two of the most commonly asked questions about unconventional religions: Why do people join religious cults? How do charismatic leaders come to exercise such enormous control over the thoughts and actions of their followers?[1]

## CLARENCE KLUG AND SELF-INITIATION

Any account of the Hollywood meeting must begin with Clarence Klug and his Self-Initiation class. Clarence had been teaching an esoteric interpretation of Revelation for over a year before Guinea and Pig appeared on the scene. In the beginning, his class had roughly 80 students, but it had dwindled to a select group of about 20 highly devoted followers. It was Clarence who introduced Guinea and Pig to his students, and were it not for him, the two might never have become cult leaders.

In a loose-leaf manuscript that he distributed to his students, Clarence claimed to decipher the symbolism of Revelation. Rather than a collection of end-time prophecies, he said the book was actually an ancient manual of spiritual alchemy. In line with Hindu teachings, Clarence claimed it revealed how one could achieve union with God by following a strict regimen of spiritual exercises. These would open the seven *chakras*, or energy centers, located at regular intervals from the base of the spine to the top of the head. Clarence said the ancients had known about this method, which he called Self-Initiation, but during the early Christian era it was driven underground and ultimately lost. The secret was preserved in code, however, in the book of the Bible known as Revelation.

By using Revelation as a key, Clarence claimed, one could unlock ''creative and regenerative forces of marvelous potency'' that he compared to electrical charges surging up the spine. Each character and event recorded in Revelation symbolized some deeper reality, and the symbols were woven together in an intricate fabric of arcane correspondences. The seven seals in Revelation 6, for example, stood for the seven chakras, and the great earthquake in Revelation 6: 12 represented the ''shock and terror'' that neophytes experience when the force released by Self-Initiation explodes in the brain.

Although his manuscript was vague about how the technique actually worked, Clarence insisted that diligent seekers could use his method of ''esoteric physiology'' to raise their vibrations until they transformed themselves into beings of divine light, transcending all physical limitations and karmic laws. ''When the Bible is read in this light,'' he explained, ''its power in life is better understood. It becomes a handbook to higher living. The mind opens to the realization that within each individual are the answers to all the questions about the wonders of man and the universe.''

To discover the hidden meaning of Revelation, Clarence claimed to have drawn on a wide range of sources, including occult mysticism, Darwin's theory of evolution, obscure Christian teachings, and recent discoveries in quantum physics. This tendency to combine themes from different traditions, called *syn-*

*cretism*, is a common feature of religious cults. The ideas in Self-Initiation were not new, but the way Clarence packaged them was. There was something for everyone, even the skeptics, in Self-Initiation.

Students were drawn to Clarence and his teachings for many reasons. Some came in search of better health, peace of mind, or companionship. Others wanted to broaden their education or pursue genuine spiritual enlightenment. A few were simply intrigued by Clarence. Yet diverse as they were, they all belonged to a subculture that today is known as the *New Age movement* (Melton, Clark, and Kelly 1991).

The name is based on the belief that humanity is experiencing a quantum leap in consciousness as our planet passes from the conflict-ridden Piscean era of dogmatic Christianity to the Aquarian age of mutual understanding and world harmony. This subculture has been called the *cultic milieu* (Campbell 1972) because it has been the breeding ground for so many unconventional religious movements, including the I AM movement, Eckankar, Ramtha's School of Enlightenment, and the Church Universal and Triumphant, as well as dozens of less well-known groups, such as Self-Initiation. One cannot understand the appeal of Clarence's teachings without first grasping the nature of this subculture.

## A BRIEF LOOK AT THE NEW AGE MOVEMENT

Although more than 20 years have passed since the Hollywood meeting, one can get a feeling for the subculture inhabited by Clarence and his students by spending an hour browsing in a New Age bookshop. The books and magazines cover Eastern religions, mysticism, the occult, psychic phenomena, UFOs, reincarnation, astrology, meditation, lost continents, Goddess worship, Native American religion, out-of-body experiences, Jungian psychology, and a wide array of unconventional healing techniques, such as acupuncture, iridology, and aroma therapy. If there is a bulletin board, it probably is cluttered with flyers advertising astrologers, tarot readings, meditation groups, psychic fairs, and whatever New Age religions are in town.

Although the New Age movement has no unifying belief system, there are common themes, all of which were present in Clarence's teachings. Together they constitute a *universe of discourse*, which means a shared set of assumptions about reality and a common vocabulary that enable people to carry on conversations without having to ask each other to explain what they mean.

At the center of New Age thought is a monistic conception of the cosmos. *Monism* refers to the belief that every aspect of creation is divine, an idea that has more in common with Eastern religions than with traditional Christianity. In Catholic dogma, for example, the absolute goodness of God stands in sharp contrast to the inherent sinfulness of humanity, whereas New Age thinking makes no such distinction. God exists within every individual, and heaven is a state of mind achieved by tuning in to one's divine essence. In the New Age cosmology there is no hell, only the absence of God Consciousness.

The spark of divinity that is thought to exist inside the individual is often called the "Christ within." The term reflects an unorthodox twist on Christianity. Jesus is seen as an enlightened teacher whose mission was to awaken our consciousness, making us aware of our own divinity. This is the message of the *Aquarian Gospel of Jesus the Christ*, a popular New Age book purporting to chronicle the travels of Jesus in Persia, India, and China, where the great teacher from the West exchanged ideas with the masters of the East. First published in 1906 and still widely read today, the *Aquarian Gospel* portrays Jesus not as a savior but as an exemplar who taught how ordinary people could transcend the physical plane by merging with the pure white light of God. This is essentially what Clarence was teaching.

Although New Agers believe Jesus was an extraordinary person, they do not see him as unique. Instead, Jesus was one of many highly evolved masters who have assisted mankind in the quest for God Consciousness. Buddha and Krishna, for example, are often held in the same high regard. In addition to these world teachers, the New Age cosmos is populated by a vast array of spiritual helpers, ranging from angels to beings from distant galaxies. Clarence claimed to have 12 spirit guides, including one named Arenda who had helped him decipher the symbolism in Revelation. He also claimed to be in regular contact with an ethereal group of Himalayan masters known as the Great White Brotherhood, whose existence was first proclaimed in the late nineteenth century by an early New Age religion known as Theosophy (Washington 1993).

The belief that space beings might be divine emissaries caught on during the 1950s, in the wake of a rash of UFO sightings around the world. These "space brothers" were thought to be spiritual messengers who had come to avert global catastrophe by helping us awaken spiritually. Clarence shared this belief. In an unpublished novel called *Worlds Apart,* which he gave only to his favorite students, Clarence described a utopian planet named Zend where the inhabitants lived in harmony with spiritual laws. The central character was Fenta, a highly evolved being from Zend, who in the 1920s was marooned on California's Catalina Island when his fellow spacemen inadvertently took off without him. As the tale unfolds, Fenta befriends a brilliant mathematics professor named Paul Bentley, and together they build a sophisticated device for contacting Zend. When Fenta is finally rescued, he invites Bentley to visit his planet, where the young professor learns the secrets of Zend's advanced state of physical and spiritual evolution.

*Worlds Apart,* like most New Age literature, has a humanistic theme. In contrast to Christians, who believe they are saved by accepting Jesus Christ, New Agers claim to be masters of their own fate. This was one of the lessons Paul Bentley learned on Zend. Avatars, such as Jesus, can help us, but they cannot save us. We have to do that ourselves. Self-Initiation was based on this idea. Clarence described it as a method his students could use to get in touch with the "holy Christ self." In that regard Self-Initiation was similar to Buddhist chanting, Hindu yoga, or Sufi dancing, but Clarence claimed his method was better suited for the Western mind.

The students who enrolled in Clarence's class were spiritual seekers. For most, Self-Initiation was the latest in a long series of experiments and explorations undertaken in search of spiritual understanding. In their free time they could be found browsing in New Age bookstores or attending lectures and study groups on an eclectic array of metaphysical topics. Cynics (e.g., Buckner 1968; Mann 1955) have characterized seekers as social misfits who get swept up in one New Age fad after another, in a fumbling attempt to come to grips with personal problems such as divorce, loneliness, or poor health. When one spiritual "path" fails to solve their problems, they readily abandon it for another. Many of Clarence's students fit this profile. As one later explained, their lives had been "a bumper car ride through a maze of spiritual trips."

However, this image is an oversimplification. Not only does it ignore the fact that many seekers are highly educated and well-adjusted (Jorstad 1990), but it fails to recognize the value placed on being a seeker in the New Age subculture. Being a seeker means reading, studying, and keeping an open mind about the possibility of other realities.

In the seeker's universe of discourse, the metaphors of "growth" and "the path" are key ideas. Growth means discovering inner Truth, and a path is anything that helps seekers in their quest for self-actualization. Most seekers view spiritual growth as an evolutionary process that continues from one incarnation to the next, as the soul progresses toward union with God. To keep growing, seekers need to explore many paths. Since God exists in all things, there is an element of truth in every spiritual path. Clarence often said, "There are many paths to the top of the mountain." Implied in this maxim is a conception of Truth that is subjective and pragmatic. In contrast to traditional Christianity, where Truth is defined by narrow interpretations of the Bible, Truth in the New Age movement is determined by the individual seeker. Any religion, philosophy, or spiritual discipline that helps the seeker along the path toward enlightenment is valid. Truth is whatever "works," and when a path no longer seems to be working, it is time to try something else.

Perhaps the greatest irony in the New Age movement is that seekers who place such a high value on the individual pursuit of truth continually fall under the spell of spiritual teachers who provide them with prepackaged sets of beliefs in exchange for their individuality. The key to the puzzle lies in a dilemma that is inherent in the subculture of seekers. In a world where almost any idea is worthy of consideration, where every path contains an element of Truth, and where reality is concealed behind a veil of illusion, seekers are apt to feel overwhelmed. The more they search, the more questions they have. When seekers flounder in their quests, they seek the guidance of someone further along the path. According to a Sufi proverb, "When the student is ready, the master appears."

## THE MYTH OF CLARENCE KLUG

Clarence was such a master. Even at age 75 he was a man of boundless energy. Despite his white hair, failing eyesight, and slight arthritic stoop, Clarence impressed his students as a man far younger than his years, and they attributed his vitality to his mastery of esoteric wisdom. Clarence was the archetypal guru, a wise but enigmatic figure. Laura explained:

Depending on the source, he was a genius, a mad scientist, a wizard, a dirty old man. To his students and a select group of spiritual groupies, he ranked second to God. To others he represented a powerful influence who exerted total control over those who came in contact with him. About the only thing everyone could agree on was that [Clarence] was a paradox.

There was a wall of secrecy around his past, but no shortage of myths. Clarence was rumored to have been a "tough punk" in the Mafia who went on to earn several college degrees and teach science at a prestigious Ivy League university. He was supposed to have been a prodigious inventor, and one account credited him with the invention of fiberglass. According to another rumor, Clarence had once enjoyed a brief homosexual liaison with the philosopher Kahlil Gibran. More outlandish tales portrayed him as a modern-day shaman. In his youth Clarence supposedly had been initiated into the Great White Brotherhood in Tibet, and now he belonged to an interplanetary council of spiritual leaders who were directing the advent of the New Age. Some even believed Clarence could dematerialize and reappear anywhere in the universe.

Clarence never confirmed or denied the rumors. Instead, when asked about them, he would just smile cryptically. When I asked a member of the Hollywood group what he thought of Clarence, he shrugged and said, "He was a sly old man. There were so many stories about him that it's hard to say. I was really nervous when I met him because he was supposed to be 2,000 years old."

Laura described Clarence as a lovable con artist, pleasant and wise but not one to pass up an opportunity to take advantage of his students. Another student called him a "first-class, triple A-number-one hip-to con man." Whatever his real motives, there is no question that Self-Initiation was a moneymaking enterprise. Among his inventions were crystals supposedly manufactured in his basement that he sold to his students for $80 apiece; he claimed that they would attract other spiritually aware seekers who were vibrating at precisely the same frequency. One must bear in mind, however, that the charges of fraud leveled at Clarence were made with the benefit of hindsight. His students had been in awe of him. "You have to understand that," Laura said. "He played us like fiddles, and we responded on key."

## THE INNER CIRCLE

For most of his students, Clarence treated Self-Initiation as an esoteric theory rather than a practical technique, like a beginning chemistry class where students learn basic principles without setting foot in a lab. He reserved the meat of his teachings for a secretive inner circle of highly devoted followers. The size of the group varied over time, but never exceeded 20. According to Clarence, these students constituted a select group of spiritually advanced beings who were ready to put Self-Initiation into practice.

To all appearances, the students who comprised the inner circle were an ordinary collection of seekers. Most had attended college and, with one exception, all were single or divorced. Nancy Gold, for example, was a 25-year-old receptionist from a wealthy Jewish family in New York. After completing an Associate of Arts degree in music and art, she moved to Hollywood in hopes of becoming an actress, a dream that was already fading a year later when she enrolled in Clarence's course. Bob Johnson, a 26-year-old model whose boyish, all-American face had been featured on cornflakes cereal boxes, was another aspiring actor. Doug Peters, 40, was also in show business. A film editor for MGM, he was one of the more successful members of the group. He also had a penchant for tall tales. A few members of the inner circle believed him when he claimed to have taken part in an undersea expedition to the lost continent of Atlantis, but most paid no attention to his stories.

Angelo Soleri, a social worker in his mid-forties with a bachelor's degree in psychology, was one of the few professionals in the group. Born a Roman Catholic, he had experimented with Mormonism and the Episcopal church before discovering the New Age movement. Angelo attributed his interest in New Age ideas to a spiritual healing after an accident that had left him paralyzed and unable to speak. Believing he would remain a "vegetable" for the rest of his life, his doctors had given up hope. However, some of his New Age friends meditated on his behalf, and he miraculously recovered. By the time he met Clarence, the only evidence of his accident was a slight limp and mild speech impediment.

Besides Angelo, only two members had professional jobs. One was a chiropractor, and another had been a schoolteacher before retiring. Mary Butterfield also had been a teacher for a while, but at 30 she still wasn't ready to settle into a career. She had been an avid hiker and skier, flitting from one job to another. After meeting Clarence, Self-Initiation became her passion, and she soon was one of Clarence's closest friends. The others either had low-level white-collar jobs or were temporarily unemployed.

Jack Pantzer, a mysterious character in his mid-thirties, was one of the few men in the group who was not gay. He was also the only person who had been involved with drugs and radical politics. Jack projected the image of a romantic adventurer. He was supposed to have been affiliated with the left-wing terrorist group known as the Weathermen, and according to another story, he had been deeply involved in California's flourishing drug traffic. More than anyone else in the inner circle, Jack was fascinated with unconventional scientific theories, such as pyramid energy, and he was attracted to Clarence because they shared an interest in quantum physics. Jack had helped Clarence design an exercise shoe called the Wedgy, which Clarence hoped to market to health-conscious southern Californians, but aside from his students, hardly anyone bought them. Married and divorced twice, Jack lived alone in his motor home, which he moved frequently to avoid being ticketed by the police.

Aside from Clarence, Laura Sutton, a 40-year-old bookkeeper and professional psychic, was the most important person in the group. After graduating near the top of her high school class, she entered college at age 16 and earned a business degree. Having rejected the Southern Baptist faith because it placed so much emphasis on the threat of eternal damnation, she felt alienated from religion until moving to Los Angeles, where, she said, "I had a sense of coming home." There she encountered New Age ideas and eventually became an accomplished tarot reader whose clients included a famous movie star. It was Laura who had recruited most of the students in Clarence's Self-Initiation class, and many of them accepted Clarence because she lent her authority to his teachings.

Although the inner circle was completely informal, like a group of college students devoted to a popular professor, its members were distinguished by certain practices that amounted to badges of membership. Most noticeable to outsiders were the crystals they wore around their necks; every member also owned a pair of Wedgies and carried a small vial of a murky concoction that Clarence called prostaglandin. Clarence claimed that a drop of prostaglandin taken twice a day would retard the aging process by opening one's chakras.

Perhaps the most important sign of being accepted into the inner circle was being given a copy of *Worlds Apart*, Clarence's utopian novel about Fenta and the planet Zend. Clarence reserved the manuscript for those he said were "ready" to comprehend its meaning. Laura explained, "Each student knew they had attained a degree of spiritual development when Clarence passed the manuscript along to them." Although Clarence said the story was just a novel, most members of the inner circle believed that Paul Bentley, the professor who befriended Fenta, was actually Clarence. According to Angelo, Clarence never said this was true, but he never denied it.

Clarence was a very clever man. He *inferred* that it was fact. He *inferred* that he was there firsthand. He *inferred* that he was the doctor in the book, but he never said he was. Clever—he just smiled that magic smile of his when someone would ask him a question.

Whereas members of the inner circle were enthralled with Clarence, the rest of his students soon tired of his rambling, abstract lectures and cryptic answers to their questions. After a few months, the class had shrunk to a point where Clarence decided to disband it. However, the inner circle continued to meet every Sunday afternoon for a potluck dinner, and they became tighter and more exclusive than ever. What happened was a *social implosion*, a term coined by sociologist William Bainbridge (1978) to describe the strengthening of in-group ties while relationships with outsiders weaken. This process plays an important role in cult formation because ideas one normally might reject become plausible when they are reinforced by friends in a social environment where competing views of reality do not intrude.

Students on the periphery of the inner circle wondered what went on in these get-togethers because an aura of secrecy pervaded the group's activities. One of Laura's friends described her curiosity.

They were always meeting at Clarence's house on Sunday. They would all bring something, always chipping in, having wine, and I wondered, what did they *do* on Sunday afternoons? It must be very important, so I wanted to go. Well, I went three weeks in a row and nothing happened. They just had dinner and sat around and talked and joked. Yet these people were together almost every single night, sometimes all night long, so I wondered. . . .

The basis for her concern was a persistent rumor that members of the inner circle were participating in sexual orgies—ritual sex in pursuit of higher consciousness. "I heard such weird stories," she said, "almost to the point of torture, although none of them would admit it."

### The Secret Life of the Inner Circle

The source of the rumors was a practice called Eugenics, the practical application of Self-Initiation. Eugenics involved learning to control orgasm during sexual intercourse. Following a regimen of sexual exercises over a 13-month period would cause the energy produced during sex to move from the base of the spine to the brain where it would ignite a spark of electricity between the pineal and pituitary glands. At this point the physical body would reach a perfected state. Claiming that each person has seven bodies altogether, Clarence taught that his students would be able to perfect one of these bodies every 13 months. Once the final body had been perfected, the student's entire being would be transformed into pure white light, and the individual would ascend and become one with God, just as Jesus had done.

Clarence introduced Eugenics gradually, revealing the technique a little at a time. He liked to make his students dig for answers and discover the significance of his teachings on their own. Full comprehension, he said, would come only when they were spiritually ready. When Laura first heard about Eugenics, she assumed masturbation was the key, but later she discovered that the method required the union of male and female energies through intercourse.

The practice of Eugenics required two individuals who vibrated at precisely the same physical, mental, and spiritual frequencies. This is where Clarence's crystals came in. Normally clear, they changed color under a black light. Each color corresponded to the owner's vibrational frequency, which Clarence determined through astrological calculations. Having found a suitable partner, the student was expected to engage in intercourse, stopping just short of orgasm in order to force the sexual energy up the spine, where it would open each of the seven chakras. Clarence claimed that the method would work only during a brief time each month, which he also determined astrologically. During the rest of the month, partners were to engage in oral sex, taking each other's "juices," as Clarence put it, into their "physiological laboratories" to accelerate their physical and spiritual transformation.

Although the ultimate goal of Eugenics was to transcend the physical plane, Clarence told his students that the more immediate result would be youthfulness and good health. He promised rejuvenation for the elderly, normal functioning for the disabled, and increased vitality and attractiveness for the young and middle-aged.

Although members of the inner circle wanted to believe in Eugenics, Clarence set so many conditions that it was virtually impossible to put the technique to the test. Laura explained the dilemma.

How do you go about finding a partner? Spiritually you are just supposed to attract this kind of person, and that makes sense to me. But you don't go looking, you can't approach men in the street. First you got to find somebody that turns you on. Okay, so they turn you on, but are they spiritually oriented? Do they have the same moon period as you do? Are they at the 700 frequency with a yellow rock? So the theory sounds good, but who in the hell is going to be able to practice it to prove him wrong?

Even without these conditions, the principles of Eugenics posed special problems for the men because most were homosexuals who found the idea of intercourse with women distinctly unappealing. To help them overcome their inhibitions, Clarence relied on Mary, the most attractive woman in the group, whose sexual appetite was legendary. Known as the "process girl," Mary had sex with nearly all the male members of the inner circle, but her efforts had no effect on their sexual orientation.

Despite the rumors about orgies, most of the sex in the inner circle involved Clarence. Members believed his semen had potent healing powers. Both women and men regularly performed fellatio on him in private sessions, and supposedly the prostaglandin they took twice a day was made from his sperm and that of his followers. Although Clarence occasionally dispensed samples to a few who were not part of the inner circle, only his most trusted students knew what prostaglandin contained. "We heard such wild stories about it," one of the recipients said. "Some said it was made out of sperm, but when I asked, they said no, it's made out of herbs." She added that when a friend threatened to have it analyzed at the police department, "you never saw anybody hit the ceiling like this group did. I mean, they were literally in a panic."

Like everything he did, Clarence introduced the use of prostaglandin a bit at a time. Angelo described how he learned about it.

He saw us all individually, and it was all done very quietly and slowly. One person and then another, and then another. You made an appointment, went in and sat down, and he gave you articles out of newspapers and magazines on research that had been done in Switzerland, how stars are always going off to get miracle injections of a hormone extract called prostaglandin.

After explaining that movie stars paid up to $500 per injection, Clarence confided that he could duplicate the process for just $30 per month. Besides using his own semen, he would have his male followers ejaculate into a bottle or, when the more attractive men were involved, he would fellate them to orgasm himself.

Even within the inner circle, not everyone was aware of all these practices. Students from the Self-Initiation class were introduced to Eugenics whenever Clarence thought they were ready to proceed, but even then, only a little at a time. "Each person," Clarence wrote in his Self-Initiation lessons, "comprehends according to his degree of development." Not only were members of the inner circle involved in different aspects of Eugenics, but they usually didn't know what others in the group were doing because Clarence swore them to secrecy. He had a way of making each person feel special by implying that his techniques were intended only for a select group of highly evolved seekers.

## Clarence's Control over the Inner Circle

Whether Clarence actually believed in Eugenics remains a mystery. "He had that wonderful, whimsical way about him," Angelo recalled. "He was really a charming guy, but you have to wonder what was real, what was kidding, and what was sheer fantasy. You could never tell." What matters is that his followers were thoroughly committed to him and his teachings. To understand their commitment, we need to examine the social processes at work in the inner circle.

Though obscure and often incomprehensible, the eclectic nature of Self-Initiation ensured that students could find elements of truth in it. Having been conditioned as seekers to keep an open mind about all things spiritual and esoteric, they willingly reserved judgment on the more implausible aspects of Clarence's teachings. The very obscurity of Self-Initiation made it appealing. By creating a sense of mystery, Clarence conveyed the impression that his students were being let in on ancient cosmic secrets that had been lost for almost 2,000 years.

Hidden wisdom is prized in some New Age circles, and Clarence capitalized on this theme in his Self-Initiation lessons.

In reading sacred literature, it is well to keep in mind that all truly esoteric works have four layers of meaning. The *surface* or *literal* meaning is evident to the general reader who accepts the words at their face value. The *allegorical* meaning becomes evident to those acquainted with the Mysteries. The *hieroglyphic* or *symbolic* meaning contributes its special keys and purpose. The *mystical* meaning not communicated even in symbols, depends entirely on the type of inspiration synonymous with the phrase "in the spirit" which is used throughout the Bible.

Once his students accepted the premise that the Bible contains deeper, esoteric meanings, Clarence became their indispensable interpreter and guide.

Like a clever salesman using the time-honored foot-in-the-door technique, Clarence introduced his ideas gradually, always preparing his students for the next stage by conditioning them to accept the premises on which his subsequent teachings were based. Eugenics followed logically from the more abstract principles of Self-Initiation, and the theory opened the door for the introduction of the sexual practices actually performed by members of the inner circle. Throughout the process, Clarence never presented his ideas in a straightforward A–B–C manner that one might expect from a college professor lecturing on his pet theory. Instead, by dropping clues along the way, he led his students to draw the right conclusions themselves. That way, Self-Initiation became a thoroughly engrossing adventure in self-discovery.

Of course, members of the inner circle were not all "true believers" who blindly accepted everything Clarence said. They included several who prided themselves on their skepticism, but Clarence was very effective at shutting down their questions. When attempting to confirm or deny a questionable claim, most people rely on empirical evidence, the tools of logic, or some independent authority that they hold in high regard. However, Clarence created an intellectual climate where each of these tests was inoperative.

Realistically, there was no way anyone could put Eugenics to an empirical test because of the multitude of stringent conditions laid down by Clarence. Even if students practiced Eugenics to the letter, it would take years for them to complete the process, and if they failed, Clarence could always say they misunderstood something or did not do something correctly. Nor was it possible to raise logical objections to Self-Initiation because Clarence claimed that genuine understanding depended on intuition, or being "in the spirit," instead of relying on the intellect. For Clarence, the rational mind belonged to the world of illusion that separates people from God and prevents them from grasping the true nature of reality. Reliance on conventional authorities, such as church leaders, was out of the question. Even if Clarence had not made esoteric wisdom the cornerstone of his teachings, his students would have rejected normative Christianity because of their deep distrust of conventional dogma.

Clarence's most effective method of stifling criticism was his skillful manipulation of a phenomenon known as *pluralistic ignorance*. The term refers to a common lack of awareness about how fellow group members are thinking and feeling. Pluralistic ignorance is caused by constraints on communication that prevent members from raising questions and expressing doubts. Because Clarence taught that only highly evolved seekers could comprehend the deeper meaning of Revelation, anyone who failed to grasp his Self-Initiation lessons obviously was not part of the elect. Like the villagers in the story of the emperor's new clothes, members of the inner circle were unwilling to reveal their ignorance by challenging the man they believed was a master of the Bible's hidden mysteries. As a result, they suppressed whatever doubts they had and worked even harder to make sense of what, in the final analysis, may have been nonsensical.

As Laura put it, Clarence kept everyone in turmoil by introducing new ideas that nobody understood but that no one was willing to challenge.

Clarence would say things up to a point and then stop. He implied that if you didn't understand, you weren't ready to go on. And we'd go through meetings among ourselves—the stuff that he didn't say but almost said, things he hinted at but wouldn't say. They drove us nuts. Each week one of us would break down and the others would have to put him or her back together again. It was one small nervous breakdown after another.

Sociological and psychological studies show that people turn to others for direction when objective sources of information are lacking (e.g., Turner and Killian 1987); for the inner circle, there was no one to turn to but Clarence.

Clarence Klug may have been a fraud, but from a sociological perspective he was a skilled social engineer who combined a thorough knowledge of New Age beliefs with an intuitive grasp of group dynamics. Ideologically he created a belief system that appealed to the seeker's ego while providing a cloak of high spiritual principles. Socially he created a tightly knit, exclusive group whose members were bound together by regular interaction, a sense of sharing secret wisdom, and a common self-conception as partners in a unique spiritual enterprise reserved for a select few. At the social-psychological level, Clarence created the conditions of suggestibility by knocking out the usual reality checks and suppressing the open expression of doubt. He then proceeded to fill the informational vacuum by introducing his teachings in a manner that made his students believe they were participating in a process of discovering ancient esoteric principles. Once members of the inner circle engaged in sex with their teacher, they implicated themselves in the group's most intimate secret. If their actions had been publicly revealed, they would have suffered ridicule and humiliation, and they knew it. Perhaps more than anything else, this committed them to Clarence because they could hardly denounce him for actions in which they had willing engaged.

The result was that Clarence had enormous control over his students. One of Laura's friends who was not part of the inner circle summed up the situation. "He had them like this," she said, making a fist, "in the palm of his hand, tightly closed. He almost had them in a stranglehold mentally, but they weren't aware of it."

Even in the most controlling cults, however, seekers tend to move on if the group fails to provide them with tangible benefits. Whatever the reason, Clarence's students believed that Self-Initiation worked, and this kept them involved even when they wondered if Clarence might be a charlatan. Angelo explained: "The conviction was that we were better off today than we were yesterday, and indeed many of us were. I personally felt like I was becoming more spiritually aware." Jack was another who thought Self-Initiation had helped him. "It brought me some really unique changes in body chemistry," he said. "I was experiencing a kind of blissfulness that I had not known before. You couldn't make me angry, you couldn't interfere with my choices. It was a period of enormous growth.'' But the feeling of spiritual progress did not last, and before long, members of the inner circle reached a turning point in their lives.

## The Inner Circle at the Crossroads

A few months after the inner circle coalesced, Clarence embarked on an ill-fated publishing venture that spelled the end of the Self-Initiation group. Enlisting the help of his students, who put up thousands of dollars in seed money, he attempted to publish his Self-Initiation manuscript. However, Clarence proved to be a poor businessman, and the effort failed after the first two lessons were printed. Everyone who invested money took a financial beating, especially Doug, who lost several thousand dollars and was pushed to the edge of bankruptcy.

The situation was even worse for Clarence. Rumor had it that he owed up to $90,000 in back taxes, and supposedly the Internal Revenue Service was planning a two-year audit of his records. Clarence stopped holding classes in his home and eventually withdrew from the group altogether, leaving it in Laura's hands. As the situation deteriorated, Clarence developed signs of paranoia, claiming that he was under constant surveillance by the FBI and CIA.

The crisis put an enormous strain on relationships in the group, and without Clarence to hold it together, the inner circle began to unravel. Tensions flared into arguments and backbiting. ''We had pitiful levels of gossip and bullshit going on all the time,'' Jack said. ''There were nasty things being said about the gay guys and vice versa. Mostly the gossip was who's doing who, and how big was Laura Sutton's last orgy. Eventually it just became too uncomfortable to hang out with those people.'' The tensions in the group coincided with other problems. Nancy, for example, lost her job during this period. Jack was dodging his ex-wife, who was seeking support for their two mentally retarded children, and Laura's partner of ten years had just left her for a younger woman.

All these factors made it impossible for members to focus on Self-Initiation, which was the reason they had come together in the first place. The inner circle continued to meet every Wednesday night, but attendance was dropping, and according to Jack, they just sat around ''doing word-package exchanges and bumping gums'' until they were ''blue in the face.'' As Doug put it, they were in a ''spiritual rut.'' The benefits they had once found in Self-Initiation had vanished.

Nancy captured the mood of the entire group when she said her life was in limbo.

I was out of a job, but I hadn't really been looking. I didn't feel interested in a lot of stuff I was into before. It was hard for me to concentrate and read the lessons I was into, or other books I was reading. It was like my mind was always somewhere else. I just wasn't growing anymore.

Other inner circle members felt the same way. "Everybody in the group was ready for a change in their lives," Nancy explained. "They weren't satisfied with the way things were, whether it was mental, spiritual, or physical. Everybody was waiting for something to happen." As Laura put it, they had come to a "crossroads" in their lives where they had to decide whether to continue on their path or make a 90-degree turn.

## ENTER GUINEA AND PIG

It was at this point that the mysterious couple who called themselves the Father's guinea pigs appeared on the scene. Shortly after his publishing fiasco, Clarence received a flyer describing two individuals who had come to help a select group of humans make the transition to the "next evolutionary kingdom." The flyer had been mailed from Ojai, a small town north of Los Angeles that had been a mecca for New Age seekers ever since the 1920s. Intrigued by what he read, Clarence decided to drive up to Ojai to meet this otherworldly pair. A short time later he asked Laura to arrange a meeting where the two people could speak. In his usual enigmatic way, he said little about the couple except to imply that they would reveal how seekers could complete the Self-Initiation process.

Besides the inner circle, Laura invited many of Clarence's former students. The secrecy surrounding the meeting generated intense excitement. Word had been leaked that Fenta had returned, bringing with him two individuals who would fulfill the prophecies of Revelation. Nancy and one of her friends searched for a hiding place where Fenta could park his spaceship. Whereas most people on the guest list planned to attend out of simple curiosity, members of the inner circle looked forward to the meeting with an uneasy sense that the message they were about to hear would change their lives forever. "All I wanted to do was hear these people," Nancy said. "It was my all-consuming interest."

On the evening of April 9, 1975, roughly 50 expectant seekers gathered in Laura's living room. The two speakers sat quietly next to Clarence at the front of the room while they waited for the audience to get settled. If anyone found their names absurd, no one said so because everybody had been prepared for the unexpected by weeks of rumors and speculation. Laura recalled, "You could almost feel the crackles of electricity running through the room."

The two aliens looked surprisingly ordinary. Wearing matching navy blue slacks and windbreakers, they could have been mistaken for a middle-aged couple on vacation in southern California. The woman introduced as Guinea had short, straight hair that accentuated her pudgy features, and she wore green eye liner that seemed curiously out of character for a supernatural being. The man who called himself Pig was tall and slender with graying hair and piercing blue eyes. He had an obvious stage presence. He did nearly all the talking while his partner sat expressionless by his side. The few times the woman spoke, her speech was marked by a mild Southern drawl that, like her makeup, seemed incongruous for an alien. Laura recalled that the man appeared to choose his words carefully, as if speaking to people who had only a limited ability to comprehend what he was saying.

Guinea and Pig spoke a language that was familiar to everyone in the room. Concepts like spiritual evolution, reincarnation, Christ consciousness, and the New Age figured prominently in their message. The man explained that the time had come for a select group of highly evolved seekers to enter the next phase of their growth. Having completed their lessons at the human level, they were ready to graduate. It was to the "twelfth graders" in the room that he addressed his words.

Beyond basic New Age ideas, Clarence's students recognized obvious parallels between Self-Initiation and what they were hearing. The process the man described entailed a physical as well as spiritual transformation. The man explained that twelfth graders could raise their vibrations cell by cell until their physical bodies disappeared from the visible world in a beam of light. He called this "human individual metamorphosis," or simply "the process." Having broken the cycle of death and reincarnation, they would be reborn as immortal godlike beings. Pig made a point of stressing the similarities between his and Guinea's message and the teachings of the man who sat next to them, nodding in agreement. "Your teacher has taught you well," he said. "Everything he has presented to you so far has been absolutely correct. All the time and effort you've put into study with him will now be put into action through this process."

However, it soon became clear that Guinea and Pig's message differed from Self-Initiation in several fundamental ways. First, there was the matter of UFOs. Rather than being transformed into light beings, the man claimed the twelfth graders would be taken to the Next Level in spaceships. However, he did not dwell on this. Instead, he focused on the process of overcoming human attachments. This required a radical break with the past, something Clarence had never mentioned.

Each true and sincere seeker of the next kingdom must walk out the door of his life. You must leave behind everything: your career, your security, your loved ones. You must leave behind every single attachment in order to open yourself for the remaining experience needed to totally wean you from any need at the human level. You have to walk out the door, close it, and never look back.

Even sex had to be overcome, because it drained vital energy needed to complete the metamorphic process. Although this idea appealed to the gay men who had struggled with Eugenics, it came as a shock to the inner circle because it contradicted everything Clarence had taught them.

It was not until the question-and-answer period that the audience began to realize that the process described by Guinea and Pig was not just another path to the "top of the mountain." The man explained that all their previous spiritual endeavors, including Self-Initiation, had been good, but twelfth graders could not hope to advance any further at the human level. "This is the only way you can make it into the next kingdom," he said bluntly. "There is no other way off the mountain."

"We were stunned," Nancy recalled. "I couldn't believe what I was hearing." Yet when she and others looked at Clarence, he simply nodded and gave them his maddening, knowing smile.

Despite all the contradictions, the message had a compelling twist. Clarence had spent the past year cultivating the belief that his students belonged to a spiritually elite group, and the man capitalized on this by comparing them to Christ's apostles:

This really isn't new to any of you. Every one of you in this room heard this message 2,000 years ago when Jesus was on earth. You were with him, worked with him, tried to carry out his mission after he left. You couldn't understand it then. You had not evolved to that level of comprehension to be able to do what he asked you to do, so you had to wait until now. This time you are all ready. You, Jesus' disciples and followers of 2,000 years ago, are back now for only *one* reason, and that is to make this conversion. You have done a marvelous job up to this point. Now it's time for the final step. You are a very special group. You are the earth's first harvest.

Then there was the element of fear.

For some of you, there will *never* be another opportunity. If you are a twelfth grader, and if you are ready to graduate from the human kingdom, and if you *do not* choose to undertake this final step, then your soul, upon death in this lifetime, will dissolve into the ethers and you will *never* incarnate again. This will be your first, *last*, and only chance.

Although, like Laura, most members of the crowd had rejected Christianity because of its fire-and-brimstone theology, the man's ability to cast the threat of eternal damnation in New Age terms made the possibility seem frighteningly real.

To make matters worse, the man added that one could be a twelfth grader and not realize it. Even the most determined seekers could be blinded to the Truth by invisible human-level spirits who manifest themselves in the form of skepticism and resistance. Clarence's students already accepted the idea of invisible entities, such as Arenda and the adepts of the Great White Brotherhood, so the notion of spirits seemed plausible. Laura was one of the few who challenged this idea, but the man deflected her questions. "You see," he told the audience, "the spirits are working right now. Many of you can feel them. We certainly can." It was disconcerting for Clarence's students to think these unseen influences might prevent them from recognizing the Truth when they were truly capable of understanding it.

Like Clarence, Guinea and Pig had a remarkable talent for shutting off criticism by getting people to question their own judgment. Clarence had spent over a year teaching his students to distrust their rational minds, and Guinea and Pig built on this foundation. When Laura persisted in challenging points in the message, the man responded in exasperation: "These questions you are asking are human questions. You can't possibly understand the answers from your level of comprehension." Guinea and Pig, after all, were appealing not to the intellect but to the higher mind of the evolved seeker. If Laura could not see the Truth, perhaps she was not really a twelfth grader.

## FROM SELF-INITIATION TO UFO CULT

When the meeting concluded, Guinea and Pig slipped out the back door with Clarence, leaving the crowd to cope with the confusion and anxiety that they had created. Laura described the questions running through their minds.

My God, were these spirit entities interfering with [our] ability to understand this concept? What if it were true? Maybe [we] were twelfth graders and didn't know it. Would this really be [our] last chance? What was "Ultimate Truth" right now? Why was Clarence agreeing with [the two people]? Everyone in the room felt as if a giant rug had been pulled out from under them.

During the next few anxiety-ridden days, Clarence arranged private meetings with Guinea and Pig for everyone who wanted more information. Most approached these meetings with a mixture of fascination and dread. Some, like Nancy, were virtually immobilized by inner conflict. She said she wished she could sleep forever, and she put off the meeting as long as possible: "I dreaded even getting up the next morning."

Almost everyone went to the meetings armed with pointed questions, especially about the contradictions between Self-Initiation and Guinea and Pig's message. Right away it became apparent that the two people did not know what Clarence had been teaching. "It was getting crazier and crazier," Nancy said.

People started asking them questions about Fenta and the spaceship and Eugenics. Somebody said, "Are you two people from [Zend]?" No. "Did you ever read the book?" No. "Do you know Fenta?" No. "What do you say about Eugenics?" We don't even know what Eugenics is.

When Laura asked Guinea and Pig why they had said everything Clarence taught was true when it wasn't, she was told, "That's your human mind asking that question." She recalled, "there were moments in time at that meeting where I actually felt my mind shut down. . . . It was like, oh yeah, that makes sense, when it didn't make any sense."

In the end it was Clarence rather than Guinea and Pig who proved to be the pivotal influence in the decision-making process. He continued to claim that all his teachings had prepared his students for Guinea and Pig's message, and he dismissed the inconsistencies by implying that his students would see the connection soon enough. It was rumored that his spirit guide Arenda had confirmed the pair's authenticity, although, as usual, Clarence never confirmed or denied the story.

Why Clarence decided to follow Guinea and Pig remains a mystery. In retrospect, his students wondered if he really believed in them or if he was just looking for a way to dodge the IRS. One thing is certain: Clarence never disposed of his house or any of his possessions, but merely locked them up as if he planned to return. Whatever his motives, when Clarence—the man Laura called "second to God"—decided to leave, he swept almost everyone in his inner circle along with him.

About a week after the gathering in Laura's living room, Clarence arranged a session that became known as the GOP (standing for Going Out Process) meeting. Guinea and Pig explained what everyone would need to bring: warm clothes, camping gear, money, cars, and food. Time was running out, and they had to act quickly. Their destination, a remote spot near the Oregon coast where the spaceships would arrive, was a closely guarded secret known only to Clarence, who remained as tight-lipped as ever.

The hour of decision came more quickly than anyone expected. Despite lingering doubts and frequent anxiety attacks, everyone in the inner circle had a sense of moving inexorably toward an inevitable finale. By now hardly anyone was talking about the unresolved contradictions with Self-Initiation. Instead, people were driven by the fear of being left behind if Guinea and Pig turned out to be right. Laura put it this way:

Our group was riddled with fear: fear of being disintegrated into the ethers, fear of not being where we were supposed to be on time, fear that we were going to lose our place on the spiritual path. . . . It was the most devastating, horrible, depressing, awful time of my life.

Laura was one of the last holdouts, but even she was caving in. "I wanted to believe," she admitted. "I tried to make myself believe." After the GOP meeting, she confronted Clarence and demanded to know why he believed in Guinea and Pig. Without answering her question, he told her the two people had projected a psychic image of her on the wall of his study; he saw dozens of spirits trying to hold her back because she was the most advanced student in his class. At the end of the encounter, Laura knew that she, too, was going, and her decision tipped the scales for most of the remaining skeptics.

As the "going out process" accelerated, word got out that Laura and her fellow students were about to join a "crazy cult." Their friends and relatives were confused and alarmed. The Manson Family murders in 1969 were still fresh in the minds of southern Californians, and some relatives did not hesitate to draw the parallel. One family considered locking up their daughter until she came to her senses. Another called the FBI, and Nancy's father and brother flew in from Acapulco to talk some sense into her. But there was no stopping the momentum. Clarence was urging them on, warning that there was even less time than they thought, and people were already disposing of their possessions. Angelo was one of the few inner circle members who decided not to leave. Although he thought his friends were making a bad decision, he saw no point in trying to reason with them: "I didn't try to talk anyone out of it. Didn't even try to appeal to them on logic, because they were beyond logic. They weren't hearing anything but what they wanted to hear."

In less than two weeks after the meeting in Laura's house, nearly everyone in the inner circle had chosen to abandon their earthly lives to follow Guinea and Pig. Months would pass before their friends and relatives had any idea what had become of them. Even as they drove out of town, they had no idea who these two people were, where they had come from, or even what their real names were.

## CHARISMA AND CONVERSION IN THE CULTIC MILIEU

In their struggle to make sense of what happened, the friends and relatives of Guinea and Pig's new devotees claimed the mysterious couple had used hypnosis to brainwash the Hollywood group. However, this explanation is an oversimplification that ignores the sociological dimensions of both *charisma* and *conversion*.

Clarence and the self-proclaimed aliens, Guinea and Pig, were *charismatic leaders*. To the average person, *charisma* refers to extraordinary personal magnetism, and there is no question that these individuals possessed that mysterious quality. However, neither the control that Clarence exerted over his students nor Guinea and Pig's sudden success at recruitment can be explained by their personal attributes alone. Charisma, like beauty, is in the eye of the beholder. I have interviewed many people who heard Guinea and Pig present their message at subsequent meetings around the country, and in every case the only ones who found it believable were those who belonged to the New Age subculture.

Charisma and conversion are closely related phenomena. The authority exercised by charismatic leaders has its roots in their followers' matrix of assumptions about reality. Once we understand this matrix, which I have called a *universe of discourse*, we can begin to appreciate why people choose to follow charismatic leaders. For conversion to occur, leaders must couch their appeals in terms that are meaningful to prospective recruits.

The term *conversion* must be used cautiously, because it often overstates the transformation that occurs when one joins a religious cult. Conversion refers to adopting a new belief system. Confirmed atheists, for example, have become born-again Christians and dedicated Communists have suddenly embraced capitalism. In conversions like these, the convert adopts an altogether different universe of discourse. However, most conversions are much less extreme. Like an Episcopalian who becomes a Catholic, the typical convert simply modifies existing beliefs without exchanging one universe of discourse for another.

Most conversions to New Age cults have this character. Clarence's Self-Initiation group is a case in point. The sexual practices Clarence introduced were new to everyone, but they were based on metaphysical assumptions his students already accepted. Clarence's seemingly uncanny knack for manipulating the inner circle was based on his intuitive grasp of the seeker's mentality. Anyone who did not belong to the seeker's universe of discourse would have found his ideas ludicrous and probably never would have embraced Self-Initiation and Eugenics.

Though far more sudden, the decision to follow Guinea and Pig was similar to accepting Self-Initiation. Although "going on the process" entailed the adoption of new beliefs and an abrupt change in lifestyle, Guinea and Pig's message, like Clarence's teachings, was firmly rooted in the New Age universe of discourse. When the two people spoke at Laura's home, they did not have to explain terms like evolution, reincarnation, spiritual growth, or the Light, because their audience already understood them. These concepts were integral to the seeker's worldview, and Guinea and Pig merely put them together in a new package. Although the two people were quite explicit about the uniqueness of their venture, claiming it was the *only* way off the mountain, they made a point of stressing the continuity between their message and the beliefs held by their audience. The process they called human individual metamorphosis was simply the next logical step in their listeners' growth. Deciding to follow Guinea and Pig may have been the most dramatic step any of Clarence's students had ever taken, but it was entirely consistent with their self-conception as seekers.

When viewed in the sociological context of the New Age subculture, the story of the Hollywood meeting begins to make sense. We also can see why this subculture is called the *cultic milieu*. Clarence's students belonged to a vast, floating clientele of spiritual seekers that supplies members for countless new religious movements, of which Self-Initiation and Guinea and Pig's UFO cult are just two examples. All that remained to transform Clarence's devotees into followers of Guinea and Pig was the right combination of circumstances.

The strange couple with the unlikely names entered the picture at a fortuitous moment when the inner circle stood at a major psychological crossroads and members were casting about for new directions in their lives. By a quirk of fate there were enough parallels between Self-Initiation and Guinea and Pig's message to make their pitch believable. In the uncertain, anxiety-ridden climate that prevailed after the meeting in Laura's house, the decisive step taken by Clarence precipitated a wave of sudden, if confused, decisions to follow his lead. Guinea and Pig literally captured a cult, but they might never have been successful were it not for the unpredictable coincidences that spelled the demise of Clarence's Self-Initiation class.

Altogether, between April 21 and May 3, 1975, two dozen seekers, nearly all from Clarence's inner circle, made their way to the secret rendezvous on the

Oregon coast. By the time they reached Oregon, Guinea and Pig had changed their names to Bo and Peep. It was a symbolic gesture that marked the beginning of their role as spiritual shepherds who expected to lead their flock aboard UFOs bound for the next evolutionary kingdom.

## EPILOGUE

The spaceships never arrived, but Bo and Peep's fledgling UFO cult lived on. About six months after the Hollywood meeting, the group burst into the news when over 20 people suddenly vanished following a lecture on UFOs in Waldport, Oregon. During the next few months more people disappeared after similar meetings around the country. Eventually Bo and Peep may have acquired as many as 200 followers.

Media reports indicated that Bo and Peep were Marshall Herff Applewhite, a former music professor, and Bonnie Lu Nettles, a registered nurse. Beyond that, little was known about them. Then, early in 1976, Bo and Peep stopped recruiting and the group dropped out of sight.

Almost 22 years passed before the group again made national news. On March 27, 1997, headlines across the country announced that 39 members of an obscure cult known as Heaven's Gate had committed mass suicide in Rancho Santa Fe, an exclusive suburb of San Diego, California. They had killed themselves by ingesting a concoction of vodka, phenobarbital, and applesauce.

Heaven's Gate proved to be the latest incarnation of Bo and Peep's UFO cult. In its first years after the Hollywood meeting, members had camped out and survived by asking for help at churches, but by the 1980s they were renting luxurious houses and supporting themselves by doing computer work. By then Bo and Peep had changed their names to Do and Ti, after the musical notes.

A crucial turning point came in 1985, when Nettles died of cancer. Until then, members had believed that the only way to enter the Next Level was in a living physical "vehicle," which was how members referred to the human body. Death was simply a ticket to another lifetime as a human. However, Nettles' death forced members to reconsider that belief. Maybe a physical ascension was not necessary after all. By the end of the 1980s, after their hopes of being picked up by UFOs had been dashed again and again, members were discussing suicide as an option for getting to the Father's kingdom.

Although the exact reasons for the suicides remain unclear, the precipitating event was the appearance of the Hale-Bopp Comet. According to a rumor popularized by radio talk-show celebrity Art Bell, a spaceship had been sighted in the comet's shadow, and Applewhite took this as a sign that his departed partner had finally returned for him and his followers. The comet reached its closest approach to Earth in March 1997.

As for the Hollywood group, all but three members dropped out of the cult before the suicides. Clarence was among the first to leave, apparently unwilling to become a follower after being a leader for so long. No one heard from him again. Laura, never able to resolve her doubts, also left within a few months, followed soon by Nancy Gold. Jack Pantzer stayed another year, and Bob Johnson and Doug Peters remained until 1991. By the time of the suicides, only Applewhite and 38 followers remained, including Mary Butterfield, Clarence's "process girl."

The fact that most of the Hollywood recruits defected should not come as a surprise. They were spiritual seekers, and seekers usually do not stay put for very long. A Canadian survey, for example, showed that over 75 percent of all those who had participated in an unconventional religion were no longer involved (Bird and Reimer 1982).

What remains to be learned is why some people chose to stay and sacrifice their human lives to board the long-awaited spacecraft. They were converts in the truest sense of the term. Shortly before the suicides, the remaining members of Heaven's Gate made a video in which they bade farewell to their relatives and friends at the human level. One parent remarked that her daughter smiled just the way she did as a little girl when she was totally happy. The suicides were the ultimate expression of commitment and a dramatic testimony to the power of charismatic leaders to command the loyalty of their followers.[2]

## NOTES

1. My most important informant was a former Heaven's Gate member who was writing a book about the Hollywood meeting and its aftermath. I am indebted to this person, who asked to remain anonymous, for allowing me to quote from her manuscript, which was never published. All names used in this chapter are pseudonyms, except for those of Heaven's Gate leaders Marshall Applewhite and Bonnie Lu Nettles.

2. For more information on the history of Heaven's Gate, see Balch 1995.

## BIBLIOGRAPHY

Bainbridge, W. S. (1978). *Satan's power: A deviant psychotherapy cult.* Berkeley: University of California Press.

Balch, R. W. (1995). Waiting for the ships: Disillusionment and the revitalization of faith in Bo and Peep's UFO cult. In J. R. Lewis (Ed.). *The gods have landed: New religions from other worlds* (pp. 137–166). Albany: State University of New York Press.

Bird, F., & Reimer, B. (1982). Participation rates in new religious and para-religious movements. *Journal for the Scientific Study of Religion, 21* (1), 1–14.

Buckner, H. T. (1968). The flying saucerians: An open door cult. In M. Truzzi (Ed.). *Sociology and everyday life* (pp. 223–230). Englewood Cliffs, NJ: Prentice-Hall.

Campbell, C. (1972). The cult, the cultic milieu and secularization. In M. Hill (Ed.). *A sociological yearbook of sociology in Britain*, Vol. 5 (pp. 119–136). London: SCM Press.

Jorstad, E. (1990). *Holding fast/pressing on: Religion in America in the 1980s.* New York: Praeger.

Mann, W. M. (1955). *Sect, cult and church in Alberta*. Toronto: University of Toronto Press.

Melton, J. G., Clark, J., & Kelly, A. A. (1991). *New Age almanac*. Detroit: Visible Ink Press.

Turner, R. H., & Killian, L. M. (1987). *Collective behavior* (3rd ed.). Englewood Cliffs, NJ: Prentice-Hall.

Washington, P. W. (1993). *Madame Blavatsky's baboon*. New York: Schocken.

*Chapter 2* _____

# Jesus People USA

## *Anson Shupe*

Anson Shupe frequently is a consultant to attorneys involved in lawsuits concerning religious liberties and clergy abuse of congregants. These interests led directly to his study of Jesus People USA (JPUSA). Ronald Enroth, a well-known evangelical Christian writer on "cults," had leveled charges against JPUSA. Based on the testimonies of disillusioned ex-members, he suggested they were an abusive group. As an objective outsider, Shupe was asked to determine if the charges were true. He visited their commune and interviewed members. His observations about JPUSA follow.

Monasteries, religious retreats, and communes are perceived by many as exotic or antisocial. After all, they reject many of mainstream society's norms. Yet the existence of such groups suggests that for some persons, a *communal imperative* exists. They have a desire to reach beyond "normal" society for something deeper and more spiritually rewarding.

The impression most persons have when they hear the word "commune," for example, is of small, self-sufficient, inwardly focused groups. Often physically isolated from the "real" world, members have abandoned ordinary privacy, personal possessions, and individual autonomy. Images of promiscuous sex (once termed "free love") and rampant drug use or, alternatively, strict celibacy and abstinence from worldly pleasures also may be conjured up.

Such stereotypes resemble some of the communitarian "hippie" experiments during the late 1960s and early 1970s. But like most stereotypes, they can be found misleading when confronted by actual examples.

So it is with one successful evangelical Christian communal group in downtown Chicago, the diverse, energetic, and outward-looking Jesus People USA (JPUSA). This commune, organized around a *covenantal* understanding of biblical precepts, overcame the demands of the blatantly *contractual* culture of one of America's largest cities.

## CONTRACT VERSUS COVENANT: A MATTER OF INTERPERSONAL COMMITMENT

Covenantal human relationships are typical of villages or moderate-sized towns in small, relatively undeveloped societies. Interpersonal bonds are not based on *negotiations* but, rather, emphasize loyalty and responsibility. Individuals respond to others as total persons, taking into account their backgrounds, experiences, and family. Covenantal communities resemble what classical sociologists such as Ferdinand Tönnies (1957) termed folk, or *gemeinschaft*, societies. Several sociologists (e.g., Bromley and Busching 1988) have argued that covenantal communities have become anomalies in our densely populated, impersonal, urban societies. Alternatively, contractual communities emphasize limited, segmented relationships. People interact with others because those others are seen as means to specific ends. They do not care about others' backgrounds, families, and experiences. Their relationships, based on limited obligations to one another, are clearly spelled out. This emphasis tends to minimize the importance and legitimacy of covenantal relationships.

Exceptions do exist in contractual communities; examples include marriage and prolonged friendships. But even these have not been totally removed from the shadow of contractualism. The logic of the contract is characteristic of urban, or *gesellschaft*, communities (Tönnies 1957). A handshake and unlocked doors were once accepted signs of trusting, covenantal relationships among neighbors. Attorneys, written warranties, and prenuptial agreements represent the contractual world in which almost every relationship has its designated prerogatives and limits. These two *ideal types* (which exist in theory but not in reality) of communities should be as antithetical as oil and water. People who voluntarily live a strictly covenantal lifestyle base their relationships on trust, obedience, sacrifice, and group social control. This presents an alien world to those who are immersed in a larger contractual world of individual autonomy and freedom.

It makes sense that social pressures against covenantal lifestyles might lead in the direction of contractualism. Indeed, the tension between these two forms of human organization, a persistent theme in American religion, has many historical and contemporary examples. Covenantal groups such as the Shakers, the Oneida community, the Old Order Amish, nineteenth-century Mormons, and the more recently arrived Unification Church of the Rev. Sun Myung Moon all have become a part of America's religious pluralist scene (e.g., Zellner 1995; Kephart and Zellner 1991; Bromley and Shupe 1979; Fogarty 1972; Nordhoff 1966;

Noyes 1966). Another contemporary example is the JPUSA movement (e.g., Shupe et al. 1989; Bromley and Shupe forthcoming).

## WHAT IS JPUSA?

This chapter's description of JPUSA's origins and development, its members' beliefs, its organizational structure, and its various ministries to the Chicago community are based on several sources. They include published social historical analyses of JPUSA by one of its members, a professional journalist (Trott 1993, 1994, 1995a, 1995b); self-descriptive materials published by JPUSA (1972, 1991); and personal observations and interviews by the author with various JPUSA leaders beginning in October 1993 and continuing since then.

### Origins

An evangelistic mission in Milwaukee, by late 1971, had recruited almost 60 members into a group of "Jesus People." Many of them were self-admitted idealistic, religious seekers who had histories of sexual and drug abuse. Almost all identified with the rock subculture of the era. By early 1972 they numbered nearly 200. That spring, they split into four groups. One went to Europe. A second headed south to Florida.

Traveling in a bright red school bus with "JESUS" painted on the sides, they performed skits, sang songs, and witnessed in the communities they visited. A third group stayed behind, forming a "home base" in Milwaukee, and a fourth contingent temporarily joined a Pentecostal tent revivalist. The Southern contingent, in particular, became important in the development of the movement. In their travels, they frequently were confused with the Children of God, a Jesus movement offshoot that became sexually aberrant under the charismatic leadership of David Berg, called "Moses" by his followers.

Because of such confusion and the fact that the secular Florida climate was never very receptive, this second group returned north in 1973 with the name of Jesus People USA (JPUSA). By 1974, JPUSA members had decided to settle permanently in a declining neighborhood of downtown Chicago. They had a vision of an urban mission serving the neglected and poor, along with a commitment to literally living in the communitarian style of first-century Christians. Much of the members' time was spent witnessing in the streets, holding Bible classes, and developing a music ministry. Their efforts were complicated by spartan living conditions in the crowded basement of a sympathetic charismatic church.

During this time, *Cornerstone* magazine, which would become a respected national publication on the order of an evangelical *Rolling Stone*, developed out of what initially had been an underground Christian newsletter.

After several "false starts" in leadership and some internal reforms, JPUSA began to seek a more secure financial base. Simple charity and the pooling of members' resources proved inadequate to establish financial stability. Other new religious movements have faced similar problems (Richardson 1988; Bromley and Shupe 1981: 157–176; Bromley and Shupe 1980). The solution for JPUSA was an evolving variety of activities including companies that did home repairs, painting, carpentry, and roofing. These came to be called their "tent-making ministries." In addition, members learned publishing skills, and produced high-quality graphics and reporting for *Cornerstone*.

In the late 1970s and 1980s, as JPUSA hung on economically and eventually began to thrive, other, better-publicized communal groups began to fade. JPUSA members did not think of themselves as among the "elect," preordained for success, but they did perceive some meaning in their survival (e.g., in contrast to the decline of Children of God and the Way International). Nationally, the Jesus movement was becoming less visible.

The widespread disappearance of nearly all the Jesus communes was a sign hard to interpret, with many commentators suggesting that such communes—along with the movement overall—had merely been a fad. . . . We interpreted disbanded communities as cases of God's plan being fulfilled; most Jesus communes had never been designed to become permanent expressions of faith. Instead, they had been halfway points between the disintegrating counterculture and the evangelical cultural mainstream. (Trott 1994: 20)

Growing in membership, through both recruitment and the increasing number of JPUSA children, the commune, by the late 1970s, was constantly short of space. This problem became more acute in 1978 when JPUSA merged with a parallel black, urban Christian communal group named New Life. After several moves, the commune settled into a former hotel in a run-down inner-city neighborhood off Lake Shore Drive in Chicago. The group still resides there.

## BELIEFS

JPUSA's members made a commitment to the original first-century Christian philosophy that "He who has two coats let him share with him who has none" (Luke 3:11), and "If a man comes to you and you send him away with empty blessings, you profit neither him nor yourself" (James 2:15–16). JPUSA members, as committed Christians, believe they are not simply to live as if they are poor. Rather, JPUSA members are to be poor, without excess wealth, pooling resources to survive and living in communitarian fashion. The book of Acts (4: 32–35) describes first-century Christians:

Now the whole group of those who believed were of one heart and soul, and no one claimed private ownership of any possessions, but everything they owned was held in common. With great power the apostles gave their testimony to the resurrection of the

Lord Jesus, and great grace was upon them all. There was not a needy person among them, for as many as owned lands or houses sold them and brought the proceeds of what was sold. They laid it at the apostles' feet, and it was distributed to each as any had need.

At the same time, JPUSA members do not go hungry or barefoot like medieval mendicants, nor do they have to forgo health and medical assistance. Rather, in a disciplined way, they have attempted to eliminate social class distinctions within the group.

According to the official JPUSA Covenant, which every adult member signs, there is a two-week trial period. Prospective members and JPUSA "size up" one another for mutual compatibility. Afterward, there is a one-year provisional membership and subsequent reciprocal reevaluation. If both parties agree that the covenant can work, then the candidate becomes a permanent (regular) member.

The attempt to preserve a biblical, egalitarian lifestyle is laid out in the Covenant. Also, the delicate issue of turning over one's material assets to JPUSA is broached. To ensure that all persons involved are clear in their purposes and motives, and not swept away by a whim of the moment, JPUSA has instituted certain safeguards. First, members are not obligated to turn over any assets. Second, married couples are not permitted to turn over substantial assets (except vehicles) to JPUSA until they become regular members. Third, any substantial assets that a member does not wish to turn over to the community should be disposed of before coming to JPUSA or stored somewhere other than the community's buildings. Fourth, members are asked not to use personal bank funds for private expenditures, unless they clear it with the financial office. This prevents a dual standard of living between members with substantial assets and those with few or none. Fifth, members may keep items such as clothing, small appliances, stereos, and recreational gear such as bikes and tennis rackets. "We are cautious in accepting a member's assets, as it's impossible to give them back once they've been used by the community. While members may terminate their membership and leave the community at any time, upon leaving, a member may not take back assets which he or she turned over to the community" (JPUSA 1972: 3).

Since few members were raised in communal settings, beliefs about equality and poverty, guided by rough biblical guidelines, evolved on an ad hoc basis into rules and directions for daily living. In this sense, JPUSA's first generation has had to "make it up as they went along" through prayer, intuition, and trial and error.

## ORGANIZATION AND LIFESTYLE

Though JPUSA is communal and democratic in orientation, by the mid-1970s members realized the need for some limited central government. When the first leaders left the movement, older members of JPUSA chose two men, previously the head deacons, to lead the group. Eventually leadership was expanded to eight and then nine persons, including males and females. They have been the senior (i.e., long-time) members of JPUSA, called to leadership but not elected. They have no specified terms of office. Directly under them are the grassroots leadership levels of deacons, deaconesses, and group leaders. Groups of 20 to 30 members are formed to socialize new members into the movement. They interpret the practicalities of the JPUSA lifestyle by using biblical principles and, thus, lend a sense of mission to the "breaking in" period of membership.

In 1989 JPUSA took another step toward institutionalization of authority, affiliating as a ministry with the Evangelical Covenant Church, also headquartered in Chicago. The present organization includes a plethora of JPUSA businesses and ministries.

While the primary oversight of the ministry rests with the council of pastors, much [*sic*] of the responsibilities for the daily running of the community and our businesses are taken by various other individuals. Such plurality in leadership is based on a mutual submission which can hear God's voice through the youngest community member as well as these who hold authority positions. (JPUSA 1991: 4)

Indeed, as a chronicler of the commune's history states, "The Book of Acts, which had provided a sort of blueprint for living in community for the Jesus People, pointed plurality of leadership as a norm" (Trott 1993: 16).

### Daily Living Arrangements

Early in its history, members were housed in either a church basement or a succession of overcrowded houses. These cramped living arrangements were understandably difficult for both single and married adults, as well as for children. The current downtown Chicago headquarters, located in a former hotel, provides more space and seems to have successfully facilitated the integration of communal and middle-class lifestyles. Put another way, the downtown commune has provided a workable meeting of covenantal and contractual lifestyles.

In the central residence building, for example, most of the individual rooms have bathrooms. To better utilize space, members have built small lofts, accessible by ladders, in a corner of each room for sleeping or reading. Most of each room can be used as a family or living room with storage areas and bookshelves under the lofts. Very small children sleep in cribs near their parents. Older children are paired in rooms near their parents' rooms, complete with bunk beds and toy boxes, much as in many middle-class homes.

Members are free to furnish these rooms as they please. My host couple for a 1992 visit had a tastefully decorated room with a number of pieces of refurbished antique furniture, complete with stereo and television/VCR. The room I lodged in belonged to a JPUSA couple absent on vacation. It was quite comfortable, though arranged differently than the hosts' room.

Both rooms were considerably nicer and more private than a room in any college dormitory. A JPUSA pamphlet described the process thus: "The married couples have all helped varnish, plaster, paint, and decorate each other's rooms. It's like an old-fashioned house-raising" (1991: 10).

Meals are cooked in a common kitchen. They can be eaten in a dining area or taken back to residents' rooms. There are phones located throughout the various floors, and a switchboard operator at the front desk takes messages and contacts persons on upper floors or in offices. While there, I detected no signs of alcohol, drugs, or tobacco. The dress code was decidedly relaxed. Both men and women wore T-shirts and jeans. Men's hairstyles were longish-to-long-plus, and many had mustaches and beards. Women wore their hair long and some wore dresses.

Any communal living arrangement must have rules about sexual relationships. In contrast to many communal groups, JPUSA's sexual practices are probably more restrained than in the larger society. Single members are to remain chaste, and married members are to practice fidelity. Violence or any form of abuse between spouses or toward children is regarded as sinful.

By the 1990s, JPUSA members had created an environment that preserves elements of community, such as frequent and informal contact, sharing, and mutual reliance. At the same time, they also preserved the outside world's values about personal property, privacy, and selective cultural enrichment. The JPUSA lifestyle is definitely not monastic. Rather, it is a blend of familial and communal traditions. While mainstream and conformist at the intimate or individual level, it is alternative or nonconformist at the community level.

JPUSA's ministries, more than its lifestyle, have prevented it from becoming a reclusive movement. This has contributed to its longevity.

## MINISTRY

JPUSA believes it has a calling to serve the world, and the world begins with its neighbors in Chicago and northern Illinois. Logically that goal should entail a host of separate programs striving to fulfill Christ's Great Commission and meet the needs of various target populations. It does. The main residence offers individuals, from a broad array of troubled backgrounds, a haven for self-reflection and spiritual growth.

In addition, JPUSA provides several hundred meals daily for the homeless in "soup kitchen" fashion and distributes food packages to those in need. In late 1994 JPUSA announced it was seeking contributions to help pay the costs of renovating its kitchen equipment. Cornerstone Community Outreach provides transitional housing for almost five dozen homeless women and their children. It also oversees parenting and life-skill classes, a big brother/big sister program, and assistance for those who need affordable housing. The New Friendly Towers program offers inexpensive rooms to approximately 90 low-income elderly citizens. They receive physician visits, housekeeping services, Bible studies, and other cultural activities.

The Leland Building, formerly the single men's dormitory, has 20 two- and three-bedroom apartments for homeless families seeking to get off welfare. These families have access to job training, education, sobriety programs, and counseling. There is a crisis pregnancy center that offers postabortion counseling and Lamaze classes, and distributes baby supplies. Other programs include a seasonal employment bureau for jobless men. JPUSA volunteers act as chaplains at the Cook Country jail and a local juvenile detention center. Internship opportunities exist for members of suburban church youth ministries. A number of diverse music ministries include the REZ rock band, which combines concerts and workshops with evangelism; a gospel choir; a hard-core punk band; an Irish-Celtic group; and a rap group. JPUSA has its own recording label, Grrr Records.

JPUSA also operates its own video company, Cornerstone Productions. *Cornerstone*, a glossy, high-quality magazine, is heavily infused with Christian rock and Jesus movement imagery. Included are music and book reviews that reflect JPUSA's countercultural origins. Much of *Cornerstone*'s journalism is devoted to cult investigations. It debunks and examines both mainstream evangelical missions (e.g., Trott and Hertenstein 1992) and controversial nonevangelical groups, such as the Unification Church (Shupe and Trott 1995). JPUSA claims that *Cornerstone*'s annual circulation ran to approximately 250,000 copies by 1978. Many distributors buy 50 to 100 copies for witnessing and church groups (Trott 1995: 44). A Cornerstone Christian rock festival, held annually at JPUSA's farm retreat near Bushnell, Illinois, invites evangelical Christian bands and speakers for a several-day gathering. By the early 1990s, over 10,000 persons were attending each year.

Many of JPUSA's adult members work in commune-owned businesses. Roofing, carpentry, painting, graphics, and retail enterprises raise revenues for the group. According to one JPUSA publication, "All finances brought in through these businesses are pooled, and all expenses, from house payments and utility bills to shoes and birthday parties, are met from this fund" (1991: 8). Thus, JPUSA challenges the popular mythology that communes are necessarily remote, reclusive, and divorced from the everyday "real" world.

JPUSA is probably more energetically and enthusiastically involved in its secular community, part of one of the most dilapidated areas of Chicago, than the majority of churches and synagogues are in their own towns and cities. JPUSA's mission is not to retreat, but to engage and serve. Its vehicle for service is a disciplined yet flexible covenantal community of evangelical Christian believers. JPUSA has learned to interact effectively with a contractual society that finds uses for the services its members can provide.

## JPUSA IN CONTROVERSY

Despite its sociological success as a struggling sectarian movement, JPUSA has experienced internal and external controversies. For example, in 1971, when the movement was still in its formative stage, John Wiley Herrin, a married pastor with a history of alcohol abuse, joined JP Milwaukee along with his wife, Dawn, and three children. By 1973 he was sole elder of JPUSA.

According to Trott (1993: 14, 16), Herrin became sexually attracted to a young woman in the group who rebuffed his repeated advances. He warned her not to tell becaues it would destroy JPUSA's ministries. Finally she informed several deacons about Herrin's adulterous suggestions. In 1974, after several tumultuous months of leadership crisis, JPUSA urged Herrin to attend a special counseling ministry for errant pastors. Counseling did not help, however; Herrin divorced his wife not long afterward and left the ministry, presumably disappearing into secular society. Another controversy was the "spanking era." Part of an experiment with internal discipline, it was thought to lead to spiritual maturity. It was the brainchild of evangelist Jack Winters, who ran his own ministry.

Following Herrin's departure, JPUSA experienced a leadership vacuum, and Winters had stepped in. By their own admission, spanking was instituted by JPUSA's elders. It was a form of humiliating social control that was practiced for about 16 months. After hearings to explore the roots of members' sins, infractions were punished by adults spanking other adults with switches (sociologists refer to such actions as *degradation ceremonies*). Disciplinarians were usually deacons of the group. Submission to spanking was purely voluntary, and more symbolic than painful. The spankings proved unpopular, however, and were no panacea for producing spiritual growth. Critics inside the movement claimed that "getting the rod" was becoming a cheap alternative to genuine repentance. It defeated the whole purpose of the practice. Trott (1993: 18) reports: "As time went on, Winters' rationale for the spankings no longer made sense, if it ever had." By 1978 the practice was waning, and the few still asking for such "ministry" didn't seem to be benefiting from it.

The relationship between Winters and JPUSA began to unravel. The breaking point was reached when Winters imperiously instructed JPUSA members either to merge into his own ministry or "go home." Members distinctly put him at arm's length and moved their ministry in a different direction.

Another scandal put JPUSA in turmoil in 1993. In 1977 Professor Ronald Enroth, an evangelical Christian sociologist at California's Westmont College, had written a book entitled *Youth, Brainwashing and the Extremist Cults*. In a letter to the superintendent of the Central Conference of the Evangelical Covenant Church (ECC), Enroth wrote in 1993 that he had interviewed approximately two dozen ex-members of JPUSA (Rev. H. W. Freedham, personal communication, June 16, 1993). He claimed numerous reports of administrative and personal abuse by JPUSA leaders. His reports cited instances of emotional damage done to ex-members in his limited sample who were (he claimed) as confused psychologically and spiritually as any of the literally hundreds of former cultists he had encountered in the course of his research (Enroth 1993).

Enroth claimed ex-JPUSA members displayed confusion, guilt, excessive dependency, fear, doubts, spiritual disillusionment, uncertainty of Christian identity, low self-esteem, feelings of abandonment, and lack of decision-making initiative. Furthermore, he stated, he had knowledge of financial irregularities involving JPUSA leaders. He reported that ex-members told him of dual lifestyle standards between the leaders and rank-and-file members. These included clothing and diets for the children. There was allegedly harsh discipline, occasionally bordering on abuse. He further stated that there were poor educational standards in the home-schooling program, and minimal and often inadequate medical and dental care for all members.

Enroth wrote to the superintendent that he had discovered these problems during the course of researching his book *Recovering from Churches That Abuse* (1994), the sequel to his best-selling *Churches That Abuse* (1992). He said this information was volunteered, not solicited.

Enroth initially told the ECC superintendent that, due to a tight publisher's deadline, he would be inclined to discuss the specifics of his findings after he completed his book. He could not possibly meet before the end of the summer of 1993. He "felt impelled," as a "Christian brother" (his words), to alert the official.

Enroth's letter set off a firestorm of correspondence between himself and officials from both JPUSA and ECC. His hearsay charges were particularly distressing for JPUSA. Leaders and spokespersons for the group were embarrassed; they had always considered the movement to be on the forefront, in opposition to cultic and questionable religious activity.

The lengthy and sometimes testy written dialogue resulted in a representative of Zondervan Press, Enroth's publisher, meeting with JPUSA leaders and ECC denominational officials. For a convoluted set of reasons, Enroth and JPUSA were never able to schedule a mutually convenient meeting. Consequently, a planned trip to Chicago by Enroth never materialized. There is no evidence that Enroth has ever set foot within any JPUSA operation or ministry. Meanwhile, JPUSA enlisted a number of academics, myself included, to evaluate this particular conflict, and all other facets of the Chicago ministry. This resulted in the publication of the first of special issues of *Cornerstone* addressing spiritual accountability. It featured a series chronicling JPUSA's history as well as outside professional critiques of Enroth's methodology.

It appeared that Enroth's accusations were based solely on angry testimonies by anonymous apostates. At the same time, those in the evangelical world, aware of the conflict, were in a serious state of confusion. How could this flagship example of communal Christian commitment be labeled as "an abusive church" by a leading evangelical social scientist? By 1995 the furor had subsided a bit.

Enroth's second "abuse" book was published, angering JPUSA's supporters and leaving those who had been unsure about his accusations no more certain than before. JPUSA had weathered the embarrassment, but felt maligned. The wounds, inflicted by an evangelical once considered their supporter, cut deep. Meanwhile, JPUSA's urban ministries to Chicago's poor continued.

## WHAT JPUSA CAN TELL US SOCIOLOGICALLY

This last controversial episode is instructive regarding the ongoing tension between covenantal and communal lifestyles. It demonstrates how a group that seems to have successfully managed the balancing act between the two never completely escapes the pull from these polar opposites. For example, there is no reason to think that Ronald Enroth, his informants, or any of the dedicated persons who make JPUSA work acted in bad faith. Sincerity is usually widespread when people of differing perspectives give their accounts of how things are. Most of the accusations of "abuse" that Enroth reported seem, in retrospect, to represent snippets of communal living that can be embellished to appear outrageous, especially to someone unfamiliar with the realities of communal life. Still other complaints come from unhappy memories of times spent in such a group. An example illustrates the point. A leader's child wore newly purchased shoes on one occasion while another member's child wore older shoes. JPUSA provides each family with a periodic modest allowance of discretionary cash to use for whatever purpose it wishes. One couple had chosen to use its allowance for a new pair of shoes, the other had not. Later, accusations of leadership favoritism were made.

Similar examples abound in Enroth's accusations of abuse. Hurt feelings and misperceptions are probably inevitable within groups whose first-generation members are exploring the dimensions of their lifestyle on a daily, experimental basis. Bitterness over larger issues elicits from angry ex-members a retrospective avalanche of minor complaints that become defined as "abuse." The pain associated with departure from a religion sometimes parallels the pain associated with some divorces.

It is important to bear in mind two points about how communitarian lifestyles are interpreted by persons familiar only with a predominantly contractual culture. First, testimonies of angry, disillusioned ex-members of intense covenantal groups always have to be taken with a grain of salt, a methodological point that Enroth basically ignored.

Second, covenantal communities are predicated on different premises and assumptions than are contractual communities. Actions that are part of the discipline and sharing of resources in a covenantal community like JPUSA can be made to sound abusive when put under the glaring light of contractual logic. Contractuals can make covenantals seem odd, deviant, even dangerous because the natures of their social organizations are very different.

JPUSA does not seem to be an internally dangerous or abusive group. It works well for the majority of its members. There is steady, but minimal, turnover of those for whom it doesn't work. Overall, JPUSA performs a number of positive functions for the broader secular community. This was acknowledged even by Enroth in his initial letter to the ECC's superintendent.

## CONCLUSION

This chapter has presented two conflicting models of human community, using JPUSA as a case study. It is inevitable that the proponents of one model will on occasion suspect or misinterpret proponents of the other. It is remarkable that JPUSA has managed to preserve its covenantal goals and lifestyle in the face of an overwhelmingly contractual environment. This balancing act makes it a sociological gem of an example. It may represent the paradigm for successful communes of the future.

## BIBLIOGRAPHY

Bromley, D. G., & Busching, B. C. (1988). Understanding the structure of contractual and covenantal social relations: Implications for the sociology of religion. *Sociological Analysis, 49*, 15–32.

Bromley, D. G., & Shupe, A. (1979). *"Moonies" in America: Cult, church, and crusade.* Beverly Hills, CA: Sage.

Bromley, D. G., & Shupe, A. (1980). Financing the new religions: A resource mobilization approach. *Journal for the Scientific Study of Religion, 19* (September), 197–203.

Bromley, D. G., & Shupe, A. (1981). *Strange gods: The great American cult scare.* Boston: Beacon Press.

Bromley, D. G., & Shupe, A. (forthcoming). *Religions in resistance: Prophetic religion in a secular age.* New Brunswick, NJ: Rutgers University Press.

Enroth, R. M. (1992). *Churches that abuse.* Grand Rapids, MI: Zondervan.

Enroth, R. M. (1994). *Recovering from churches that abuse.* Grand Rapids, MI: Zondervan.

The Family. (1993). *An overview of our beliefs and practices as expressed in our statements.* [Brochure]. Zurich, Switzerland: World Services.

Fogarty, R. S. (1972). *American utopianism.* Itasca, IL: F. E. Peacock.

Jesus People USA. (1972). *JPUSA covenant.* Chicago: Jesus People USA.

Jesus People USA. (1991). *Meet our family.* [Brochure]. Chicago: Jesus People USA–Evangelical Covenant Church.

Kephart, W. M., & Zellner, W. W. (1991). *Extraordinary groups* (4th ed.). New York: St. Martin's Press.

Nordhoff, C. (1966). *The communistic societies of the United States.* New York: Dover. (First published 1875).

Noyes, J. H. (1966). *Strange cults & utopians of 19th-century America.* New York: Dover. (First published 1870).

Richardson, J. T. (Ed.). (1988). *Money and power in the new religions.* Lewiston, NY: Edwin Mellen Press.

Shupe, A., Busching, B., & Bromley, D. G. (1989). Modern American religious conflict. In J. B. Gittler, (Ed.). *The Annual Review of Conflict Knowledge and Conflict Resolution* (pp. 127–150). New York: Garland.

Shupe, A., & Trott J. (1995). Cobelligerents or co-opted? Sun Myung Moon's ties with conservatives and evangelicals. *Cornerstone, 23* (105), 36, 42–44.

Tönnies, F. (1957). *Community and society—gemeinschaft und gesellschaft* (C. P. Loomis, Trans.). East Lansing, MI: Michigan State University Press.

Trott, J. (1993). Life's lessons: A history of Jesus People USA Covenant Church, part one.'' *Cornerstone, 22* (102–103), 11–14, 16–18, 21.

Trott, J. (1994). Life's lessons: A history of Jesus People USA Covenant Church, part two.'' *Cornerstone, 23* (104), 19–23.

Trott, J. (1995a). Life's lessons: A history of Jesus People USA Covenant Church, part three. *Cornerstone, 23* (105), 38–41.

Trott, J. (1995b). Life's lessons: A history of Jesus People USA Covenant Church, part four. *Cornerstone, 23* (106), 43–46, 48.

Trott, J., & Hertenstein, M. (1992). Selling Satan. *Cornerstone, 21* (98), 7–19, 30.

Weber, M. (1947). *The theory of social and economic organization* (T. Parsons, Ed; A. M. Henderson & T. Parsons, Trans.). New York: Free Press.

Zellner, William W. (1995). *Countercultures: A sociological analysis.* New York: St. Martin's Press.

*Chapter 3*

# *The Farm*

## *Michael Traugot*

Michael Traugot, while enrolled at Harvard, was a leader of Students for a Democratic Society, a group adamantly opposed to existing political and economic policies. He moved to San Francisco after graduation in 1967 and became involved in the youth movement. His future wife, Myra, encouraged him to attend rap sessions led by Stephen Gaskin. The message there was simple: world peace could be achieved only by first finding peace within oneself and then living life as a positive social activist. In Gaskin's group he found purpose and social acceptance. The group journeyed to Tennessee to establish a communal, independent lifestyle. Michael was one of the founding members of the Farm and currently works as a psychological counselor. He has written *A Short History of The Farm* and has lived there since 1971.

A social movement is organized collective behavior aimed at changing or re-forming "social institutions" or the "social order" itself. Such a movement, viewed as a "revolution" by some and an "aberration" by others, surfaced among the "baby boom" generation of Americans, those born between 1947 and 1962.

After World War II, the blessings of a "middle-class lifestyle" had extended to a larger proportion of American citizens than ever before. Ironically, the white, middle-class baby boomers, those who had benefited most from these improved circumstances, became protesters. They experimented with an innovative lifestyle including longer hair, a different style of clothing, and new living arrangements with modified sexual roles.

Spiritual insights, aided by marijuana and other psychoactive substances, were explored. In the early 1960s, a large group of young people, called "hippies," flocked to San Francisco, looking for adventure and a new lifestyle. At the same time, practitioners of all sorts of Eastern religions, among them Hindu gurus and Buddhist Zen masters, were setting up shop in San Francisco next to new homegrown "religions" like Scientology and EST (Erhard Seminar Training). Esalen Institute, in Big Sur, was fast becoming famous for encounter groups and other exercises designed to explore the "true self." The pursuit of personal enlightenment and empowerment became a religion to many.

## ORIGINS OF THE MOVEMENT

Stephen Gaskin, one of the many individuals influenced by this tide of new ideas, was a little older than the baby boomers. Born in 1935, he grew up in the southwestern United States. A Marine veteran of the Korean War, he had earned a master's degree in creative writing and was teaching at San Francisco State College. Stephen watched many of his students leave school to live a different lifestyle. He followed them, drawn into the Age of Aquarius.

At his twenty-seventh birthday party, he experimented with marijuana. It opened new doors of consciousness for him. Soon he was tripping on LSD. Stephen found the "hippies" to be sweet, innocent, and naive, full of hope and energy, and easy prey to all kinds of manipulators. Concerned about this, he started teaching classes at the new Experimental College at San Francisco State. It included courses in all sorts of new subjects, some for credit and some not, mostly dictated by the interests of the students and faculty. His curriculum included major world religions, magic, telepathy, parapsychology, phenomena of the mind, sociology, and psychology. Among the titles of courses were "North American White Witchcraft," "Magic, Einstein, and God," "Group Experiments in Unified Field Theory," and "Meta PE."

During the next two years, enrollment in the classes grew, and soon they moved off campus. They also outgrew their titles, eventually becoming known simply as "Monday Night Class." It was the largest regularly occurring public meeting in the Bay Area, attracting between 1,000 and 1,500 people every week.

During these three years, Stephen increasingly became the counselor, role model, and minister to an evolving community of young adults. At one point he declared he would henceforth be a full-time "spiritual teacher," and he would continue in that position as long as the community was willing to support him. During these years, Stephen and his classes developed a philosophy of life that was to serve as the underpinnings of the community that followed.

The classes' most basic belief, "We Are All One," is an integral assumption of many religions. They concluded that every person is made of the same materials and in the same fashion as all other humans, all other life on Earth, and

Earth itself. The effort by individuals to relate to this "All" is a natural function of human existence. We are members of this church, whether we acknowledge it or not. "Your membership button is your belly button," Stephen would say. They believed all people have a "higher self," an extension of their earthly being. An individual out of touch with this self makes poor decisions and is insensitive to the needs of others. Making love and taking psychedelics can be exercises in learning to hear one's inner voice and expand one's consciousness to see things as they truly are. Real changes, the ones that make things better both in personal life and in the life of the community, stem from spiritual decisions.

Entire societies, like Nazi Germany, can lose touch with this reality. On the other hand, groups of people and entire cultures can sometimes reach a high spiritual level together and achieve miraculous results. In the 1960s, the civil rights movement accomplished much, and many people were inspired to action through the spiritual nonviolence of Martin Luther King. The community that sprang up around Stephen Gaskin grew directly out of this philosophy. It was a conscious, up-front agreement to try to better the world. Members further believed each person is a fountain of energy, a valve from which universal life energy is metered into the world. We can direct our energy toward whatever goal we want to achieve. We add life force to our surroundings.

The new religions were becoming increasingly popular, and by the summer of 1969, a "Holy Man Jam" was scheduled for Boulder, Colorado. Stephen was invited, along with various yogis, swamis, Zen masters, Sufis, and others. Many of his students traveled to Boulder to be at the Jam, and their experiences whetted their appetite for more travel.

Stephen was gaining a reputation among some liberal churches as one who could articulate the social and political changes going on among the young. In 1969, the American Academy of Religion held its annual meeting in San Francisco. When the delegates learned about Monday Night Class, many decided to attend. Impressed by what they saw, they invited Stephen to speak at various sites all over the United States. Stephen's family at the time included four adults, who were together in a "four-marriage," and two children.

Stephen and his family were living in a converted school bus. He thought he would adjourn the Class and make the tour. After a number of requests from students, he invited those who could arrange transportation and be self-supporting to accompany him on the road. The trip ballooned beyond anyone's expectations and came to be called the Caravan.

## THE CARAVAN

Some Class members owned homes on wheels, and now more of them wanted them. With Stephen's encouragement they bought secondhand buses for a few hundred dollars each. Beds were installed, shelves were built, toilets (wooden boxes with seats and buckets to be emptied) were nailed together and painted.

They learned to drive the buses as the Caravan progressed. People joined at many points along the route, far more than Stephen had anticipated. Eventually the Caravan grew to about 300 people. At its peak there were about 100 vehicles, many of them full-length school buses, sometimes carrying as many as 10 or 12 young people each. The Caravan spread out along the freeways, sometimes for 20 miles, driving slower than the rest of the traffic, the young people waving at everyone. It attracted a lot of attention. Besides accompanying Stephen, the Caravan's members had a mission to make peace between the generations. Stephen would talk to the crowds, often numbering several hundred, and members would mingle with the audience and discuss topics including sex, dope, rock 'n' roll, war, peace, age, and the environment. Stephen encouraged each Caravaner to visit his or her parents during the trip and try to personally "bridge the gap."

Rules were enforced. "If you're sleeping together, you're considered engaged, and if you're pregnant, you're considered married." Another rule prohibited accepting welfare, food stamps, or any other kind of public assistance. The Caravan was entirely self-supporting; members looked for work wherever they stopped. This proved to be very popular with the public. When the Caravan really did need help, people responded. The entire Caravan became stuck in a snowstorm in Nebraska, for example, and the members were given milk, eggs, and bread.

One of the greatest changes Stephen made in the interest of the "big picture" was to give up LSD. "I'm willing to have my name associated with pot," he said, "but not acid." This was quite a change for the man who had been known as the "acid guru," who had sworn that LSD had changed his life for the better. Other highlights of the Caravan were Sunday morning services at a National Grasslands in North Dakota and, two days after Christmas, at the Washington Monument. Only in Colorado did the Caravan run into locals who didn't like the idea of long-haired hippies camping in their neighborhood. They were treated badly. Stephen decided to end the trip early and drove back to California without stopping. The Caravan had taken four months and covered 7,000 miles.

## TENNESSEE

Once home, it was difficult for Caravan members to resume business as usual, even though they were mostly the same group of people who had begun the journey four months previously. The idea of going back to their "normal" lives was not exciting to Stephen or to many of his students. There had been talk for some time, even before the Caravan was formed, about getting land where they could live together, along the lines of the Buddhist or Hindu *ashram,* a spiritual community with a teacher. Stephen realized the time was ripe. There was a critical mass of young, energetic students, seasoned from their time on the road and eager to pursue their spiritual awakenings together.

They wanted to settle in the country, raise families, and continue to work toward changing the world for the better. Stephen knew it could not happen in California. Land prices were too high, and too many gurus and spiritual teachers were already plying their trade there.

Some Caravaners had met people from Nashville, Tennessee, who had been especially nice. Within two weeks of returning to the Bay Area, Stephen announced that a new Caravan would be leaving for Tennessee to seek land. The trip was completely open-ended. There was nothing solid to go on, just a few personal connections, plus Stephen's intuition and the spirit and energy of the young Caravaners. At the last Monday Night Class in California, Stephen said:

After services the Caravan's going to take off to Tennessee and get a farm. Because what you put your attention into you get more of, and I need more grass, more wheat, more soybeans, more healthy babies, more good-looking sane people, people that can work. That's why I want to go out and really get into it with the dirt.

Upon reaching Nashville, teams of Caravaners fanned out to different parts of Tennessee, looking for land. The media spread word of the group's intent, and many landowners were reluctant to sell. While shopping for a guitar, a group member met a woman in Nashville who owned land in Lewis County, one of the poorest and most backward rural counties in Tennessee. Impressed with their sincerity, she agreed to rent them her land for one dollar a year until they could find a permanent spot. The Caravan thanked her profusely and headed for Lewis County, about 65 miles from Nashville.

The land included 680 acres of hilly scrub oak and hickory on the western edge of the Highland Rim, a geological feature that surrounds the Nashville Basin. Folks in nearby Maury County—a phosphate-rich, much wealthier farming area—called the Summertown area "the Barrens." From camps and caves in the Barrens, highwaymen had raided inns on the Natchez Trace and waylaid farmers returning from New Orleans with gold after floating their goods to market. The most famous victim was the explorer Meriwether Lewis, who was murdered only seven miles from the Farm.

The Barrens was noted for its poor soil, its wild residents, its feuds, and its moonshining. While exploring the deep hollows, members of the Caravan sometimes found old barrels in the woods, remnants of moonshining operations. Besides moonshiners, the area contained a great many devout Christians, who viewed the new arrivals with suspicion. The group stayed at this farm for only seven months, but they were very eventful.

People from the surrounding area came to check out the new arrivals. Many were friendly, some were hostile, all were curious. Members of the Caravan spent a lot of time introducing themselves and explaining the philosophy of the group, where they came from, and how they intended to live. Many of the first people to visit the Farm at this crucial time have remained good friends of the community. Stephen continually emphasized that in contacts with neighbors, everyone should be treated with respect. He encouraged the Caravaners to speak for their values and explain why they were pacifists and vegetarians, why they believed in integration, and why they wore their hair long.

Stephen asked Leslie Hunt, another former Marine who had assisted him on the Caravan, to be in charge of security. Leslie recruited a crew who put up a barbed wire fence around the property and established a gate at the head of the new dirt road. The gate was manned 24 hours a day for the next 12 years both on the first farm and the present farm. During that time most of the men and women in the community did at least some "gate duty."

The neighbors laughed at the fence. One rumor going around was that it was "mating season" on the Farm, and the fence was to ensure privacy as the hippies went about their "business." In some ways this was true. The settlers were mostly in their early twenties, and though some neighbors may have envisioned orgies, many couples were getting together and starting families. Within a year, the first wave of the Farm's "baby boom" was taking place. Within four years, half of the Farm's population consisted of children. Several hundred of these early Farm children are now in their late teens or early twenties, and some of them are starting families of their own.

The rule from the Caravan, "If you're sleeping together you're engaged, and if you're pregnant you're married," carried over to the Farm. Marriage was accomplished in a very traditional way, with a marriage license and a minister. Stephen found all that was necessary to be a minister in Tennessee was a congregation and services. He became the minister. To those few Farm folk who objected to the licenses, he said, "If you're willing to tell the universe that you want to stay together, you might as well tell the county." This was part of the Farm's becoming a "real" place, or, as Stephen put it, "Utopia with a zip code."

There had been a few babies born on the Caravan, and Ina May Gaskin, who was part of Stephen's "four-family" (and is still his wife and partner), had assumed the important and challenging task of becoming community midwife. Born and raised in Iowa, Ina May had earned a master's degree in English, and had served two years in the Peace Corps in Malaysia. She taught herself midwifery from scratch and practiced the art with some assistance, at crucial times, from various doctors.

It was determined that midwifery was unregulated by state law in Tennessee. State officials "gave us a stack of birth certificates and a stack of death certificates and told us we were on our own," Stephen related later. Ina May found a local physician who was willing to help and advise the community. His experiences included delivering babies for the Amish community located a few miles from the Farm. He was very knowledgeable about home birth without anesthesia and high-tech intervention. With the physician's help, Ina May and her assistants developed a tremendously successful midwifery program that is still operating in 1998.

## THE FIRST GARDEN

As soon as possible, a garden was started. This was perhaps the best garden in the entire history of the Farm, and certainly the most intensively tilled. The settlers had been waiting to get their hands into the soil for some time. Many of them had been carrying trays of seedlings on their buses. Beds were carved out of the sod by hand; manure and rock fertilizers were turned under. Every lump of hardpan clay was broken up.

The crops were all a great success. Plenty of rain and the fact that the soil hadn't been farmed for some time helped. This first garden started a tradition of community farming that continued well into the middle years of the Farm.

Besides gardening, the settlers capped a spring and installed a pump, the beginning of a water system. They constructed a small building for food storage and distribution, and erected sheds, tents, and shacks. They soon found themselves in demand as workers in the local economy, planting and picking pimiento peppers and doing other agricultural work, as well as construction. This gave them the chance to earn much-needed revenue. Many Tennesseans met the Farm this way, and in general, the Farm made a good impression.

The area around the Farm was still primarily an agricultural area, but it was starting to change. Many of the local young people were seeking work in town, leaving the rural older generation without enough help. The Farm fit right into that niche. In the first years, neighbors taught apprentice Farm folks much about farming, logging, building, and just about anything one could do for a living in rural Tennessee. Until the garden began to produce, a wild vegetable crew was organized to keep the settlement in greens. There were abundant supplies of lamb's quarters, purslane, and poke salad scattered across the countryside, and watercress grew in many of the local streams. There was trouble, however, when the members of the group unknowingly picked watercress downstream from an outhouse. The result was a hepatitis epidemic that left about one-third of the group sick for up to several weeks. Somehow the group managed to survive this epidemic and other obstacles—rain, sometimes hostile neighbors, and the generally primitive level of resources. This was partly due to the fact that they were mostly young adults with lots of energy and few children, and partly a tribute to their idealism and dedication. These settlers were serious. Many of them could have been enjoying a much higher standard of living with their parents, or as college students.

The leadership of Stephen and Ina May was crucial at this point, inspiring and rallying everyone to the cause. The Farm was like a heart transplant, Stephen said, and for a while there was some doubt about whether it would be accepted into the body of Middle Tennessee, or rejected. The single event that most threatened to trigger rejection had to do with one of the Farm's agricultural ventures.

## BUSTED

Among the flora lovingly carried to Tennessee in the buses were some marijuana plants. After all, this was a self-styled "grass church." Members depended upon marijuana for insight, for ceremonial purposes, and to enhance lovemaking. The group was generally against dealing pot, however. Stephen and the group felt that if money was not exchanged for pot, then pot could be distinguished from the hard drugs peddled by gangland types. Also, in using a substance as a sacrament, as an aid to consciousness, they believed one absorbed some of the karma of those who produced and distributed it. Now that they were on their own land in the country, Farm folks wanted to grow their own.

One day in late August 1971, a raid took place. Pot crew members who went out to tend the crop were arrested. The main force arrived at the gate, police cars along with television camera crews, and what followed was one of the friendliest pot busts on record.

Farm members, alerted to the situation, massed around the main road and watched a line of police cars drive slowly down to the garden meadow. They smiled and waved at the police and at the TV cameras. Someone got out of a press car, stuck a microphone in front of Stephen and, asked him, "Are you growing pot here?" Stephen replied, with a grin, "Who, me?" and directed the cameras' attention to the okra patch, six feet tall and loaded with flowers, to the cucumbers, and to the tomatoes. The police took Stephen to his bus and questioned him, and Stephen admitted he knew the pot was being grown. He and those arrested in the patch were taken to be booked. By telling the truth, admitting that he knew about the pot, Stephen established a reputation for telling the truth that served the Farm well in the future. Even today, if the police or FBI inquire about someone at the Farm and are told that person is not there, they go no further.

A local landowner had come to Stephen shortly before the bust and offered to sell the group 1,000 acres adjacent to the land they were renting. It was mostly covered with scruffy oak and hickory that had been logged several times over. Nevertheless, it did have about 300 acres of cleared fields right down the middle of the property.

With the acquisition of the land, settlers knew they had a big job ahead. They were going to have to build the infrastructure of a community from scratch while bringing in enough money to keep the operation afloat in a backwoods area of underemployment. They would accomplish this while hosting visitors and adding new members. The feeling of "community" was never lost in the process.

Meanwhile, Stephen and the Farm's legal crew managed to postpone jail on the marijuana conviction for two years, appealing the case all the way to the United States Supreme Court. During this time, the groundwork was laid that would keep the enterprise going during Stephen's absence, and through the years of tremendous growth that occurred after his return.

## THE FARM FAMILY

Some have observed that the Farm family structure looked remarkably like that of traditional America, and there is some truth to that. Most of the Farm families have always been one-couple families or single parents with kids. Even the four-marriages, for which the early Farm was famous, extended to only a small portion of the population. These were not just "swingin'" or "swappin'," but serious attempts at a new, more inclusive kind of family. The four adults considered themselves married in all ways, including raising and providing for all their children, and were sexually faithful to each other. They purposely varied sexual partners to "split fields," to get to know both opposite-sex partners as well as possible. They were expected to be very close to their same-sex partner through sharing and "manifesting together" as a team.

Marriage was taken seriously at the Farm. Ceremonies took place on Sunday mornings, in front of the entire congregation, which usually included most of the adult members of the community. Vows were simple: "... for better or for worse, for richer or for poorer, in sickness and in health, as long as we both shall live." The energy glowed at those marriages. The combined attention of 200 folks in a worshipful mood, after meditating silently for 45 minutes and singing a long "chant" together, was like bonding with everyone present. The community protected marriage in various ways; couples were given a lot of help and advice in sorting out their relationships, and those who allowed themselves to become romantically involved with someone else's spouse could wind up having to leave the community for 30 days.

Farm family life was different, however, from that of most Americans. The Farm was like a large extended family. Sometimes mothers would nurse each other's babies, blurring the line a little between the nuclear family and the "clan" or "tribe." Children were cared for in groups known as "kid herds," different adults taking turns watching them. In this atmosphere, the kids seemed to bond with each other, and many of the children who grew up on the Farm are still interacting closely with each other.

Most Farm families lived in housing units with several other persons. Households got as large as 60 people. Often a makeshift arrangement—a central building containing a living room, kitchen, and bathroom—was surrounded by satellite bedrooms—a bus, a van, a small cabin. There were no flush toilets initially—in fact, no running water to homes for quite some time. Especially at first, with no electricity, no TV, and hardly any radio, visiting, playing music together, and related activities were quite popular. Consequently, the children of Farm folks had a feeling of being part of a much larger identity group.

In later years, these living patterns changed, partly for economic reasons. Growing families needed more space. Families became directly responsible for their financial upkeep and got to spend their own money. They became more independent. Each family had different needs and work schedules. Many people living together in a single household became inefficient. Houses that used to serve many individuals became single-family dwellings, and kids were raised in a more conventional manner, going to school while their parents went to work.

## SEX AND REPRODUCTION

Sexual behavior on the Farm appeared unorthodox, especially at the beginning, when most of the women didn't wear bras and everyone seemed to emulate the image of the "loose hippy," with long hair, colorful clothes, and a disarming openness. In reality, it was a lot of couples roughly the same age getting together, marrying, and starting families.

Sex wasn't just for reproduction, but was for meditation and ecstasy, the achievement of a state of openness and grace. Like birth and death, lovemaking was considered a holy sacrament, to be practiced with as few distractions as possible. Thus, sexual union was a time for cleansing oneself of psychic debris, making the subconscious conscious, and dealing with any disagreements the couple may have had during the day. This promoted solid marriages. Hence, making love was at the core of the community.

At one point early in the Farm's existence, Ina May called a women's meeting to talk about sex. Some of the men had been complaining that their partners were holding back. Ina May encouraged the women to try to satisfy their men—assuming, of course, the men had been considerate and supportive—because that would make for happier families, better relationships, and a more harmonious community. Approximately nine months after this meeting, there was a definite surge in the population of the Farm, a mini baby boom.

A little later, Ina May convened another meeting, this time to talk about birth control. Since chemical and mechanical means were not acceptable, the topics included various methods of achieving satisfaction apart from intercourse. Cuddling and oral sex were alternatives.

## NATURAL BIRTH CONTROL

Several of the Farm women asked Margaret Nofziger, a nutrition expert, to find a method of birth control that would be acceptable to the community. Following some leads she had been given by an infertility specialist, Margaret developed a method of determining when a woman is fertile and when she is not. This method included keeping track of a woman's cycles (the "rhythm method"), recording her basal body temperature every morning before rising, and checking cervical mucus at various times during the month. Margaret's book, *A Cooperative Method of Natural Birth Control*, published in 1976, has sold 700,000 copies and has been translated into six languages. Some of the biggest purchasers were the Catholic Church, Planned Parenthood, and the federal government's family planning division. Her method was widely adopted by Farm couples who were interested in birth control.

The midwives emphasized the mother's participation in the birth process.

They also made sure basic dietary and medical information circulated around the community. Nearly all the children born on the Farm were born at home without anesthetic, were breast-fed, and were raised as vegetarians. Most of these kids were taught an intensive sex education course when they were older. At the time, all these things were very progressive.

## HEALTH CARE

The Farm's health care service, developed in a frontier situation, predated some of the ideas suggested today by leading medical reformers. The emphasis was on prevention, good diet, exercise, and the elimination of bad habits. Primary medical care was handled at the grassroots level. Physicians were consulted for serious problems. Midwifery is a good example. It provided cheap, quality care in a low-tech environment. The key to this system was effective screening, knowing which cases to refer to more highly trained personnel.

## GENDER ROLES

Early on, the Farm developed fairly traditional gender roles, but not because of ideology. Many of the women wanted to spend time with their small children. Consequently, they chose jobs that allowed them to see their children during the day. From the very beginning, however, women held important positions on the Farm. They were midwives and clinicians, and some were involved in the financial affairs of the community. While attitudes varied among families, the men usually tried to do their share of the housework, many of them enjoying quality time with their babies and young children. As the children have grown older and more independent, many women have found employment in town. Their decisions are made on the basis of job availability and individual preference rather than of rigid sex roles. And today, quite a few of the Farm businesses are headed by women.

Each Farm household functioned as a team. People took turns doing the dishes, cleaning, and cooking meals. They used the advantage of numbers to get things done. Members of both sexes covered for each other, took care of the kids while others went to work, built additions, and made improvements in their ''spare'' time. For the first few years, there wasn't running water in the houses, and electricity was provided by car batteries. Lighting was by kerosene or a few small car lightbulbs. Direct AC power was run only to the public workplaces: the laundry, the motor pool, the construction offices, and other Farm businesses and facilities.

## ECONOMY

The Farm was entirely communal for the first 12 years of its existence. All income went into a central bank. It was spent according to need. Food was bought or grown and distributed equally, one share per person. Pregnant women, nursing mothers, children, the infirm, and people on the "skinny list" were often given special portions. Someone who needed money for something personal or for a work crew went to the bank and made a request. Decisions on which requests to honor were mostly made by the Bank Lady, with some help from the bank crew, Stephen, the heads of Farm work crews, and occasionally by the entire community in an open meeting. The method changed as the Farm grew and evolved.

The Farm was granted nonprofit standing by the Internal Revenue Service, which allowed the group to pool income but did not allow them to receive tax-deductible donations. This meant that from the start, the Farm would depend entirely upon the efforts and resources of its members. All the assets of the Farm were held in common, and all the income of the Farm was distributed among the members equally for tax purposes. If the total income rose to a level where each share was over the threshold of taxable income, then the community had to pay. In the 12 years this practice was followed, the income level never came close to the taxable threshold.

Work crews, the other significant organizational unit of the community besides the household, could be as large as 50 persons. They took care of business on the Farm and worked for income outside the community.

At first Stephen appointed the heads of crews. These straw bosses would meet from time to time to plan strategies and compare notes. Usually there was an overall "Farm straw boss" who organized the crews. As the Farm grew, Stephen had less to do with the daily operations. Decisions were made by combinations of the Farm straw boss and other crew chiefs. This tendency continued, and by the time the Farm reached its peak population in 1980, there was quite an elaborate bureaucracy that managed the work of several hundred individuals.

## INCOME

Two of the main sources of income for the Farm were construction and book publishing. Income from both was irregular. The Book Publishing Company had hits in *The Big Dummy's Guide to CB Radio*, *A Cooperative Method of Natural Birth Control*, and *Tofu Cookery*, as well as a steady long-term seller in *Spiritual Midwifery*. However, in between, it could only pay for the labor of its personnel. It takes a while for a publishing company to issue enough titles to make a steady profit, and The Book Publishing Company today, still community-owned, is starting to achieve that status. Revenues from construction varied according to the local and national economy; high interest rates or a recession hurt the Farm's construction business. At times the Farm Building Company had high profits, and at other times there was barely enough work to keep a small crew occupied.

Other moneymakers, including a painting crew and Farm Hands, a labor pool that sought jobs of every description, made money, but income varied according to season and economic conditions. The farming crew brought in quite a bit of money through sales of produce, but most of that had to go back into the farming operation. The real benefit was the food they grew. In season there were abundant vegetables and fruits, and even in winter there was usually something homegrown in the diet, depending upon how much the community had managed to preserve that year. It would be difficult to estimate the total value of the food produced by the farming crew, but in terms of bringing dollars into the community, agriculture did not prove to be a big moneymaker.

The absence of seed money to buy state-of-the-art equipment resulted in the workers struggling with old or jury-rigged machinery. It was necessary to make up for the lack of mechanical advantage by expending extra human effort. Another problem preventing crews from making sustained progress was that no crew got to keep its own income. All money went through the common bank and was apportioned according to need in the community.

The community was growing fast, taking on new people and new projects, and there was always an acute need somewhere. A crew chief might request some of the money the crew turned in to the bank, but there was no guarantee the crew would get it back. Some of this hardship led to great innovation. Farm folks developed a rough-and-ready, hands-on attitude that served them well.

Farm people, though mostly from cities and without much prior trade experience, managed to build an entire community from scratch: houses, businesses, public buildings, water system, swimming hole, sound stage, recording studio, radio station, clinic, food-processing areas, machine shop, motor pool, and junkyard. Much of the construction was done with salvaged materials.


## SPIRITUAL LIFE

Sunday morning services were the focal point of the Farm's spiritual life and, for many individuals, the highlight of the week. They were regarded as a chance to relax and open up, reflect on the cares of the week and then transcend them, to touch base with the rest of the community. Just about everybody attended services, the adults taking turns staying home and baby-sitting. Originally services were held at sunrise, as they had been in San Francisco, but after a while they were changed to a later hour to give people who rose early every day and worked hard a chance to stay in bed. Services took place outdoors whenever possible. After meditating silently for an hour or so, the entire group chanted a long, powerful "om," and, after another short silence, Stephen would speak.

He usually started with a lecture on some topic of spiritual interest that was relevant to what was happening on the Farm or in the world at the time. For many, this was a chance to catch up on the global aspects of the Farm, which was gaining a reputation worldwide for its programs and lifestyle. Members were encouraged to comment, add to the discussion, and bring up their own topics. Sometimes the meetings were more down-to-earth and material, focusing on specific problems or challenges facing the community.

## DIET

Most Boomers had been brought up on the standard four food groups. Many Americans now recognize this diet as being weighted very heavily toward the consumption of high-cholesterol meat and dairy products. Today many people in the United States are vegetarians, and many fast-food restaurants now offer vegetarian options. The Farm helped bring these changes about by disseminating, through its publishing company, information on a vegetarian lifestyle and by demonstrating how to raise healthy children on a nonanimal diet. The primary reason the Farm developed a vegetarian diet, however, was efficiency. Far more vegetarians than meat-eaters can be fed on an acre of land, and it is less harmful to the environment.

The Farm built a soy dairy and developed an original recipe for soy ice cream called Ice Bean, which is marketed under that name. Farm people also are part of the wave of development of new sources of protein, including mushrooms and yeast. In addition to innovation in food, the Farm pioneered solar home construction, use of wind power, radiation detection, solar-powered radios, and other technology.

## EDUCATION: THE FARM SCHOOL

The Farm school grew from a one-room schoolhouse with a few kids to a bustling school with over 350 students. In some ways the school was mainstream. There were regularly scheduled classes, homework assignments, and letter grades. But there were also differences. It was much friendlier than most public schools. Students knew teachers from the community, and called them by their first names. Classes included conventional academic studies but emphasized the visual and performing arts to a greater extent. Teachers tried to offer as much hands-on experience as possible, including frequent field trips. The Farm high school was especially innovative, with an emphasis on apprenticeships and real-world experiences. High schoolers attended classes in the mornings and worked in the afternoons. They learned to grow food, repair cars, provide health care, construct buildings, and operate ham radios, video equipment, and an FM radio station.

## RECRUITING

The Farm continued the mission of the Caravan: to rally the baby boom generation to create new ways of living and get straight with the older generation so that, together, they could work toward ending war, poverty, and environmental destruction. To help spread these ideas, the Farm had transcribed the audio tapes of the Monday Night Class meetings. It sold 100,000 copies. These sales had provided a significant portion of the money necessary to move the

Caravan and to keep the early Farm afloat. They had also provided the foundation for The Book Publishing Company.

Another recruiting method was for Stephen to go on speaking tours. He was in demand after the Caravan, and received offers to speak all over the country. Stephen took the first of many road trips in the fall of 1972. These trips exposed many people, especially those of college age, to Stephen personally and to the Farm philosophy. These and other recruiting efforts resulted in rapid expansion of the Farm. From an initial population of about 300 in 1971, the Farm grew to approximately 600 in 1974, 1,200 in 1978, and a peak of 1,400 in 1980. In 1998 the population is about 250.

## THE GATE

All visitors and aspiring members had to pass through the gate. The Farm attracted over 10,000 visitors per year during the mid-1970s, which was ten times the average population of the community. A gate crew of five or six welcomed visitors and introduced them to Farm philosophy. Any visitor who was not overtly hostile could stay for a day or two. Visitors were expected to work alongside Farm crews. In exchange they received three vegetarian meals per day, a place to sleep, and, usually, a shower.

Prospective members learned what to expect if they joined: hard work, no cigarettes or alcohol, no weapons or violence, no sexual ''hunting'' or harassment, and no ownership of property. Members could keep their tools, musical instruments, and clothes, but nothing as large as a car; that would become community property. Also, members had to agree to be Stephen's spiritual students.

Having declared that they might want to live on the Farm, prospective members became ''soakers'' who got to stay around and ''soak it up.'' Soakers lived on the Farm just like members, finding out through participation what the community was like. They met regularly for ''soakers' meetings.'' At first, Stephen ran these meetings personally. He would ask the soakers if they were ready to join. Each new member made a personal agreement with Stephen to be his student, as well as an agreement with the community to be peaceful, work hard, and be helpful in every way possible.

The Farm attracted many new members through its midwifery program. It offered pregnant women a choice. For those considering abortion, the Farm promised to deliver the baby, keep him or her with Farm foster parents, and give the child back if the mother changed her mind. The promises, of course, were based on the community's ability to give effective services. This offer attracted hundreds of women, and the midwives figure that, over the years, the Farm gave over $1 million worth of free birthing services.

The Farm constantly had to differentiate between itself and other communities that practiced either violence or some form of brainwashing. The policy was always ''The gate swings out easier than it swings in.'' No one was ever kept on the Farm against his or her will. If parents showed up at the gate to see their child, gate crew members immediately summoned him or her. The Farm would not take in runaways, and harbored no fugitives knowingly. Runaways were told to call their parents. If someone showed up who was in trouble with his draft board, the gate crew would tell him to clear it up and then join the community. This policy created goodwill with police and the local FBI office.

## PLENTY

By 1974 the Farm was doing well. New, strong, talented young people were flocking in. A few good crop years in Tennessee helped, and the local economy supported many Farm workers. In accordance with the Farm philosophy, Stephen and others decided to launch a charitable relief and development organization to help people whose needs were greater than their own. Called Plenty and chartered as a charitable organization, it was able to receive tax-free donations for its projects.

Plenty started locally. A tornado in northern Alabama caused much damage. The Farm, hearing about it and having many laborers on hand, sent a busload of people to help. On other occasions, neighbors needed help and the Farm responded. The Farm clinic was already helping neighbors in need—this was a medically underserved area. Plenty solicited volunteers and raised funds for these kinds of projects.

## GUATEMALA

In 1976, a devastating earthquake hit Guatemala. Power sources were cut, and the only news out of the country came through independent ham radio operators. The Farm had been training radio operators, and some of them became involved in the initial efforts to get news out of the stricken area. Canadians soon donated a shipload of plywood and other materials for rebuilding, but they supplied no laborers. The Farm had large crews of carpenters, and this seemed like the perfect opportunity to participate in international relief and development. Plenty volunteers were soon headed for Guatemala.

This became one of the most spectacular and successful of Plenty's projects. The group's services branched out from construction to include agriculture, nutrition education, primary health care, and development of sources of clean water. At one time the Farm had over 100 volunteers working in Guatemala, all of them supported by charitable donations. The money didn't come from the Farm, but the personnel did.

Many of the Guatemalans who had come to be known by Farm people were killed in the government repression that raged in Guatemala throughout the 1970s and 1980s. At one point, Plenty folks helped some Guatemalans construct and operate the first native-language radio station in Guatemala. The government closed it down and machine-gunned the people who were operating the station.

Plenty left Guatemala in 1980, not because the projects were finished but because of the danger to its personnel and to Guatemalans directly associated with them.

## AGRICULTURE ON THE FARM

Agriculture on the Farm went through several stages. The first year's garden, very labor-intensive, proved that more efficient means of food production would be necessary to support the community. A vigorous discussion ensued about how this should be done. One group held that the operation should use only natural fertilizers and cover crops, avoiding the use of chemicals and poisonous sprays. This meant the operation would be small, because there wasn't enough organic fertilizer available to treat huge numbers of acres. The other camp wanted to grow enough food to feed the entire Farm, plus some to sell. In general, they wanted to plant as many acres as possible, using chemical fertilizers and sprays. Through compromise, a hybrid farming operation developed. Both tractor power and horsepower were utilized. Chemical sprays and fertilizers were used in conjunction with manure and cover crops. During the next few years, the program grew in size and efficiency, covering a significant portion of the food needs of the Farm.

The Farm often sent small crews to different parts of the country, especially to parts of the South, to earn money. Some farming crew members visiting Florida reported that vegetables and fruits could be grown all winter in south Florida. The community decided to farm in Tennessee in the summer and Florida in the winter, keeping a small crew active during the off-season in each area. It was an ambitious project, eventually growing to well over 100 Farm people living in at least three locations around Homestead, Florida, farming hundreds of acres, working for other farmers, and doing construction work. There were many positive aspects to the Florida Farm, winter vegetables and contacts for Plenty being two of them. Financially, however, the Florida excursion was a disaster. Farming in the Homestead region was risky. To compete, farmers would invest as much as possible to plant as many acres as they could. If the crops did well, the price of the produce would fall. If it was a poor year, the price of the produce would be high but there was little yield. The Farm, with limited capital and machinery, would have to borrow money to plant, and if a good crop ensued, they could not compete with their neighbors who were highly mechanized. If the crop was poor, there was no money to pay off the loss.

## CHANGES IN GOVERNMENT

Throughout the early years, the conviction of Stephen and three others for growing marijuana hung over the community. A legal crew, including two lawyers who were Farm residents, was formed to handle the case. The case was appealed to the Federal District Court, where the convictions were upheld, and then to the United States Supreme Court. Their case was based on the rights of United States citizens to practice their religion in peace. The precedent was a decision permitting the Native American Church to use peyote in its religious ceremonies. Since the Supreme Court refused to hear the case, it became inevitable that Stephen and the others would go to jail.

In Stephen's absence the Farm underwent a gradual transition from "charismatic leadership" to a "rational system" of government. The Farm straw boss and the group of crew bosses who had kept things going while Stephen was in prison continued in that capacity after his return. They came to be called the Board of Directors. As the Farm ballooned in population and complexity, government functions grew increasingly formal. It became more difficult to keep track of the cash flow, and accurate records were not always kept. After the Florida farming disaster, the board of directors gained control over all the checkbooks on the Farm. They assembled a picture of ongoing projects and the debt the Farm faced. As a community the Farm had a yearly cash flow that grew from approximately $125,000 in 1971 to approximately $1,000,000 in 1975. At the same time overall debt rose to approximately $600,000. They determined the Farm needed a net income of $10,000 per week to cover the bills. Throughout the years, the Farm's weekly income had ranged between $6,000 and $8,000.

## ECONOMIC CRISIS

Although several factors contributed to the Farm's worsening financial situation, the main problem was that too many ongoing projects stretched resources too thin. The Farm continued to expand membership, including people who needed help, while simultaneously supporting Plenty projects and a multiplicity of functions on the home front.

Another important factor was the deterioration of the national and local economies during this period. The Farm was largely self-sufficient in meeting food needs, but income from its businesses declined. The passage of time also was playing a major role. Originally the community was seen as an experiment, a project to help the world. Now the focus shifted to raising children. Many members felt they needed more space and more resources to care for families adequately. Along with all this came a loss of confidence by many members in Stephen's judgment and his ability to lead the community. Competition between groups over scarce resources developed: between Plenty and the Farm, between individual households, between projects. At one point, it was a choice between providing running water to the residents of one area of the Farm or putting in a cable communication system for the community. The cable system got priority—communication was determined to be more important than basic conveniences—a decision that caused bitterness among the folks who didn't get running water. The hardy pioneers who had hung together over 7,000 miles on the Caravan, faced down and befriended angry and suspicious neighbors, and birthed babies in buses, were becoming tired of poverty conditions they did not seem able to overcome. The lack of opportunities and basic services prompted many people to leave. In addition, some needed to go on with their careers, live nearer their parents, or live in a different climate. Primarily they left for economic reasons. The Farm population, in a six-year period, declined over 70 percent.

## THE CHANGEOVER

The community was seriously looking for a different way to manage its finances. Seeking a financial solution, the board of directors suggested that each adult member pay monthly dues. The amount, to be established at budget meetings at which all qualified members voted, would go primarily toward debt reduction. The remainder would be used for basic community necessities: roads, the water system, and taxes. All other expenditures would have to be voted into the budget by the members. Each member would have to be self-supporting. Anyone unable or unwilling to pay the monthly dues would have to leave. This was a radical change from the communal arrangements of the preceding 12 years, but after much discussion, the plan was overwhelmingly adopted by the community. The plan did preserve some of the Farm's communal nature. The land and other assets of the community were still held in common. The fact that each family was now on its own led, not unexpectedly, to another exodus.

The changeover put many people in a shaky position. Those who had worked in jobs taking care of the community were now jobless because the communal economy could no longer support their positions. These included clinic personnel, midwives, and schoolteachers—in short, functionaries the community had considered extremely important. Those who wanted to stay had to figure out how to do so as individual families in a depressed rural economy. Many Farm members now had to go to school or take entry-level jobs, doing what most other Americans their age had already done.

People daily left the place in which they had invested a significant portion of their lives, taking with them their experiences but no material wealth. It was a difficult time for many, both emotionally and financially. Individuals and families found different solutions to new challenges. Many Farm services were turned into private businesses: the clinic, the motor pool, the Farm store, the soy dairy, the bakery, and the school. The Ice Bean business was sold to some departing members, the electronics business was sold to some of its workers, and The Book Publishing Company found an investor and reorganized, with the community maintaining ownership.

A popular and successful solution for many was nurse training. The local community college had an excellent two-year Registered Nursing program. Many of the women, who had worked for the Farm clinic, enrolled in this program. Some took out loans or got help from their parents. They all did well in the program, and most of them are now employed as health professionals.

Even today, a considerable percentage of Farm members live close to the official poverty line. Many don't have health insurance. Nonetheless, the Farm today has the overall appearance of prosperity. There are quite a few successful businesses, and a bunch of healthy-looking teenagers and young adults, raised on the Farm, are obviously well-fed and intelligent. Former members returning for visits often comment on how good everything looks. The remaining members have managed to stretch their resources, live cheaply, and organize themselves to make the best of their situation. Despite the abruptness of the changeover, and the population loss, the Farm people managed to pay off the total debt of $1,200,000 in a little more than three years, securing the land for themselves and for the future.

## THE FARM TODAY

About 250 people lived on the Farm in 1996, roughly half of them under 21 years of age. About 120 adults comprise the voting membership. At an open town meeting, a simple majority of voting members determines an annual budget. The land and assets are still held communally, whereas individual members own their personal possessions and the value of any improvements they have made to their dwellings since the changeover.

To rejoin the community, former members must undergo a six-month provisional membership—it's twelve months for new people—and then be voted in by two-thirds of the current voting members. A joining fee of $3,000 per adult has been set for both new and returning members. The primary requirement—that one have a means of making a living—is still difficult to enforce in rural Tennessee. Members must pay dues and follow other community rules, including the agreement to be nonviolent. Stephen and Ina May Gaskin continue to live on the Farm, where their status is that of any other member. Stephen writes for a national magazine and goes on the lecture circuit, talking about the 1960s, the Farm, and what has happened since its establishment.

Ina May has continued as a leader in the midwifery movement, through public appearances and her quarterly journal, *The Birth Gazette*. She is active in national and state midwifery organizations, and was invited to testify before Hillary Rodham Clinton's health reform task force. She practices midwifery with the Farm Midwifery Center. Ina May is also widely known for handling "difficult" births, like breeches, twins, and shoulder presentations. Her instructional videos of such cases are used by midwifery and medical schools. Recently the Farm Midwifery Center's statistics for almost 2,000 births over a period of 24 years were published in the *Journal of the American Public Health Association* and the *Journal of Family Practice*. More than half of the births were for non-Farm residents. Over 95 percent were done at home. More than 98 percent were accomplished without anesthesia. The cesarean rate was 1.7 percent, whereas the national average is over 20 percent.

Most of the several thousand individuals who are estimated to have lived at the Farm have gone on to other pursuits. Farm people are deeply involved in the midwifery movement in all parts of the country. One man owns a company that manufactures solar and hybrid electric cars. Another sells solar equipment throughout the Caribbean area, and several install communications equipment in the Caribbean and in Central America. Several Farm folks were involved with the *Whole Earth Catalog*. The WELL, a popular computer network, was started by Farm people. One Farm person is a leader in interactive learning videos, and several are inventing ever more sensitive and useful electronic devices. A few are writers, and there are at least 20 physicians who have lived on the Farm; many of them had their first contact with the health professions in the Farm's health care program. Several Farm people have earned their law degrees, and one has opened an environmental law practice in Oregon. Many of the best practicing tie-dye artists in the country are Farm-trained. One person runs a popular vegetarian café in Florida and does radio call-in shows about diet, the environment, and related topics.

## THE FARM IN RETROSPECT

Ferdinand Tönnies, writing in the nineteenth century, felt that communities— homogeneous, tight-knit groups, largely rural, and based on kinship and common beliefs—were genuine expressions of group life. As such, they met basic human needs for interpersonal interaction and belonging. Such *gemeinschaft* societies, according to Tönnies, were dominated by community themes. *Gesellschaft* societies, in contrast, were predicated on artificial social arrangements created by specialization, and emphasized individualism and competition.

The Farm was an attempt by young persons in the 1960s to recapture the essence of a gemeinschaft community. They rejected the emphasis, prevalent in America in the 1950s and 1960s, on individual competition, success, and acquiring material possessions. To this end, they established an "intentional" community emphasizing interpersonal relationships formed along noncompetitive, communal lines. As the Farm grew, specialization was necessary to perform the multiplicity of tasks efficiently. The resulting division of labor dissolved the bonds of the community, creating competition among individuals and families. The Farm people had been forced by circumstance to abandon their relational emphasis, and the financial survival of individual nuclear families became the focus of attention. One of the most commonly heard statements during and after the changeover, as many Farm people cut their hair, shaved, and sent their kids to public school, was "I didn't want to be so different from the rest of the society."

In the short span of 25 years, Farm people have gone on a dizzying ride from capitalism to communism and back; from a first-world economy to a third-world economy and back; and from society to community and back. Yet things are not as they were before the Farm. Almost universally, people who have lived on the Farm report that it changed their lives for the better. The fact that the Farm still exists, that the networks still exist, and that people still are working for the causes they believed in over a generation ago attests to the sticking power of idealism, of working together. If the Farm's purpose from the start was to provide a graceful, long-term lifestyle on one piece of land for all who lived there, then it could be said the early Farm had failed to reach its goal. It took the changeover, plus most of the people leaving, to approach that. On the other hand, if the purpose was to promote new ideas, form bonds with many individuals, stimulate interest in positive social change, and have a real impact on the culture, then the Farm has been a definite success.

# Chapter 4

# The Love Family: Its Formative Years

### Robert W. Balch

Rob Balch's first contact with the Love Family came in 1979, at a gathering designed to promote world peace. A visit to their ranch north of Seattle the following year further heightened his interest in the group, one of the most successful communes in the United States at that time. He investigated them over the next several years and discovered that they were undergoing tumultuous change. His relationship with the Love Family deteriorated quickly in 1985, after he sent Love Israel a draft of a paper he had written about the community. The situation illustrates a problem common in fieldwork. When group members allow a sociologist to study them, they expect the researcher to reciprocate by portraying the group in a positive light. If that does not happen, resulting hard feelings can spell the end of the relationship. "To the Love Family's credit, however, the door is still open," Rob notes.

I first saw the Love Family at a Rainbow Gathering in 1979. The location, a high, forested plateau in Arizona, could be reached only by a three-mile hike over a hot, dusty trail. Rainbow Gatherings had been held every year since 1972, when a small group of hippies, who later became the Rainbow Family, organized a celebration for world peace high in the Colorado Rockies.

In 1979 almost 10,000 people attended the Gathering. It was a colorful, chaotic collage of tepees, sweat lodges, trading circles, and outrageous characters wearing beads, feathers, tie-dyed shirts, or nothing at all. The days were filled with informal workshops on Rolfing, past-life regression, rebirthing, massage, and dozens of other New Age topics. Each night the air reverberated with the primitive, tribal sounds of drumming that lasted well into the wee hours of the morning. At times the entire encampment overflowed with love and brotherhood, but the mood could change in an instant. A single incident, like the time a Navajo man accused the hippies of being make-believe Indians, could make the harmony evaporate faster than a puddle in the Arizona sun.

One afternoon toward the end of the Gathering, I attended a council hosted by Love Israel, the 39-year-old leader of the Seattle commune known as the Love Family. The purpose of the meeting was to decide where next year's Gathering would be. On the floor of Love's spacious, octagonal tent was a huge Persian rug. The white tent flaps had been rolled up to let in the sunlight, and crystals dangling from the wooden frame sent rainbows dancing around the space. Seated on a pillow that elevated him above everyone else, Love Israel resembled an Old Testament patriarch. He was tall and slender, with clear blue eyes, long brown hair, and a full beard. He wore a spotlessly clean, sleeveless robe tied at the waist with a red sash. His neatly combed hair reached down to the middle of his back. As the meeting got under way, beautiful women in long, handmade dresses poured mugs of freshly ground coffee with honey and cream, taking care to serve the most influential guests first. It was, I thought, a magical scene out of a Hollywood version of *The Arabian Nights*. I wondered who these people were, and I wanted to see them again.

My chance came the following year. In the spring of 1980, I spent a weekend at the Love Family's 292-acre ranch north of Seattle. The ranch, even more enchanting than I had imagined, was in a secluded, wooded valley in the foothills of the Cascade Mountains. It conveyed an impression of order, tranquillity, and harmony with nature. A muscular, long-haired man was plowing a field with two Belgian horses, and several women were singing a song about New Jerusalem while working in the garden. On the far side of a meadow, children were laughing as they splashed in a lake framed by alder and fir trees. At the center of the valley stood a large white tent on a wooden platform with colorful flags rippling overhead. This, I was told, was where Love Israel lived when he visited the ranch.

The most prominent structure on the ranch was a weathered barn that had been remodeled for Family meetings. Outside, a few people were talking, including an attractive woman with long, brunette hair who was wearing a brightly embroidered dress. She took my hand, smiled, and looked intently into my eyes for several moments, then welcomed me to the Family. Her name, she said, was Together. I was taken inside the barn, where hand-painted banners hung from the walls and Persian rugs covered the floors, conjuring up images of an ancient, mythical kingdom. At one end of the central meeting room, a large window in the shape of the Star of David symbolized the Family's belief that members were the true Israelites, God's chosen people.

The Love Family was almost 12 years old in 1980. Out of hundreds of communal experiments started in the late 1960s and early 1970s, it was one of the few success stories. Most of these groups failed within a year or two, but the Love Family had survived and prospered. With approximately 300 members, it was one of the biggest communes in the United States. Besides the ranch, the Family owned a cannery and a horse ranch in central Washington, a rural homestead on Lake Roosevelt in the northeast corner of the state, and several houses on Queen Anne Hill in Seattle. After being attacked as a dangerous cult for more than a decade, the Family had earned the support of neighbors, local businessmen, church leaders, and even Seattle's mayor and chief of police.

Over the next three years I made several visits to the Love Family, and every time I went back, I could see signs of change. At first there were just small intrusions from "the world," which was how members referred to everything outside the Family. They included clocks, calendars, nail polish for girls, and jeans for women, none of which would have been permitted a few years before. By 1982 there were indications that some people were unhappy with the way Family life was changing, and the next year one of Love's elders confided to me that the Family was in serious trouble. Trying to be honest without revealing too much, he explained a little about the community's economic problems and disagreements about how money should be spent. His comments, however, did not prepare me for what happened just a few months later.

In the summer of 1983, the Love Family suddenly broke up. According to the Seattle papers, most of Love Israel's inner circle of elders had left the Family after a dispute with Love over money, power, and drugs. People who had steadfastly supported Love for almost 15 years were accusing him of turning into a power-hungry cocaine addict whose drug habit had brought the Family to the brink of bankruptcy. Over the next eight or nine months, about 85 percent of Love's followers defected, and the Love Family seemed to be on the verge of total collapse.

The breakup prompted me to start collecting systematic data on the Love Family. I wanted to know why, at what appeared to be the peak of its success, this seemingly harmonious community was falling apart. I felt it was important to interview Family members while the breakup was still fresh in their minds and before they tired of talking about what had happened.

## STUDYING THE LOVE FAMILY

I had thought about doing research on the Love Family ever since my first visit in 1980, but the idea for a full-blown study did not begin to take shape until several months after the breakup. In 1984 I moved to Seattle with Janann Cohig, a sociology student from the University of Montana. Together we drew up a plan for an *ethnography* of the Family. An ethnography is a detailed descriptive study that uses direct observation and in-depth interviews to document a group's way of life. What made our study unusual was the fact that the group we wanted to investigate had all but disintegrated. Most members had defected, and the Family was struggling to survive. The ranch that had so captivated me on my first visit was nearly deserted. Defectors had carried off almost everything of value, and the place had taken on the look of a ghost town. We arrived at a time when the Family was split into three factions calling themselves groups A, B, and C.

Group A consisted of about 40 members who were still loyal to Love Israel. Most were living in Love's house on Queen Anne Hill, and the rest were in southern California with Love, who had left town because of bad publicity. Group B was composed of angry defectors whose accusations against Love Israel had made sensational headlines in the Seattle papers. Two were suing Love to recover money they had given to the Family. One eventually acquired Love's house in an out-of-court settlement that forced Love's followers to move back to the ranch. Group C was less sharply defined. It consisted of members who had defected only after it became clear that the Family was disintegrating. Although they held Love responsible for many of the Family's problems, they still considered him a friend and preferred not to take sides in the conflict.

The loyalists were struggling to hang on to the Family's lifestyle in the face of bankruptcy and lawsuits, whereas the defectors were trying to cope with the formidable problems of readjusting to life in the outside world: finding jobs, paying bills, establishing credit, and getting birth certificates for their children.

With Love Israel's permission, we moved into the Family's guest house, the Front Door Inn. Before the breakup, the Inn had hosted thousands of visitors every year. By the time we arrived, it had become a boarding house for Love Family fringe members and wannabes. Our housemates included a kleptomaniac, a manic-depressive who had been kicked out of the Family for chasing a woman around the ranch with an ax, and a paranoid schizophrenic who once barricaded the house so thoroughly that the other residents had to climb in through a second story window. Most of these people hoped to find a place in the Family now that so many had left, but the only reason they were allowed to live in the Inn was that the Family desperately needed money to pay its bills.

At first, Janann and I spent most of our time with Group A, but our attention soon shifted to the defectors because they were more willing to talk about the Family's internal dynamics. Most ex-members still lived on Queen Anne Hill, where they partied together, baby-sat each other's children, and traded goods and services in an effort to help each other get back on their feet. With few exceptions they were open to our study and went out of their way to help by providing us with Family documents, pictures, and tape recordings of music and meetings. They even let us stay in their houses after we moved out of the Front Door Inn. Except for a week with the loyalists at the 1984 Rainbow Gathering in California, Janann and I spent the next nine months in Seattle. Then I had to return to work. Janann withdrew from the study because she had fallen in love with an ex-member and was finding it too difficult to maintain her objectivity. I continued collecting data for the next three summers.

Because we were mainly interested in the Family's history, most of our data came from interviews. Rather than asking a set of fixed questions as survey researchers do, we had people describe in detail how and why they joined, what their lives in the Family had been like, how they had perceived the events leading to the breakup, and why they had decided to stay or leave when the Family started to collapse. Most interviews lasted about two hours, but some involved several lengthy sessions stretching over days or weeks. Our shortest interviews were with members of Group A because the loyalists didn't want to talk about problems in the Family except in very general terms. The defectors were more open, but in some cases their memories were colored by the extreme hostility they felt toward Love Israel. Sometimes people embellished their accounts for the sake of a good story or tried to save face by downplaying their involvement in events they now found embarrassing. However, because the Family was such a small, intimate community, it was relatively easy to verify information by checking stories against each other.

Altogether, we interviewed 97 people from the three factions, as well as many others who had been connected with the Family in one way or another. Among them were neighbors on Queen Anne Hill, members' parents, police officers, local politicians, spokesmen for anti-cult groups, friends of the Family, and people from other *counterculture* groups, including several from the Rainbow Family. Love himself never granted a formal interview, but I did have a few conversations with him about the breakup. What emerged from these interviews was an intriguing picture of the rise and fall of one of the most successful communal experiments in recent American history.

## AN OVERVIEW OF THE LOVE FAMILY

Not everyone shared my enchantment with the Family. Even within the hippie counterculture the Family had a mixed reputation. Some thought it represented the highest ideals of the 1960s, but many others, especially in the anarchist Rainbow Family, believed Love Israel was an autocratic dictator. One member of the Rainbow Family, who had worked closely with the Love Family when plans were being made for the 1981 Gathering in Washington state, complained that Family members could not make even trivial decisions without first getting approval from one of their elders.

For many parents, the Love Family appeared to be a cult in the worst sense of the word. Curt and Henrietta Crampton, whose daughter Kathe joined the Family in 1973, were alarmed when one of their letters was returned with a printed stamp that read: "Return to Sender. Eye to eye, hand to hand, we'd love to see you in our land."

Later they received a letter from a Family member named Strength who said Kathe was about to be baptized. This meant she would "die to the past" and become a "new creature in Christ." When Mrs. Crampton visited the Family a few weeks later, Kathe had become Corinth Israel. She looked emaciated and was covered with sores from an outbreak of scabies. Worse yet, Mrs. Crampton was never allowed to talk with Kathe alone. When she asked her daughter if she missed the biking, sailing, and backpacking she used to love, Kathe replied flatly, "In heaven those things don't matter anymore." Mrs. Crampton claimed her daughter's personality had undergone a radical change. "It was as though we were not speaking the same language," she said. "I just couldn't break through the shell. . . ."

In the anti-cult movement that developed during the 1970s, the Love Family was compared to the Manson Family and the People's Temple. Ted Patrick, one of the Family's most outspoken critics, called it a "collection of drugged-up, spaced-out, wired-up mental zombies" (Patrick and Dulack 1976: 152), and a *National Enquirer* story was just as damning (Baker 1979). The headline read, "America's Most Dangerous Cult—A World of Violence, Drugs and Child Abuse."

The article quoted a prominent psychiatrist who claimed the Family's indoctrination methods could cause irreversible psychological damage. But not all the experts agreed. Sociologist William Bainbridge, one of the few social scientists who actually visited the Love Family, wrote in a *Seattle Times* article that Love's followers were "effective, rational and happy" (1976: A13). The Family, he said, came from a long tradition of religious innovation that "goes back to the original Christian community created by the Apostles."

At the center of the controversy was Love Israel, formerly Paul Erdmann, a Seattle television salesman who dropped out of the mainstream along with thousands of other young people during the mid-1960s. After moving to San Francisco's Haight-Ashbury district, where the hippie movement began, he started to experiment with psychedelic drugs.

One night, after taking a powerful dose of LSD, Erdmann and two of his friends had a vision. Although I never heard Love's account of what happened, I interviewed the other two and their stories were nearly identical. In a statement written several years later, one of them described what he experienced when he and Erdmann stared into one another's eyes:

I began to feel that our thoughts were flowing together, it was as though we were thinking the same thoughts at the same instant. Then even closer than that, like we had one mind that we were both thinking in. I felt the last barriers breaking down and fears exploding into nothing as we let go. Then, as I looked at him, I saw myself, his face turned into my face. I felt like I had been turned inside out. Still looking into his eyes, I began to see many faces, all with the same quality or spirit. I knew that I was seeing God behind all the eyes, even mine. Finally, I realized I was seeing the face of Jesus Christ, totally real and looking right at me. We were taken to a place of golden light, above bodies, above male and female, beyond time and space, right to the source of all—one with each other—one with God, one with everything. . . .

This vision became the keystone for the Love Family, whose uncomplicated belief system was expressed in three fundamental principles: We are all one, Love is the answer, and now is the time to create heaven on Earth by living together in perfect harmony. In 1968 Erdmann returned to Seattle and rented a house on Queen Anne Hill where he started a small commune with three other people. He immediately took on the role of spiritual teacher and soon adopted the name Love, which he claimed to have seen inscribed in gold on a white stone during another LSD trip. Just over a year later, his small group of followers anointed him as their king in a special ceremony.

Love was a classic example of a *charismatic leader*. "Charisma" is Greek for "divine gift." The concept of charismatic authority was introduced by Max Weber, a German sociologist who pioneered the study of new religions. Weber concluded that charismatic leadership is fundamentally different from other types of authority. In societies dominated by tradition, leaders are either born into positions of authority or they are chosen because they exemplify traditional values. In urban-industrial societies, people become leaders because of their ability to perform specific tasks, like being good administrators. Leaders are essentially interchangeable parts. They can be replaced with nothing more than the inconvenience of a job search. But charismatic authority is different. Charismatic leaders are not bound by traditions, constitutions or bureaucratic job descriptions. Instead, they can do whatever they want as long as they can persuade others to follow them.

Love was one of those rare individuals who possess the powers of charisma. He was smart, handsome, articulate, and consumed by a sense of mission. But more important than that, he was supremely self-confident. Even though his followers had seen visions of Israel and Jesus Christ before joining the Family, they didn't know what to do with their revelations. However, as an ex-member put it, Love was always "110 percent positive." He knew what they felt, and he was willing to take action when they were still trying to make up their minds.

In the beginning, most members were attracted by Love's personal magnetism, but as the Family developed into a full-fledged community, its unique culture and the warmth of its people became the group's strongest selling points. The community became a major stopover for hippies and spiritual seekers traveling through the Northwest. It was widely known in the counterculture as one of the most "together scenes" in the country. Contrary to the stereotype that cults always use aggressive recruiting tactics, the Family didn't need to proselytize to attract members. Instead, the problem was screening out people who wanted to join but would not fit in, usually because they were looking for a free ride or they had psychological problems that might disrupt the Family's harmonious way of life.

Sociologically the Love Family can be described as a utopian society. A *utopia* is an idealistic community whose members believe in the possibility of creating a perfect social order where all human failings can be overcome. The United States has a long history of utopian experiments, starting in the eighteenth century and continuing to the present. Like the Love Family, many of these groups have seen themselves as the true Israelites.

One of the most striking parallels to the Love Family is Benjamin Purnell's

House of David, a religious cult that thrived in Benton Harbor, Michigan, during the first half of the twentieth century (Fogarty 1981). Its male members dressed in robes, had full beards, and wore their hair long, after the fashion of Old Testament times. Like Love Israel, Purnell claimed his followers were the new nation of Israel whose mission was to create heaven on Earth.

Love, however, went far beyond Purnell in his efforts to make ancient Israel a model for social organization. The Family was a patriarchal kingdom based on Love's image of the tribe of Judah. Even in Seattle, where most members lived in ordinary middle-class houses, I was impressed by the Family's Old Testament imagery—oil lamps, Hebrew names, handmade robes, long hair and full beards, and hand-painted tapestries depicting biblical scenes. The men in the Family learned how to use slings, and archery became a popular sport (giving rise to a baseless rumor that the Family was stockpiling weapons). Every spring the Family celebrated Passover, which was considered the holiest event of the year.

Despite the trappings of Old Testament life, members of the Love Family saw themselves as a Christian community. They were, to borrow a term from Purnell, Christian Israelites. According to the Family's Charter, their purpose was to fulfill the prophecies of the New Testament by following the example of Jesus Christ.

The Love Family's brand of Christianity was based on a *monistic* conception of God. Monism means we are all part of God or, put another way, that there is a spark of divinity in each of us. Monism is basic to Buddhism and Hinduism, whereas orthodox Christianity teaches that God is a separate entity and that humanity is fundamentally sinful. Members of the Love Family believed that because God is in all of us, we are essentially one being, separated only by our egos and selfish desires. They regarded this understanding as the true revelation of Jesus Christ. Through his example of perfect love, Christ represented the spirit of God in man, but when Jesus died on the cross, the essence of his vision was lost and mankind succumbed to the forces of darkness and separation.

Love claimed that during the 1960s the spiritual consciousness of mankind had reawakened, and once again people had begun to recognize their oneness with God and each other. By dropping their worldly egos, loving each other, and living in agreement instead of conflict and competition, people could manifest the reality of Jesus Christ. For members of the Love Family, this was the real meaning of the resurrection. They were the body of Christ, forgiven for their sins, and they expected to live forever in a state of perpetual harmony and bliss without experiencing disease or death. Living in the present was all that mattered. On my first visit to the Family, when I asked children what time it was, they would say, ''Now is the time,'' reflecting the Family's belief that worldly conceptions of ''past'' and ''future'' were merely illusions.

From a sociological perspective, the Family's unique theology is what made it a *cult*. For sociologists, the word ''cult'' is not a pejorative term, but simply a label for a group of people bound together by beliefs that fall outside a society's dominant religious tradition. However, for most people the "cult label" evokes images of a leader who uses powerful *mind control* techniques, often described as "brainwashing," to coerce his followers into accepting bizarre beliefs.

Contrary to the brainwashing stereotype, nearly everyone we interviewed who had belonged to the Family told us they had experienced revelations similar to Love's even *before* they heard of Love Israel or the Love Family. In most cases, their revelations occurred under the influence of LSD or some other psychedelic drug, and their experiences were typical of acid trips during the heyday of the hippie counterculture. They included loss of ego, a sense of oneness with God, and a recognition of the essential unity of all creation (Masters and Houston 1966).

Although drugs were a regular part of Family life, they were never used indiscriminately, and only certain drugs were acceptable. Ironically, given the Family's reputation in the anti-cult movement as a drug cult, some defectors who had been heavy drug users before joining the Family credited Love Israel with getting their lives back on track by providing them with a sense of purpose and a structured lifestyle.

Except for LSD, which was used only when it was provided by guests, synthetic drugs like angel dust were discouraged, and I never met anyone who had used amphetamines or barbiturates while in the Family. The most common drug was marijuana, which members called "mashish." It was smoked almost every day, usually before the morning meetings or after dinner. Mashish and psychedelics were referred to as "sacraments" because they reinforced the Family's feeling of being one.

One exception to the rule against synthetic chemicals was the solvent toluene (nicknamed "tell-you-all"), which members used on a daily basis in 1970. Believing they could create any reality they wanted, if they were all of one mind, members would sit in a circle and decide on what they wanted to experience. Then they would put plastic bags containing napkins dipped in toluene over their faces and breathe the fumes together while concentrating on their common goal. A defector I interviewed described an occasion when he and several others decided they wanted to go to the moon:

We closed the doors to the sanctuary . . . and that was our spaceship. . . . It was so real you could feel the house go up. . . . We were really there. It was something! That's the way that stuff was. It could really dissolve the reality we sit in right now. . . .

When we came back down from the moon, opening the door to leave was such a trip, to open the door and see the rest of the house there. . . .

It was toluene that first brought the Family to national attention. Early in 1971 two members died from suffocation after passing out with plastic bags over their faces. Love prayed over their bodies, expecting them to revive, but his vigil was cut short when someone called the police and the bodies were taken to the morgue. Later the Family issued a press release claiming the men had died because of "disobedience" to Love, meaning they had been breathing toluene alone, without his approval.

The press release reflected the Family's belief that following God takes precedence over conforming to worldly laws. This belief, known as *antinomianism*, the priority of God's laws, has a long history in American society, dating back to the seventeenth century, when Anne Hutchinson challenged the orthodoxy of Puritan New England by claiming that it was God's will that all people should be able to worship as they pleased.

Rather than disavowing the use of drugs, the Family's press release praised the "potential these chemicals have for bringing a man into closer relationship to his brother and to God." The statement went on to say that police interference in their lives only served to demonstrate that "it is impossible to deal reasonably with the existing system." Before the toluene incident, hardly anyone had heard of the Love Family, but after the headlines in 1971, the Family became a major target of the anti-cult movement.

The Love Family mellowed throughout the 1970s, but it continued to resist worldly laws and regulations. One example was the Family's stand on birth dates. Because members believed they were eternal, they refused to tell anyone how old they were, making it impossible for them to get drivers' licenses. Many members were sent to jail for not having worldly ages. In one case, a woman from the Family was pulled over for running a stop sign while riding a bicycle. Since she had no identification, the police officer started questioning her. When she said her name was Understanding and told the officer she was eternal, she was arrested and taken to jail. When the booking officer tried to enter her name in the computer, the machine responded by printing out hundreds of pages of random numbers. As a result, it took several hours to complete the paperwork and get her locked up. The next day the *Seattle Times* described the incident in a comical story entitled "Jail? It's a MisUnderstanding?" The Seattle police eventually got used to the Family's unusual customs and started to let members off the hook for driving without licenses, but in other parts of the country, police officers weren't nearly as sympathetic.

Some members spent weeks in jail for hitchhiking, and a few were beaten up by policemen who thought they were just playing games when they refused to give their birth dates. Confrontations with the law helped to unite the Family against the Satanic forces of the world. Satan was seen as the spirit of separation and disharmony, and his presence was manifested inside the Family, just as it was in the outside world.

Satan stood for anything that threatened the Family or its collective mind. The Love Family called itself the Church of Armageddon because the battle between God and Satan was an ever-present reality in their lives. Love used to say, "Armageddon is happening now." In the event of a serious crisis like the day the two members died from inhaling toluene, members would run from house to house, shouting "Armageddon!" to alert their brothers and sisters to possible danger.

The most graphic example of Armageddon was *deprogramming*, a technique pioneered by Ted Patrick to get cult members to renounce their beliefs. The most famous case was Patrick's attempt to deprogram Kathe Crampton in 1973. He and two of his henchmen, who had been hired by Kathe's parents, grabbed her off a sidewalk on Queen Anne Hill, dragged her into a car, and drove her to a motel, where she was locked in a room and subjected to a constant onslaught of attacks on her belief in Love. Patrick was so sure he could deprogram her that he allowed a CBS news crew to film the entire episode. When she escaped and found her way back to the Family, Love rewarded her by giving her the name Dedication. It was Patrick's most embarrassing failure.

Another member was captured by deprogrammers three times. The last time was in Alaska, where he was living with several members at a remote homestead on the coast south of Anchorage. A plane suddenly landed on the beach, three men climbed out, wrestled him into the cockpit, and flew off. His parents took him to the nation of Israel, where they left him, without a passport, in the custody of relatives. But, like Kathe Crampton, he escaped. After hitchhiking across Europe, he stowed away on a ship to America and then hitched rides back to Seattle. When he reappeared on Queen Anne Hill several months later, Love gave him the name Sure, and he eventually became an elder in the Family.

One deprogramming had tragic consequences. After being kidnapped by deprogrammers who were unable to get him to renounce Love Israel, one member was locked up in several mental hospitals, injected with tranquilizers, and given at least 20 electroshock treatments. Although he never went back to the Family, the man suffered through years of mental anguish about God, Satan, and the Love Family as a result of the experience. It was his own personal Armageddon.

Only a few parents resorted to deprogramming to get their sons and daughters out of the Family, but many others thought about it, especially in the 1970s, when the Family was receiving so much bad publicity. Not all parents were upset, however, and some were even grateful to Love for giving meaning and structure to their children's lives.

Nevertheless, even though there was a measure of acceptance, most parents were disturbed by the Family's belief in a collective mind where individuality seemed to have no importance. Their visits to the Family convinced them that Love Israel had succeeded in transforming the concept of a single mind into reality. Members made a conscious effort to drop their egos and submit to the group's collective wisdom. They tried to keep themselves in what they called a "high place" at all times by "staying present" and eliminating worldly "thoughts" from their consciousness.

To parents, these were just code words for not thinking, not questioning, and doing what they were told. Deviance in the Family was equated with "being separate," not just physically but socially and, most important, mentally. Anyone who clung too strongly to a contrary viewpoint was likely to be severely criticized in Family meetings. He or she might be warned not to think with a "small I." Thinking with a "small I" was viewed as ego indulgence, whereas thinking with a "big I" meant submitting to the will of the group.

If Love noticed that someone seemed preoccupied, he might ask why the person looked so "dark" and add a reminder not to trust "separate" thoughts. "If you think you see something wrong here," he would say, "it's probably you."

People who couldn't deal with the constant pressure to conform usually left the Family in a few months. Those who stayed made a deliberate effort to fit in.

As I got to know the members, it was easy to see the differences in their personalities, but still there was a remarkable uniformity in their expressions, inflections, tone of voice, and way of relating to each other. Members spoke softly, went through their routines quietly and efficiently, and always seemed cheerful about whatever they were doing. At the 1984 Rainbow Gathering someone warned me, in all seriousness, not to eat with the Love Family because they laced their food with a drug that made them perpetually happy.

The ideal of being "one" was reflected in virtually every aspect of Family life. Members believed that Israel was a state of mind sustained by agreement, and they constantly reaffirmed their oneness through communal meals, collective work projects, and morning meetings.

On Sundays in Seattle, members often walked around Queen Anne Hill. They followed a predetermined route called "the circuit," which required them to pass by all the Family's houses, thereby keeping them in touch with friends they otherwise might not see. Inside their houses, there were no mirrors. When I asked about this, I was told that mirrors were unnecessary because members were expected to see themselves in their friends. In effect, the community was their mirror. At night, members on "nux watch" (nux being Hebrew for "night") would circulate from house to house, gently waking each of their brothers and sisters to say, "I love you," and ask what they had seen about New Jerusalem in their dreams. Privacy was virtually nonexistent.

In Seattle it was common for 10 to 15 people to share a house, and quarters were even more cramped on the ranch, where everyone lived in circular tents known as yurts. The typical outhouse at the ranch (there was only one flush toilet, located in the barn) consisted of a three-sided, open-air structure with three holes side by side. The open side always faced a trail so members could talk to their friends while relieving themselves.

Although many of the defectors I interviewed wondered in retrospect if they had been brainwashed, they still had fond memories of the Love Family. Ironically, some of their best memories were of situations that anti-cult writers cited to show how oppressive Family life was. At one time, for example, 16 people lived in eight tiny cubicles in a small, windowless room in the basement of Love's house, where they shared virtually everything but toothbrushes. When I asked an ex-member what it was like, he replied: "Wonderful! It was like summer camp. It was very cramped, but we had a lot of fun. Those people are still my best friends."

Many defectors nostalgically recalled the blissful feeling of merging into the group's collective consciousness while singing, chanting, or meditating together. Even without the help of drugs, members often had deep spiritual experiences on these occasions, ranging from intuitive revelations to dramatic visions that became part of the community's folklore. A typical example was this vision, which Love recorded in the Family's book of visions and revelations:

While meditating together [with Love] I saw Love's face turn into mine. I then saw the face and character of a lamb. The lamb turned into the Lion of Judah. I then saw the faces of my brothers cross Love's face until I saw the face of Jesus Christ. Love's face then reappeared as my King. He looked totally royal with a jewel studded crown on his head. As I looked at the crown I saw a city. Looking into the center of the jewel of the crown I saw the land and people of Israel singing and dancing together.

Some ex-members admitted they embellished their stories to please Love, usually by making him more central than he really was, but almost everyone still believed their visions had been genuine revelations from God.

The Family's cohesiveness was reinforced by rigid boundaries separating believers from the world. Members were set apart by their unusual names and appearance, and social contacts with outsiders were very limited. They rarely went anywhere alone, and hardly ever without an elder's approval. Radios, televisions, clocks, watches, books, and newspapers were conspicuously absent, and children's storybooks were censored by blacking out passages that were considered too worldly. For years there were only two telephones in the Family, one at the Front Door Inn and the other in the Family's business office. Besides serving as a crash pad for transients and visitors, the Inn kept outsiders at arm's length. By channeling guests through the Inn, the Family tried to screen out people who might prove disruptive, and I was impressed by the community's ability to maintain a tranquil, village-like atmosphere in the middle of a densely populated urban neighborhood.

In spite of the Family's belief that Satan controlled everything outside the community, members never completely cut themselves off from the outside world. They tried to cultivate friendships with their neighbors on Queen Anne Hill, and they developed strong ties with other counterculture groups such as the Rainbow Family. Love made a concerted effort to develop relationships with people in high places, and by the early 1980s the community had many influential friends in Seattle. The Love Family had been granted observer status on the Church Council of Greater Seattle, and on the Family's behalf a state senator from Queen Anne Hill introduced a bill that would have made it possible to get a driver's license without a birth date. Although the bill failed, the Seattle Police Department defused the licensing issue by issuing members special identification cards bearing their Israel Family names and the word "legal" in the space reserved for their ages.

More parents were visiting, too, although many did not like the community's controlling lifestyle. Three parents even moved in with the Family, but none of them joined. In 1982 Hollywood entertainer Steve Allen, whose son Logic was an elder, published a book about the Family that was generally positive. Symbolic of the members' growing desire to have their parents visit was the new outhouse they built at the ranch. It was the only one on the property with a door.

The Family was able to remain insulated for so long because members never took jobs in the outside world except to harvest fruit in eastern Washington, and then they always worked as a group. The Love Family was financially independent because new members were expected to turn over all their assets to the "Commonwealth of Israel." Although most had little to give, a few donated substantial amounts of money. One of them "brought home" nearly two million dollars' worth of cash, real estate, and other assets. In recognition of his commitment, Love gave him the name Richness.

Although the Family's culture was based on the belief that "we are all one," members did not believe in social equality. The Family's social structure was symbolized by a golden pyramid, and Love Israel, as head of the body of Christ, stood at the apex. According to the Charter, Love was "a parent in all spiritual things, a minister and guide worthy of all respect and obedience." Even as the Family grew and Love turned over more responsibilities to the elders, he continued to have the last word on every important decision.

In a statement issued by the council of elders almost ten years after the Charter was written, Love was described as "the point of agreement between us, the central thought in our mind, the mind of Christ, [and] the point of final resolve in all matters that concern us." As the central thought in the mind of Christ, Love had absolute authority, and members were not supposed to have any thoughts but his.

Because Love was the king of Israel, he was allowed more privileges than anyone else. Even in the early days when everyone was crowded into two or three houses, Love had his own room. He had sexual relationships when everyone else was celibate, and he enjoyed eating cheese and eggs for breakfast while his followers ate sprouts and brown rice.

Love's lifestyle became more luxurious as the Family grew, and his household contained the best of everything in the kingdom. One of Love's "priests," as his personal servants were called, described what it was like.

Love's house was bigger than anyone else's house. It had more people in it. For the most part, it had very attractive, intelligent people living in it, hardworking people in it. We had nicer clothes than anybody else. . . . The people were fun. . . . They were interesting, they were upbeat, they were exciting. Elders came and went from our house. We got to hold the pipes [for smoking mashish] at the morning meetings, and the other guys got to clean out his stash and get high in the middle of the day. [The women in the house] were the ladies that got to go through all the clothes when they first came. These were the ladies that got all the jewels. They got to sleep with Love, and have his babies. . . . If you got to go over to Love's house, you might be in the front room with 20 people and me and [my brother] playing music in the back. You might get to get high. If there were any visitors, they would be there. If Love was high and into one of his talking moods, you'd get to hear your leader speaking the word of God. He was the center of the action.

When critics in the anti-cult movement compared Love's lifestyle with living conditions elsewhere in the Family, they couldn't understand why members put up with the discrepancy unless they had been brainwashed. But Love's followers believed his special privileges were justified. He was, after all, their king. Even most defectors believed that Love set a good example for them in the beginning. A former elder explained why.

There were a lot of things I admired about what Love was doing, things that in comparison to myself, I thought he was doing better than me. . . . He would really get up [early in the morning] and meditate. He really would get up and read the Bible for hours. . . . He really would totally pay attention to you while you were with him. . . . If a problem arose . . . , his first recourse would be to stop, calm down, eliminate the panic, wash away the fears, meditate, try to get clear, try to get loving, get back to a positive frame of mind, remember God, have confidence, have faith, trust that it will work out. Those were admirable things. Those were pluses in my mind. I respected him for it. I emulated him for it.

In other words, Love's followers gave him authority because they believed he embodied their highest ideals. From their perspective, Love deserved the privileges he enjoyed.

Beneath Love was the council of elders, which handled most of the family's day-to-day administrative jobs. It consisted of men who were energetic, talented, and charismatic in their own right, but most of all they were men who were exceptionally devoted to Love. Each elder was in charge of a household, where he had basically the same authority that Love had over the entire Family.

On my first visit to the ranch, I stayed in Logic's household, where I was the guest at a formal dinner in a sparsely furnished army tent erected on a wooden platform. Logic, the perfect embodiment of his name, was a pleasant, articulate man in his mid-thirties who seemed totally dedicated to the Family. We sat across from one another on embroidered pillows while Logic's wife, Simplicity, and another woman, a servant in the household, served our dinner on a hand-carved table, lit by candles and oil lamps. While we ate, the women stood off to the side of the room, never speaking unless I asked one of them a question. They did not eat until after Logic and I had finished our meal.

Women were admitted to the elder's council sometime during the mid-1970s, but their position was mainly symbolic. In practice, their authority came almost entirely from their relationships with men on the council. All but two were paired with elder men, and the more influential their partners, the more authority they had. One of the exceptions was Understanding, who once had been married to Philip Rockefeller, and the other was Wisdom, an attractive, white-haired woman who had rented a house to the Family before she joined. Wisdom and Understanding lived in Love's household, where they helped take care of his children.

Rank-and-file members were known as "youngers," regardless of how old they were. The youngers' job was to serve the elders. They had little freedom to come and go as they pleased, and their lives were absorbed by the demands of day-to-day survival. This was especially true at the ranch, where everyone lived in tents—army tents at first, and later yurts mounted on wooden platforms. Except in the barn, there was no electricity or running water. People cooked on wood stoves and lit their quarters with kerosene lamps. The men handled all the heavy labor while women tended to the domestic chores. Life was especially hard for younger ladies, as the women were called. In a typical day a woman might spend 15 hours cooking, cleaning, washing clothes by hand, and taking care of the elders' children.

Status distinctions permeated the Love Family. One of the most important was the distinction between people with Bible names and people with virtue names. When people joined the Family, they would adopt Hebrew names from the Bible. Then, after they had demonstrated their commitment, which might take years, Love would give each person a virtue name, such as Humility, Patience, Trust, or Courage. Receiving a virtue name was a holy event because one's name stood for the part of Jesus Christ that the person exemplified in his or her relationships with others. There was high turnover in the ranks of people with Bible names, but until the 1980s, few members with virtue names defected.

Virtue names were extremely important in the Love Family. Besides defining the Family's core membership, they shaped the roles people played and the way members related to each other. A former Family member observed:

Watching the Family was like seeing all the thoughts [of Christ] interacting, relating to each other as if they were those thoughts, concrete manifestations of a real, godly personality. There were light thoughts, like Fun, Simplicity, and Bliss, and heavy thoughts, like Righteous, Serious, Courage, and Reverence. There was this great pressure, from both within and without, to be that thought.

The pressures that came with getting a virtue name were intense. Receiving a virtue name was an honor, but living up to it could be like climbing a mountain of sand. An ex-member named Fun remembered being out on a hike with Love in the Cascade Mountains. Everyone was hot, sweaty, and tired. "Hey, Fun," Love shouted, "what's wrong here? We need some more fun!" And it was Fun's responsibility to make everyone happy again. The former elder named Strength recalled similar incidents. Once, when he was so sick he could barely stand, Love caught him lying down. "[Love said] 'What are you doing? I just heard two people in the neighborhood are sick and it's your fault. You're their *strength* and you're making them weak. Right now, get up!' I did rise up and walk.''

On another occasion, despite turning "bee amber yellow" from hepatitis and having just been stitched up without an anesthetic after a head-on collision, Strength spent several hours driving a tractor during an apple harvest because he felt compelled to live up to his name. Looking back, he thought his dedication bordered on insanity, but "on the positive side," he said, "I did find out that I had powers that I couldn't have discovered any other way.''

Differences in rank were reflected in the practice of bowing. Members used to greet one another by bowing their heads while holding their palms together in a prayerful fashion. By watching who bowed to whom, one could unravel the web of status relationships that structured the Family's social life. Youngers bowed to elders, women to men, children to adults, and everyone to Love Israel. Once Love loaned one of his robes to a visitor from another community known as The Source. When the man stepped out of the house, several members mistook him for Love and bowed in unison. "It was a strange feeling," he recalled, "to have them all bowing to me just because of what that piece of cloth symbolized.''

One of the most important privileges of rank was sexual freedom. In the anticult movement, the Love Family was often called a free-love cult, but that image was inaccurate. Love discouraged the formation of exclusive romantic relationships, and many members did change partners frequently, but sexual relationships were much more structured than the free-love image suggests. Before 1971, everyone was celibate except Love and two or three women. Later, Love allowed a few couples to "get together," which was the Family's euphemism for having sex.

By the end of the 1970s, the Family had developed a complicated set of informal "agreements" governing sexual relationships. New members were expected to abstain from sex for at least a year, and some people I interviewed had been celibate for as long as nine years. The celibacy rule weeded out the less committed and forced new members to get to know other people in the Family as brothers and sisters.

When two people wanted to get together, they would first approach their elders, who would usually discuss the idea with the people in their households. If there were no strong objections, one of the elders would take the idea to Love, who nearly always approved. There was no wedding ceremony, and members never used the terms "husband" and "wife" (although I do for the sake of convenience).

The men who were closest to Love—his elders and a few men in his household—had much more sexual freedom than anyone else. Although the elders were expected to form stable relationships to "build the Family," as Love put it, they were encouraged to have sex with other women, and a few elders had two or three wives. Jealousy was a common problem in these polygamous households, but women were expected to submit to their husbands and keep their thoughts in "a high place."

Love was the only person with virtually complete sexual freedom. He had two wives, Honesty and Bliss, by whom he had 11 children. In theory all the women were his wives, and most considered it an honor to get together with Love. There were other benefits, too. Love's favorites lived in his household, wore the nicest clothes, accompanied him on trips, and generally enjoyed more freedom than other women. Every day a "priestess of the day" (jokingly called the "lay of the day" behind Love's back) was selected to be his personal servant. Most women, however, chose not to get involved with Love because they thought of him as an older brother or a father figure.

Because almost everyone in the community was celibate in the early 1970s, there were very few children. The only kids in the Family had come with their parents. Members had little experience raising children, and they had cut themselves off from parental role models in the outside world. These factors, along with Love's belief that Satan worked through children because they were "weaker vessels," led to extreme forms of discipline. Children who cried were locked in closets, and misbehavior was punished by spankings with a wooden rod. Several times a boy, a chronic bed-wetter, was forced to sleep on the floor or in a bathtub without blankets. Children who weren't old enough to feed themselves were expected to sit quietly while an adult held the food in front of them and said, "This is the body of Jesus Christ," before putting each spoonful in their mouths. If they reached for the food, or even acted hungry, they were not fed.

Children were not the only ones subjected to harsh discipline during the early 1970s. One member was expelled for stealing bread from the refrigerator. Nobody owned up to the crime, so Love had members draw lots to determine who the culprit was. It wasn't until years later that the real thief confessed and people realized Love had kicked out the wrong person.

Like the children, some adults were given swats for "disobedience," such as having sex with someone outside the Family. One ex-member recalled, "It was living hell. A one-inch oak rod, right across the buttocks and lower legs. Oh, my God, indescribable pain. I don't think I've ever felt more pain inflicted on me in my life."

In the early days Love also had members kneel with their foreheads on the floor as an exercise in self-discipline. Three men spent almost three full days in that position, wetting their pants rather than getting up to use the bathroom because they were afraid Love would kick them out of the Family if they got up. One got kicked out anyway.

I just keeled over. I had no more muscular control. I tried to struggle to get up on my hands and knees, and just couldn't do it. So he comes over and throws my coat at me and says, "Get out and stay out! You're no good, you're weak." I crawled down the stairs on the front of the house, and I crawled down the sidewalk.

In the early 1970s, life with the Love Family was like Marine boot camp taken to an extreme. Like a drill sergeant, Love used severe methods to strip members of their old habits and attachments. Although he was attacked for this by the Family's critics, sociological studies have shown that strictness in religious groups is correlated with commitment (Iannaccone 1994; Kanter 1972). The more a group demands from its members, the more committed its members are. One reason is that the less committed drop out when they realize what is expected of them. Another is that members who endure intense tests of commitment become even more committed as a way of justifying their sacrifices to themselves (Festinger et al. 1956). Whatever the reason, the men who spent those three days kneeling on the floor all became elders, and they remained some of Love's strongest supporters until the breakup. One of them still belongs to the Family, where he functions as Love's business manager and second in command.

Most new religions go through a "red hot" phase when they begin, but they usually mellow with age. The Love Family was no exception. Members believed God's kingdom was being established on Earth, and they were the vanguard of the new age. Satan was waging war against them, and he worked in subtle ways, even through the thoughts of people who sincerely believed in Jesus Christ. This was Armageddon, and it called for extreme measures, like martial law in wartime. However, as the Family grew and became successful, the intensity diminished. The practice of giving swats to disobedient members was dropped, and Love banned corporal punishment for children. Kids who cried were no longer locked in closets, although they might be told to sit outside until they could "be happy again."

One reason for the change in child-rearing practices was that more people were becoming parents. The Family experienced a baby boom in the mid-1970s, and mothers who were close to Love managed to soften his stand on discipline. Another reason may have been an influx of new members from The Source family in Hawaii, whose leader had been killed in a hang-gliding accident.

Source members introduced many of their customs into the Family, including a gentler approach to bringing up children. In contrast to the outside world, where children are segregated from adults and grow up in age-graded peer groups, kids in the Love Family were integrated into adult activities and given responsibilities at an early age. The community had its own school that was accredited by the state of Washington, but since children didn't have birth dates, students were divided more by ability than by age.

To make up for the lack of birthdays, the Family started an annual celebration called the Golden Egg Party, which featured an elaborate egg hunt at the ranch. The child who found the golden egg had a party in Love's house, and all the other children were invited. Christmas was primarily a children's holiday, and members would spend days making toys, baking treats, and decorating the barn for the festivities.

By 1980 the Family had evolved into a child-centered community where children were treated with love and respect. In 1982 a cover story for *The Weekly*, a Seattle arts and entertainment tabloid, proclaimed the Love Family "a roaring success" (Downey 1982). Based on what little I knew then, I had to agree. The extreme practices of the past, like breathing toluene and locking children in closets, seemed irrelevant to what was happening in the 1980s. Family members appeared genuinely happy and loving, and the self-imposed barriers that had separated them from outsiders for more than a decade were eroding rapidly. Dozens of parents and neighbors now came to visit and take part in the Family's joyful celebrations. Beneath the facade of smiles, however, the community was simmering with discontent.

## TROUBLE IN THE KINGDOM—MONEY, POWER, AND DRUGS

The turning point came in 1979 when the Family's fishing boat, a war surplus mine sweeper, burned off the coast of Alaska. To pay off the boat mortgage, Love decided that members should get jobs outside the Family. Some found low-paying work as housekeepers, waitresses, gardeners, or factory workers, while others banded together to form their own businesses. The most successful ventures were the Israel Brothers Construction Company and the McGraw Street Store, a corner market on Queen Anne Hill.

To encourage members to find jobs, the council of elders decided to let workers keep 10 percent of their earnings. The rest, turned over to Love, was drawn on to pay bills and take care of household needs. Before long, each household was expected to pay its own rent, utilities, and food while continuing to give a fixed percentage to Love.

The effects of working in the world were almost immediate. For outsiders like myself, the most obvious change was the appearance of worldly luxury items. On my last visit to the Family before the breakup, I saw men drinking canned beer, women wearing blue jeans, and girls with lipstick and painted nails. Now newspapers and telephones were necessary to find jobs; mirrors and haircuts helped members present an acceptable image at work; and clocks and watches kept them from being late. When I asked a boy for the time, expecting the usual answer ("Now is the time"), he pulled out a pen with a digital clock in it and told me it was 3:56 P.M. These changes were more noticeable in Seattle than on the ranch, where limited job opportunities kept members at home, but even there the signs of change were unmistakable. When I visited the ranch in 1982, for example, I found the elders watching the NBA playoffs on television in Strength's yurt.

It wasn't long before the demands imposed by work schedules began to take their toll on the community. It was hard to hold down a nine-to-five job and still have time for Family meetings, community work projects, Rainbow Gatherings, or even Passover. By 1983 the traditional practice of holding daily morning meetings had been abandoned in Seattle, and for Christmas most children were given store-bought presents because there wasn't time to make toys by hand.

The fundamental problem posed by working for money was a conflict between economic goals and communal values. In the past, work projects had been communal efforts that kept members woven together. An ex-member explained:

People were literally happy, enjoying the life of riding in the back of a pickup truck with no protection against the weather, and holes in their boots, and going out to harvest grapes together. There was a lot of *fun* in it.

As soon as the emphasis shifted to earning a paycheck, the Family's communal fabric began to unravel. The Love Family was hardly unique in this respect. As sociologist Rosabeth Kanter points out in her book *Commitment and Community* (1972), most utopian societies in American history have struggled with the same dilemma. Kanter describes this dilemma as a conflict between two antithetical forms of social organization, *gemeinschaft* and *gesellschaft*. The terms were first used by the German sociologist Ferdinand Tönnies, to describe changes caused by the industrial revolution. *Gemeinschaft* refers to a community whose members are bound together by common values and intimate relationships. Commitment to tradition takes precedence over individuality, and social relationships are valued for their own sake. In *gesellschaft* societies, social relationships are organized around specific tasks, and tradition and intimacy take a backseat to getting a particular job done. Relationships tend to be impersonal, and individualism is valued more than group solidarity.

Kanter's study showed that even the most successful nineteenth-century communes gradually took on *gesellschaft* characteristics, mainly for economic reasons, until the communal bonds that held them together finally dissolved. Signs of the transition from *gemeinschaft* to *gesellschaft* could be seen throughout the Love Family after 1980. One was an increase in personal autonomy. Now members could walk to work alone and even visit friends on the way back without having to get permission from their elders.

Thanks to the new policy allowing them to have their own spending money, workers enjoyed the freedom to treat themselves to a cup of coffee or stop off for a beer on the way home from work. Logic's wife, Simplicity, who had stood meekly in the shadows when I visited the ranch in 1980, started her own sewing business without Love's approval. During the 1970s, she probably would have been kicked out of the Family for showing that kind of initiative, but now, because her business was bringing in money, Love was willing to look the other way.

Another sign of *gesellschaft* was increasing specialization. It had been developing for years, beginning with the formation of the elders' council, but the pace accelerated once members started working for money. The most conspicuous example was Sure's household, which ran the McGraw Street Store. Sure developed an internal marketing system in which he bought food in bulk and sold it at discount rates to individual households.

Considering the importance the Family placed on visions, the most interesting example of specialization was a group called the Prophets' Council, which was made up of people known for their frequent visionary experiences. Love formed the group because not many people were having visions, and he thought the Council's spiritual insights would help keep the Family on track. The group met on a regular basis and kept minutes of the discussions, but it had no impact on the direction the Family was taking, and hardly anyone, including Love, took it seriously.

The decline in spirituality was reflected in the Family's music. In the past, songs emphasized spiritual themes and communal values, and they were meant to be sung in intimate Family gatherings to the accompaniment of acoustic instruments. After 1980, however, electronic rock 'n' roll began to dominate the musical scene. Bands were organized to make money, the biggest and best-known being the National Band, which played at local concerts. Songs continued to stress the ideals of love and brotherhood, but religious themes were downplayed to broaden the band's appeal to the general public.

Not everyone liked the trend toward secularization. The council of elders split into two factions that represented the "physical" and "spiritual" sides of Family life. On the physical side were the liberals, who favored economic development and greater involvement with the outside world. They wanted to change the Family's stand on birth dates, which constantly got in the way of making money. Logic, for example, had to rely on Family friends with connections in government to get licensed, bonded, and insured as a building contractor without having to give his Social Security number.

On the spiritual side were the conservatives, who resisted every encroachment of worldly influence. They invariably sided with Love, but it was hard to say where Love stood in the controversy. He continued to talk about the importance of "sticking with their agreements," such as holding to their stand on birth dates, but at the same time he pushed the Family deeper into debt by taking out high-interest loans even when the elders advised against it.

The conflict was reflected in a deepening rift between members in Seattle and those living on the ranch. People on Queen Anne Hill, who were bringing in most of the money, saw the ranch as a financial burden, whereas those on the ranch thought the people in Seattle were becoming too worldly. The standing joke was that Satan lived between Seattle and the ranch.

The joke reflected growing resentment between the people who were earning money and those who were not. The moneymakers tended to look down on members without jobs. Said one member:

Not everybody worked, you see. Only a few worked, and that built resentment. Subtly—it was never blatant. It was only the few really talented people that had their nose to the grindstone that were making it happen and paying the bills, while everybody else was living their spiritual life.

On the other hand, the people who did not have jobs resented the high priority given to making money. Even when they worked hard to support the Family in other ways—as teachers, for example—they had almost no spending money of their own. The difference often meant nothing more than the ability to buy an occasional six-pack, but after living without any money at all for over a decade, even a beer was a luxury.

These changes were well under way in 1981 when Richness received an inheritance worth more than $1,000,000. At first, Love told everyone to quit their jobs. "We'll never have to work again," he said. He then spent most of the money on a horse ranch in eastern Washington and more houses in Seattle. Within six months more people were working than before. Even though they were bringing in thousands of dollars every month, it was obvious to everyone that living conditions were not improving, and in some respects people were worse off than before.

As late as 1983, food expenses averaged just 65 cents a day per person (Israel 1983). The responsibilities of holding down a job, raising children, and tending to the needs of the community offset the benefits of having small amounts of cash for personal use. A former elder described his own situation this way:

I was required to come up with about $800 a month to cover my end of things. . . . And if I wasn't working, I was expected to be upstairs in this grungy, filthy, horrible attic full of the itchiest insulation I've ever been around, putting a room up there to make more room. So it's like I either had to be out making money, or I had to be working around the house, putting in an eight-hour day here.

Meanwhile, Love was distancing himself from the Family's everyday life. By the 1980s the community had become so big that it was impossible for him to to be anything more than a symbolic figurehead for most members. Beyond that, his lifestyle now included luxuries that would have been unthinkable a few years earlier: handmade suits, expensive whiskey, Cuban cigars, a credit card, ski trips, and membership in an exclusive Seattle health club. When Love took a vacation, he still took along other members of the Family, but the circle of people he invited was getting smaller and more exclusive.

Love's most expensive habit was cocaine. He had used it occasionally since the 1970s, and at first no one objected. In keeping with a long-standing Family agreement, members never bought drugs. Love used cocaine only when it was offered by a guest, and he made no attempt to hide his use from his followers. It didn't take long, however, before Love started freebasing. To support his growing habit, he secretly recruited a few members to buy cocaine for him, sometimes leading them to believe they were the only ones doing it. Most members knew Love used cocaine, but hardly anyone knew how much. The only time they saw him use it was when he shared it with them in the privacy of his room. What they didn't realize was that Love was doing coke almost every night with a different group of people. His personal habit reportedly cost somewhere between $200 and $600 a day, and when guests were included, it could reach as high as $2,000 for a single night.

The more Love got into cocaine, the more isolated he became. He started staying up all night and sleeping late into the day. A priest sat by his door to make sure he was not disturbed, and people who wanted to see him might be told that he was meditating or reading the Bible. This happened to me just before the breakup in 1983. I had brought a group of students to visit the Family, and we were talking with Logic, who by then had moved into a house next to Love's. When I asked Logic if we could see Love, he apologized, saying Love was too busy. But throughout our conversation I had been watching Love through the window, standing by himself on his balcony, staring vacantly into space.

Eventually Love closed the area around his house to everyone except members of his household and a few special friends. The children who lived there were sent to the ranch, and the few people who remained were instructed to see that the area was quiet at all times. What had once been the hub of Family life, so full of fun and excitement, now seemed empty and lifeless.

Even before the elders realized the extent of the cocaine problem, it was clear that Love was making bad decisions. The clearest example was his purchase of an abandoned brick factory in eastern Washington that he wanted to turn into a Family retreat, complete with palm trees and irrigation canals. Counting the purchase price and renovation costs, the total bill might have exceeded $175,000, and that didn't include labor that would have been taken away from the Family's moneymaking efforts. The elders thought the idea was totally unrealistic, but Love bought the property anyway. The brick factory came to symbolize the council's impotence. "No matter how excited we got," a former elder told me, "no matter what decisions we made, nothing really changed because Love maintained financial control of everything." Despite the fact that Richness had donated enough money to pay all the Family's debts, Love was still taking out loans. Another elder described the predicament this way:

We're sitting on a million dollars, cash, and [I'm] going down [to the bank] borrowing money. I don't get it. It was like watching more money than we would ever have, just run through our fingers. It used to drive me nuts, but [Love] didn't care. He was always impatient. He'd always have a new idea. He'd always want me to run down to the bank and swing another loan.

The Family's economic problems were aggravated by the fact that now almost half the members were children. Many parents, especially at the ranch, worried about not having enough money to buy milk or shoes for their kids. Love, however, was largely unaware of their concerns and less available than before. Most members kept their feelings to themselves because of the constant pressure to avoid negative thoughts. The few bold enough to complain directly to Love, however, usually got a chilly reception. One woman from the ranch who confronted him, claimed he told her she just needed to be more resourceful—the woods, he said, were full of edible plants. Then, she claimed, he offered her a line of cocaine.

Not surprisingly, people were starting to leave the Family. What made the exodus different from defections in the past was that now, prominent members were leaving. But it was not until two highly respected elders, Diligence and his wife, Joppa, defected that most members realized something was seriously wrong. They left in the middle of the night without telling anyone, and their departure stunned the Family. When I interviewed her later, Joppa was very clear about why she left.

I couldn't live in that society anymore because I knew the truth. He was not perfect. He was selfish. And he was degrading other people, and trying to bring everybody down with him, and I loved my children too much to drown them for his selfish pleasure. It was really because of my kids [that I left]. I probably could have stayed there another 20 years if I didn't have those kids. . . . I had a baby and I couldn't even afford to buy a pair of shoes for her.

By the time the Love Family held its annual Passover celebration in the spring of 1983, the community was a powder keg ready to explode. The irony is that hardly anyone knew it. Even in the council of elders there was widespread ignorance about Love's behavior. On his way back from a vacation in Mexico, for example, Love had given his real name and birth date to a customs agent, but the people who overheard him kept it a secret. Except in private conversations with their closest friends, the elders generally kept what they knew about his cocaine habit to themselves. They almost never told their households about the gravity of the Family's financial problems. A defector who taught in the Family's school told me he didn't even hear about the cocaine situation until two months before the breakup, and then he refused to believe it because he thought the Family was too poor to support such an extravagance.

The situation that existed in the Love Family is a classic example of a sociological phenomenon known as *groupthink*. Sociologist Irving Janis (1972) borrowed the term from George Orwell's novel *1984* to describe a highly conformist way of thinking that prevents the free exchange of information. The ingredients of groupthink include (1) belief in the inherent morality of the group, (2) shared rationalizations for questionable actions, (3) strong pressures to conform, (4) self-censorship of members holding divergent views, (5) "mind guards" who reproach anyone challenging the apparent consensus, and (6) a resulting illusion of unanimity.

All these conditions existed in the Love Family. Not only were members convinced of their moral superiority, but in their eyes, Love Israel stood at the top of the spiritual pyramid. They believed they could "make Love right" by eliminating their egos and giving him their unconditional support. It followed that Love's failings were caused by lack of agreement. Even when Love stepped out of bounds, his transgressions appeared minor when compared with the materialism, corruption, and violence in the outside world. Because of the importance attached to oneness, members at all levels were reticent about expressing their reservations, often blaming themselves for not "getting it." Those who spoke out, even in private conversations, were admonished to "be positive" or "stay present." Outspoken members were considered too "thoughty," and their ideas were dismissed as worldly "conceptions." When gentle reminders didn't work, dissidents could expect to find themselves on the "hot seat" at the next Family meeting, which could be very humiliating.

The end result was a pervasive reluctance to communicate one's true feelings. By 1983 Love's authority was sustained by a fragile facade of normalcy that concealed an enormous amount of discontent. It is not hard to imagine the effect that the facade of unanimity had on Love. He lived in a protective bubble that insulated him from negative thoughts and dissenting views. The response to Love's drug use was a prime example. "Once in a while," an elder recalled, "he would ask if I thought he was too far into it, but I usually said no. We all did. I'd say, 'No, Love, I think you can handle it.' In point of fact, I didn't always believe that."

Early in 1983 the facade suddenly collapsed. Sensing that trouble was brewing in the council, Love called an elders' meeting in eastern Washington. To help everyone relax, he passed around a bottle of whiskey, but the alcohol unleashed a backlog of resentment. The cocaine situation was on everyone's mind because one of the elders had just been given a tip that the Family was about to be raided by the Drug Enforcement Administration. During the meeting someone posed a question for Love: Given their agreement to submit to the collective wisdom of the body of Jesus Christ, who would be right if the elders agreed that Love was wrong? Love responded that he would be right, because he alone represented the mind of Christ. His unwillingness to admit any part in the Family's problems split the council apart, and one elder stormed out of the meeting, muttering obscenities.

Love did make one concession. He agreed to stop buying cocaine, but the next day a rumor spread that on his way back to Seattle, he had stopped off to make another drug deal. The fiasco in eastern Washington proved to be the final straw. One by one the elders began confiding in each other, sharing information about Love's private life that they had been keeping secret for years. As they did, it became obvious that the extent and depth of dissatisfaction were much greater than any of them had realized. It was during this time that one of the people who had been with Love in Mexico revealed that Love had given his worldly name and age to a border guard. For people who had spent time in jail for claiming to be eternal, or who had struggled to get jobs without legal identification, Love's disregard for the Family's agreements was seen as a fundamental betrayal of trust.

Secretly a small group of elders, including Logic, Strength, and others who had been with Love since the beginning of the Family, drafted a petition outlining their concerns. The letter accused Love of abusing his authority by making himself an exception to Family agreements, deceiving the community, and overtaxing the Family to feed his "insatiable appetite" for selfish pleasures. "At the root of all these problems," it read, "is a gap between absolute authority and unfulfilled responsibility. We believe this exists because we have been trying to perpetuate a belief in Love Israel's infallibility, which is not true." The petition asked Love to apologize for his "gross self-indulgence" and turn over authority for running the Family "to those who are responsible," meaning the council of elders. The final draft was completed on July 14, 1983, and within a week it had been signed by all but three elders.

However, when the elders confronted Love with the petition, he tore it up and accused the council of giving in to the forces of Satan. Love took the position that people were either with him or against him. He gave them two choices: they could submit to his authority or leave the Family. Almost immediately the group's collective resolve caved in, and when it became clear that Love still had the upper hand, the elders who had drafted the petition decided to leave. When Logic and Strength, who had been two of Love's strongest supporters, left the Family, the news swept through the community like a tidal wave. Most members could hardly believe it. Then other elders started to leave, and suddenly people were forced to take sides in a conflict most of them knew nothing about.

At first most of the youngers stood behind Love, but now the rules that had kept people from sharing negative thoughts with each other were giving way. For the first time, many of the elders held frank discussions in their households about Love's cocaine habit and the Family's financial problems. During these meetings, and in dozens of informal conversations that followed, everything else that had been bothering people came to the surface.

Before long, many youngers were leaving, too. As the pace of defection accelerated, it became clear to everyone that the Love Family was falling apart. Even members who still supported Love had to consider their options—they could stay on what seemed to be a sinking ship, or they could swim for shore. By the end of February 1984, when the tide of defections had finally subsided, almost 85 percent of the members had left.

## EPILOGUE

The breakup was over by the time Janann and I started our research in 1984. Most defectors, then mainly in their thirties, were still living in the Seattle area and they kept in close contact with each other. With few exceptions, they said they still believed in the visions that brought them together, but religion no longer played an important role in their lives. Except when reminiscing about the Love Family, they didn't talk much about it, and very few had become involved in any kind of religious activity since the Family broke up.

On the whole, the ex-members looked and acted much more like typical middle-class Americans than like the hippies they used to be. Some of the Bible name members had kept their Hebrew names, and a few still lived communally, but the majority were trying to blend into the world around them. Most of the men had cut their hair, shaved their beards, and taken conventional jobs.

In contrast to the Family's fluid sexual relationships, monogamous, nuclear family households had become the norm. Their children were enrolled in public schools and generally were doing well. Parents let their kids choose new names for themselves, and some experimented with two or three names before finding one they liked. Only a few remnants of the Family's culture remained among the defectors. Social relationships, for example, tended to reflect the positions they had occupied in the Family's hierarchy, so that distinctions between elders and youngers, virtue names and Bible names, were still visible. To some extent, even their economic success reflected their former standing in the Family. Most of the youngers had taken blue-collar jobs, whereas the elders were more likely to have found white-collar positions. Logic, for instance, was on his way to becoming a successful real estate salesman, and Strength had taken a job in one of Seattle's major stock brokerages.

One might have thought that the readjustment process would have been traumatic, and for some it was. But after years of adapting to Love's unpredictable behavior, most ex-members were adept at making abrupt changes in their lives. Even more important was the fact that so many members had defected at the same time. They supported each other by talking through their anger and disappointment, finding each other jobs, and trading services. Especially during the summer months, groups of ex-members partied at each other's homes almost every weekend.

About forty members, not counting children, had stood by Love during the breakup. Most were living in Love's Queen Anne Hill house when Janann and I arrived in Seattle; Love and a few others had moved to southern California. Strange as it seems, Love had gone to work as a mortgage banker for an old high school friend. Although he kept his beard and long hair, and continued to go by the name Love Israel, he wore suits to work and quickly adopted the trappings of upper-middle-class life. He rented a large house in an exclusive suburb by the ocean, sent his children to a private school, and spent nights on the town with friends outside the Family. Although many defectors refused to believe it, Love apparently had kicked his cocaine habit.

Meanwhile, the loyalists in Seattle tried to hang on to the Family's culture. They kept their long hair and beards, continued to wear robes, and organized themselves according to the Family's traditional household model. But there were signs that the boundaries separating the Love Family from the outside world were continuing to break down. On a visit to Love's house, for example,

Janann and I watched women dance to Michael Jackson's "Thriller" album while doing housework.

The loyalists claimed the defectors either had lied about their visions or had turned away from their spiritual understandings for selfish reasons. In fact, a few defectors admitted to us that they had made up visions to be accepted or that they had embellished what they had really seen to make their experiences more acceptable to Love. On the other hand, the defectors derided the loyalists as unproductive fringe members and opportunists who saw the breakup as their chance to move up in the hierarchy. Although they acknowledged that a few competent people had stayed with Love, they dismissed them as pie-in-the-sky idealists who never really understood the problems facing the Family.

Richness, whose money had supported the Family for so long, had filed a lawsuit to recover his assets. Love settled out of court, ostensibly because he did not want "to be against anyone," but more likely because several key witnesses were ready to testify against him. Twelve defectors had filed affidavits, charging Love with drug-dealing and sexual abuse, that could have proved very damaging in court. Richness was awarded most of the Family's property, including Love's house on Queen Anne Hill. Love, however, kept title to the ranch.

Tension between the factions ran high during the first months Janann and I spent in Seattle. We even heard rumors about death threats against the most outspoken defectors, although we never had any reason to believe them. Instead, it seemed that people on both sides were genuinely saddened by the way old friends had turned against each other. On our first visit to Queen Anne Hill after the breakup, we stood by as two members, who hadn't seen one another for months, met for the first time on the street. One was clean-shaven and the other still had a full beard. They approached one another tentatively, shook hands, and exchanged some small talk. "What name do you go by?" asked the clean-shaven man. "Encouragement," the other said. "And you?" "Bruce," the other replied. With that, the encounter ended. They said goodbye, turned, and walked in opposite directions.

Despite the Family's uncertain future, about half the remaining members attended the 1984 Rainbow Gathering in northern California. Love drove up from Los Angeles with Honesty and one of his elders, although he stayed for only three days. The breakup of the Love Family was being talked about all around the Gathering, so it was important for Love to make a good showing. The Family's encampment was dominated by Love's sanctuary tent, but Love and Honesty slept in an ordinary camp tent that was barely big enough for Love to stand up in. During the day, Love hosted members of the Rainbow Family, and at night, people from all over the Gathering crowded into his sanctuary tent to play music. Privately, however, many Rainbow people were glad the Family had broken up, because in their eyes, Love had always been a dictator. Most defectors did not believe Love had the nerve to return to Washington, but he surprised them by moving back to the ranch in the summer of 1985. Although he claimed to have more than 80 followers, only about 40 adults and their children were living at the ranch by the end of the summer.

Nevertheless, the community was slowly beginning to take shape again. Work crews were organized to clean up the grounds and renovate the barn, while others went to work in the surrounding area to pay off the Family's debts.

The last time I visited the Love Family was in 1996. The ranch was as beautiful as ever. Two exotic-looking houses had been built near the barn, new flower beds had been added, more trees had been planted, and a long set of rough-cut stone steps now connected the barn with a neighboring yurt. The first floor of the barn had been turned into a lodge for informal gatherings, complete with a kitchen, bar, pool table, and television where the children watched videos on the Family's VCR. Love's area was upstairs where the offices were, and what had once been the common meeting area now served as his living room. It was tastefully decorated with Persian rugs, antique furniture, and pictures painted by Family members during the 1970s. Old Family banners, including one depicting a vision of Jesus Christ leading his people into New Jerusalem, hung from the walls.

Draped from the high, arched ceiling were purple and white streamers left from a birthday party. Birthdays were just one of many signs of change. Decorating the downstairs hall were pictures of Family teenagers in tuxedos and formals taken at the high school prom in nearby Arlington.

Love's oldest son, Life, wore slacks and a sport shirt, and drove a bright new 4x4 pickup truck. Many men, including Love, had cut their hair to conventional lengths, and their beards were much shorter. While we were taking a walk together, Love told me about their troubles with local zoning authorities, but mostly he talked about the Family's teenagers. He was especially proud of his son Clean, who had starred on Arlington High School football teams and had been runner-up in the homecoming king competition.

At first glance, the Family seemed to be prospering again, but there were hints that the community was still struggling to survive. In contrast to the showplace character of the area around the barn, some of the yurts hidden in the forest were shabby and in need of repair. Hardly anyone had joined the Family since the breakup, and except for children and a few teenagers, most members now were middle-aged. A few members were missing teeth, and some of those who were not, obviously needed dental work. Aside from three or four paintings donated by an ex-member, all the artwork in the barn was at least 15 years old—most of the Family's artists had left during the breakup. The few artists who remained were so absorbed by taking care of children and making ends meet that they had little time for artistic endeavors.

During my visit the Family threw a Saturday night party for a young member who had just returned after being gone for a year. A band from Arlington High played rock music in the barn, and Family members joined in with their drums and maracas. At least half the crowd consisted of young people who had grown up in the Family. They were attractive, extroverted, and clearly admired by the friends they had invited. The women wore stylish skirts and blouses, and most of the men dressed in slacks and sport shirts. To an outsider the scene would have looked like an ordinary college party, except that many of the partyers were in their forties and fifties, and were wearing robes and sandals. Sometime after midnight the party moved to the meadow, where young and old alike danced and sang until dawn to tribal drumming reminiscent of the Rainbow Gathering where I first met the Family. I was impressed by how comfortable the two generations were with each other. In conventional American society, invisible boundaries separate the worlds of teenagers, young adults, and the middle-aged; those lines were virtually nonexistent at the party.

Yet hardly any of the young people at the party still lived at the ranch. The few who did were teenagers, and most of them were planning to leave after they finished high school. Despite their obvious affection for the Family and respect for Love Israel, the clothes they wore symbolized their independence from Love and their parents. For them, the Love Family would always be their home, but they had others worlds to explore. By Monday morning nearly all the young adults were gone, back to college and their worldly jobs; their parents on the ranch went back to work, trying to pay their bills and keep the Family afloat financially. It seemed doubtful that the Family would be any more successful at keeping its kids at home in the future than it had been so far.

In 1998 the Love Family is 29 years old, making it one of the oldest counterculture communities in the United States. Out of thousands of communal experiments started in the late 1960s and early 1970s, the Family is one of a tiny handful of survivors. In her study of nineteenth-century communes, Kanter found hardly any that survived more than a generation, which she defined as 25 years. From that perspective, the Love Family is a success story. But when I looked at the ranch on Monday morning after the party, I had to wonder what would become of the Family's utopian dream in another 25 years.

## BIBLIOGRAPHY

Allen, S. (1982). *Beloved son: A story of the Jesus cults.* Indianapolis: Bobbs-Merrill.

Bainbridge, W. S. (1976, June 18). A sociologist's view: Love family deserves tolerance. *Seattle Times*, p. A13.

Baker, R. (1979, October). America's most dangerous cult—a world of violence, drugs and child abuse. *National Enquirer*, p. 16.

Downey, R. (1982, December 1). All in the Love family. *The Weekly*, pp. 31–35.

Festinger, L., Riecken, H.W., & Schachter, S. (1956). *When prophecy fails.* New York: Harper & Row.

Fogarty, Robert S. (1981). *The righteous remnant: The house of David.* Kent, OH: Kent State University Press.

Iannaccone, L. R. (1994). Why strict churches are strong. *American Journal of Sociology, 99,* 1180–1211.

Israel, S. (1983, Spring). Bringing the vision down to earth. *In Context*, 22–25.

Janis, I. (1972). *Victims of groupthink: A psychological study of foreign policy decisions and fiascos.* Boston: Houghton Mifflin.

Kanter, R. M. (1972). *Commitment and community: Communes and utopias in sociological perspective.* Cambridge, MA: Harvard University Press.

Masters, R. E. L., & Houston, J. (1966). *The varieties of psychedelic experience.* New York: Holt, Rinehart and Winston.

Patrick, T., & Dulack, T. (1976). *Let our children go!* New York: E. P. Dutton.

# Chapter 5

# El Niño Fidencio and the Fidencistas

## Antonio N. Zavaleta

Antonio Zavaleta grew up in the Lower Rio Grande Valley between Texas and northeastern Mexico. As a young man, during summer vacations from school, he stayed with his grandparents on their ranch. They employed many migratory Mexican farm workers, with whom he spent many hours. "My lifelong love for Mexican folklore and of Mexico in general was kindled around the campfires and the endless evening stories. It was there that I first heard the stories of El Niño Fidencio." After receiving his Ph.D. in anthropology from the University of Texas at Austin, Tony began teaching and served as a Brownsville City Council member. He had been studying a well-known native healer in Brownsville, and the idea of comparing these techniques with those of Fidencio was exciting. He made several trips to Espinazo, the home of El Niño Fidencio. On one such trip he met Maria, a follower of Fidencio, and together they worked to learn the details of the healer's life. "It is rare that an anthropologist has the opportunity to have firsthand, day-to-day knowledge of the inner workings of a religious cult and to be accepted by it. They are as sincere and profound as any religious group I have ever encountered."

Known as a land of mystery and paradox, Mexico today is the product of a conflict between two distinct cultures, Native American and Spanish. In the sixteenth century, Spanish explorers, seeking adventure and wealth, brought to Mexico a mixture of medieval chivalry and religious devotion (Boone 1989).

Many of the Spanish military were members of lay religious orders and hoped to re-create the crusades. Religious leaders, on the other hand, hoped to establish a utopia and prepare for the second coming of Christ (Darley 1968).

## A CLASH OF CULTURES AND ACCULTURATION

Spanish Catholicism included a plethora of medieval practices. These ideas meshed with and enhanced the superstitious world of the Native Americans. The friars, zealous in their desire to spread Catholicism, quickly recognized that their success depended on tolerance and acceptance of native beliefs and practices. Over time, many Indian religious ideas were brought into the Catholic Church, both symbolically and physically. This ultimately opened the door for the *acculturation* of some of these beliefs into the official Catholic Church in Mexico.

Acculturation occurs when one culture blends with another, losing its distinctive traits in the process. The result was the creation of an unofficial as well as an official Catholic religion. Today, after nearly five centuries, there exists rich diversity between the practice of Catholicism and of its alter ego, Mexican or folk Catholicism (Madsen 1967).

Beliefs common to both Catholicism and folk Catholicism include the concept of the incarnation of God in the form of man, his life and teachings on earth, his death or departure, and his promise of return followed by the establishment of a utopian society (Morinis and Crumrine 1991). In addition, the concept of a virgin goddess is essential to both belief systems, as is the belief in the existence of a pantheon of lesser gods or ''saints,'' who are believed to be physically capable of affecting the lives of the living. Finally, the existence of sacred or holy sites dedicated to the saints and the requirement of the faithful to make pilgrimages to these sites are central features of both belief systems. Although the two religions coexisted and shared similar beliefs, they served different populations.

Traditional Catholicism met the needs of the Spanish, their descendants, and the affluent. Folk Catholicism was more responsive to the needs of the poor, the Indians, and the racially mixed descendants of the Spanish and Indians. Now, as then, the majority of the Mexican people are spread across the country, living in small towns, villages, and settlements. Their extended kinship groups live, for the most part, a subsistence existence in isolation from the major religious, cultural, and economic centers. It is among these largely rural people that the practice of folk Catholicism flourishes.

## SOCIAL STRATIFICATION IN MEXICO

The distribution of wealth and power in a society describes its system of *social stratification*. Societies vary tremendously in the extent to which people share, or refuse to share, societal resources. An important feature of any stratification system is the opportunity for individuals to better themselves materially.

Such movement is called *social mobility*. Rates of social mobility differ considerably among societies. For example, *caste systems*, such as those that exist in India, have very little social mobility. Birth determines the shape of human existence, what jobs members can hold, whom they can marry, whom they can interact with and how. Rules are reinforced by the Hindu religion. Individuals born into a caste, die in that caste. Moreover, their children will live and die in the same caste. *Class systems*, characteristic of industrialized societies, such as the United States, are those in which people have the opportunity to experience upward or downward mobility. Another system of stratification that has more opportunity for social mobility than a caste system but less than a class system is called an *estate system*. Mexico had such a system.

Estate systems are typically rural, with those at the top owning or controlling most of the land. Because such societies are not heavily industrialized, and because educational opportunities are limited to the wealthy, most people are poor and will remain so.

Race can also influence the degree of social mobility in a society. In Mexico, Spaniards and their direct descendants occupied the upper strata and Indians were at the bottom. Mexicans, or mestizos, a racial mix descended from the Spaniards and Indians, constituted the lower and middle classes. The upper classes, living in Mexico City, controlled huge provincial landholdings as absentee landlords. They led lives of privilege, insulated from the middle class and especially from the lower classes of Indians and poor mestizos. In spite of the early emergence of a mixed class, there was little or no social mobility allowed in the system (Ricard 1982). Limited economic and political opportunities for the Indians and mestizos created a climate of frustration and hopelessness.

Mexico's history is filled with the oppression and exploitation of the many by the few. The Spaniards, with their twin missions of gold and God, subjugated the native population. And often those who suffered the most turned to religious and "otherworldly" beliefs for comfort.

## ENTER A MESSIAH

By the mid-1920s, Mexico's underclass had endured over four centuries of suffering. The country was rocked to the core by revolution, civil war, death, and destruction. At the same time, President Plutarco Calles (1924–1928) brutally attempted to rid Mexico of the Catholic Church (Krauze 1987).

It is noteworthy that messiahs usually appear during periods of oppression or economic catastrophe in order to fulfill people's longing to end their suffering. Such a situation is characterized as *structural strain*. Strain occurs when individuals' needs are not being met through existing social structures. Such strain can produce a number of different kinds of social movements that are categorized by sociologists as *collective behavior*, some of which are messiah-led.

Messianic leaders are universally *charismatic*. People follow them because they have personal characteristics, distinctive appearance, or mannerisms that galvanize an audience.

Most messiahs are heralded by unusual or unexplainable natural phenomena, such as "the star of Bethlehem" signaling the birth of Christ. In Mexico, volcanic eruptions and the appearance of a comet in the skies over Mexico City set the stage for the Mexican Revolution of 1910–1917. These occurrences were thought to foretell a messiah.

In 1926, unearthing of a monolith in the central plaza in Mexico City was believed to prophesy that Indians would regain their ancient rights (Brenner 1929). This prophecy had been made some 475 years earlier by native priests who had witnessed the monolith's burial by the Spanish. The priests concluded that after some indeterminable period of penance, the foreign invaders would be expelled, and native culture and religion would be restored. What they could not have foretold was that the actual rediscovery of the monolith would coincide perfectly with the appearance of a Mexican messiah in the desolate deserts of northern Mexico.

### Nature of the Redeemer

Fulfilling the Mexican image of a redeemer, José Fidencio Sintora Constantino came to the attention of the Mexican press in 1928. This coincided with president Calles's persecution of the Catholic Church.

His followers called him El Niño, "the child." He was a peasant, as poor as the people who sought deliverance at his hand. He claimed that his power was derived from God, through the soil and native plants of the desert. His spiritual gift, or *don*, had been granted to him, through a direct revelation by Christ and the Holy Spirit, beneath a sacred pepper tree in the center of Espinazo, a small village in northern Mexico. Fidencio adhered to a simple credo: "Those who suffer have the Grace of God. By suffering, health is reached, and it is necessary that this should be so, because those who desire to be well, should be strengthened by sorrows and pain" (Brenner 1929: 21).

Fidencio came to be regarded as a living folk saint during his lifetime (Macklin 1973; Spielberg and Zavaleta 1997). Media interest in his healing power waned in a few years, but Fidencio showed no more concern about the loss of newspaper attention than he had shown interest in his previous celebrity status. He often said that his mission on Earth was not to be famous, but to ease the pain of suffering humanity. In the end, numerous attempts to exploit him failed. He died as he had lived, a simple, barefoot peasant.

### El Niño's Childhood

Since the arrival of the Europeans, Mexico has been home to a parade of prophets and miracle workers. All have appeared during times of crisis. All have claimed supernatural powers, all have had cultlike followings, all have had short-lived popularity, and have all paled to insignificance when compared with El Niño Fidencio (Brenner 1929).

There are only sketchy facts known about the early life of Fidencio. He was born in 1898, near the village of Yuriria, in the Mexican state of Guanajuato. He and a younger brother were orphaned as children. For a time they were removed from the village, but by the age of 11, Fidencio was back in Yuriria, assisting the local priest as an altar boy.

From an early age he showed a great fascination with religion (Quiros 1991). At the age of 13 or 14, he was contracted to work for a wealthy family as a kitchen boy. It is curious that he was selected for household work because work in the fields was traditional for Mexican boys at that time. He attended elementary school for a short time; it was neither common nor expected for a peasant boy to continue schooling beyond the age of puberty. As an adult, Fidencio was semiliterate.

Around 1921, at the age of 23, Fidencio, in the company of his brother, settled in Espinazo, a small community in northern Mexico. He never left this area.

### El Niño the Healer

Fidencio's first attempt at healing was the spontaneous act of setting his mother's arm, broken in a fall. Although the splinting of an arm hardly seems remarkable, Fidencio was said to be eight years old at the time (Quiros 1991).

At Espinazo, Fidencio developed a considerable reputation for treating animals, especially assisting at births. But it was not until he was called upon to assist with a human birth that his ability and fame as a healer and midwife began to unfold.

During the course of his lifetime, El Niño Fidencio had several supernatural experiences in the form of revelations or visions—some, he claimed, were visitations by Jesus Christ.

In an early vision, Fidencio was visited by a strange, bearded man who imbued him with the spiritual gift of healing, which included profound knowledge of medicinal plants. Although Fidencio never had any formal training in the healing properties of plants and home remedies, he was expert in their use.

A second supernatural visitation occurred in 1927. This mystical event played a significant role in Fidencio's life. He felt it authorized him to share his gift of healing with the masses of needy and, thus, begin his mission on Earth. From this time on, Fidencio adopted the persona of a holy man and lived the life of an ascetic. He achieved fame as a healer in 1928, at the age of 30. He died ten years later, a few days short of his fortieth birthday.

### EL CAMPO DEL DOLOR

In the early days of 1928, Mexico was in the throes of the post-Revolutionary government's persecution of the Catholic Church. Catholic clergy were expelled, imprisoned, and executed, and church property was confiscated. During these troubling days, Mexico turned her eyes to the northern desert as the first reports of miracles began to emerge.

The earliest news coverage of the strange young miracle worker described a man who neither claimed to be a doctor nor prescribed any patent medicines. He nevertheless performed healing miracles, including making the blind see and the dumb speak. Talk of the young healer previously had been confined to northern Mexico, but in 1928 virtually all the major dailies in Mexico City carried articles on the miraculous cures in Espinazo.

Throughout 1928 and 1929, articles, supported by dozens of eyewitness testimonies, touted Fidencio's healing abilities. News spread rapidly, and soon his fame extended throughout Mexico and to the United States and Europe (Ha traspasado 1928; "The Worker of Miracles" 1928).

*El Universal de México*, one of the leading newspapers and among the first to give national exposure to the phenomena in Espinazo, sent its top reporter, Jacobo Dalejuelta, and photographer, Casasola, for a firsthand look. In February 1928, the paper reported that the demented, the paralyzed, and the leprous, a thousand strong, had formed a little town of makeshift huts and tents around the home of Fidencio. More than a hundred small wooden huts had been erected to rent to the growing crowd of miracle seekers. El Niño Fidencio worked near a sacred tree, and the ill gathered around him for public healing sessions that ran day and night for several days at a time. This scene eventually became known as the healing circle or *el círculo de curación* (Dementes, paralíticos y leprosos 1928).

*El Universal de México* described Fidencio as a "young man of few words, muscular with a sort of yellowish color and very simply dressed" (Dementes, paralíticos y leprosos 1928). His room contained a crude wooden bed, a table, and a chair. However, according to reports, he used these infrequently, preferring to sit and sleep on the floor. He did not eat or drink with regularity, and mostly consumed liquids. In spite of these abstemious habits, El Niño Fidencio worked for days and nights without interruption, seemingly unaffected by fatigue (El curandero de Espinazo 1928).

Significantly, from the earliest days of his fame as a healer, El Niño Fidencio was a public man. He performed his cures in the midst of thousands of onlookers, always allowed photographs, and gave numerous interviews. During one of the public healing sessions, El Niño reportedly turned to Dalejuelta and said, "Open your eyes, go wherever you want, tell the people what you have seen, and be sure to tell the truth." To the photographer, Casasola, he quipped: "Take pictures of whatever you like, but be sure to give me copies, because if you don't, none of them will come out" (Dementes, paralíticos y leprosos 1928). As a result of this openness, hundreds of photographs document his life and work. With the national press focused on El Niño Fidencio, a massive response was predictable. The needy, the sickly, and the terminally ill, people from every walk of life and social class, began converging on the little desert village of Espinazo.

For the majority of the year, the town bakes in unrelenting heat. When it is not hot, a desert chill descends on the landscape and its inhabitants. As hundreds and then thousands of sickly and dying people arrived in 1928, this desolate and unforgiving spot was turned into the field of pain, *el campo del dolor* (El campo del dolor 1928). The hopeful created their own accommodations by improvising shacks, stacking thorny desert plants into the shapes of huts and leantos. The crowds, suffering from insanity, paralysis, cancer, leprosy, and syphilis, were so large their members had to wait for weeks, even months, to be seen. Thus, many virtually became residents of Espinazo.

### Famous Cures

The newspapers' accounts contained many case histories of El Niño's miraculous cures. One famous case, retold many times, involved a young blind boy, the son of a Spanish immigrant. The boy, age two, was the victim of a firecracker accident that caused him gradually to lose his sight until he was completely blind. The doctors had given him no hope of recovery.

As tales of the miraculous El Niño filtered throughout Mexico, the child's parents decided to take him to Espinazo, an arduous journey that required two weeks. The family lived in a brush shack that they constructed, using their clothing to cover the many openings. Weeks passed as they waited patiently. When the day finally came for Fidencio to see their son, he would not allow the mother to explain the cause of the boy's blindness. "It's not necessary that you explain it to me," he said (Dementes, paralíticos y leprosos 1928). Asking them to be patient, El Niño Fidencio massaged the boy's eyes for a few minutes. Then he lifted his head to the heavens in an ecstatic state for several minutes, as if he were having a vision. When some time had passed, El Niño lowered his head and continued to massage the boy's eyes. Finally he said, "*Ya estás curado*; . . . [you're healed; bring me a handkerchief to cover his eyes and be sure not to remove it until the early morning light" (Dementes, paralíticos y leprosos 1928). The family returned to their shack. Early the next morning, as day was breaking, the boy's mother began to remove his bandage. The boy exclaimed, "*Ya veo* [I can see]" (Dementes, paralíticos y leprosos 1928). This documented case of restored sight was later judged to be an extreme case of *autosuggestion*, which it very well may have been. Such cases, however, caused frenzy among El Niño's followers, adding to his fame and popularity.

Another interesting case typified the cures for which El Niño Fidencio was famous. A woman reported that her husband, who suffered from chronic dyspepsia, had consulted numerous doctors. He had undergone unsuccessful surgery, and his condition was so serious that he was expected to die. With no other hope available, the couple decided to go to Espinazo. El Niño came into their tent and, without asking any questions about the man's illness, began to massage his stomach. When he departed, Fidencio, who often used fruit as a medicine, left a large bunch of bananas for the patient to eat. The wife remarked that her husband could not eat them because fruit made him very sick. However, having begun to feel a little better, the patient asked for a small piece of banana and, to his wife's great surprise, asked for more a short time later. Within two hours, he had eaten four bananas, causing him to vomit violently. Fidencio returned the next day and massaged the patient's stomach with a paste made from fruit, soap, and medicinal plants. By the second day, the man had improved remarkably, and by the fourth, he was able to walk for the first time in months (Curaciones hechas por El Niño Fidencio 1928).

Among the early curiosity seekers was a medical doctor from the city of Torreón who was afflicted by paralysis. Fidencio cured him after only one week of treatments. While in Espinazo, the doctor witnessed many cures, which he later reported, including the notable cure of a young man from Monterrey who had gone insane. The doctors had declared his insanity incurable, so his father had brought him to El Niño, who immediately began to extract the young man's teeth. Following this procedure, the youth rapidly regained his lucidity. The young man's insanity, the doctor from Torreón reasoned, had been due to an infection in his teeth that had affected his nervous system. The young man, grateful for his cure, stayed on to work in El Niño's household. It was a familiar pattern in Espinazo for the healed to volunteer service to the community (Aspectos de el campo del dolor 1928).

## THE MYTH OF EL NIÑO

If the press played a large role in spreading the news of El Niño's cures, it may have played an even larger role in promulgating the myth of El Niño. He was said to have had special powers, particularly clairvoyance, since childhood. According to some reports, when an incurably ill person approached, Fidencio would remark to the crowd, "A person is coming who is wasting his time; tell him to go off and prepare for his death; I can't help him except to pray for him" (Aspectos de el campo del dolor 1928). Dalejuelta reported in *El Universal de México* that the well-known General Peraldi came to Espinazo with an incurable illness. El Niño told him to stay if he wanted, but that he could not help him. He must make peace with God because "Your sufferings are going to take you on an eternal adventure" (Curaciones hechas por El Niño Fidencio 1928). According to the report, General Peraldi died before the end of that day.

Followers and observers alike reported that El Niño Fidencio often seemed to enter a trance while healing. He denied being part of the spiritist movement that was common in the early part of the century and was popular in Mexico (Kardec 1989). A very religious person, Fidencio asserted that he was in communication with the Heavenly Father, who healed through him. He seldom referred directly to the supernatural, but simple comments like the one he made to the photographer Casasola—about the photographs not coming out if he were not given a copy—were passed on by word of mouth. The press repeated the stories, greatly enhancing the belief that El Niño had the supernatural ability to affect the outcome of events.

Not all the effects of notoriety, of course, were positive. The growing reports of miraculous cures enraged the medical community, and claims of fraud and deception grew more common. In Mexico City, Dr. Neumayer, a professor at the national medical school, gave a public demonstration on the types of psychic cures performed by El Niño Fidencio. Neumayer claimed that Mexico was fertile ground for these types of healings and predicted that El Niño's ability would soon wane (Opinión de un médico 1928).

## A PRESIDENTIAL VISIT

The media reports of miraculous cures in Espinazo reached a fevered pitch in the early months of 1928. On February 8, 1928, the presidential train *Olivo* made a special stop at Espinazo so that President Plutarco Calles could have a private consultation with Fidencio. The president's visit came at the height of the government's persecution of the Catholic Church, and naturally led to speculation that Calles intended to expand his efforts to control the church. However, eyewitness reports indicate that Calles suffered from a serious skin ailment and came seeking relief from El Niño Fidencio. Calles's visit protected El Niño from serious interference by local and state governments, as well as by the church and medical communities (Condal 1977.)

Medical associations called for immediate intervention, not on the basis of Fidencio's practice but on the basis of what was not being done to protect the community at large. So many seriously sick people had congregated in Espinazo that the fear of contagion became an increasingly valid issue. Many believed that the situation posed a serious health threat to all of northern Mexico (Dos veces por semana habrá caros por Espinazo 1928).

## FRIENDS AND ENEMIES OF EL NIÑO FIDENCIO

Because of the thousands of seriously and incurably ill people flocking to the village, it was inevitable that the death rate in Espinoza would rise. In fact, so many people had died that two new cemeteries had to be created. "A New Cemetery for the Miracles of Fidencio," reported the Monterrey newspaper (Un nuevo panteón 1928). How could the president of the Republic go there and not see the truth of what was happening? "Was some deal made to protect Fidencio?" asked *El Universal de México* newspaper (Pretende ser mejor 1928). In a small village where one death might be recorded every year, 44 persons had died in less than one month (Un nuevo panteón 1928). The focus of the Mexican press turned from reporting the issue to hosting a debate between the medical and spiritist communities (Kardec 1986). With such negative publicity, the governments of the northern states of Nuevo León and Coahuila experienced extreme pressure to resolve the case of the young healer.

The early newspaper accounts also were among the first to mention El Niño's cult following that emerged from among the loyal masses of the healed (Dementes, paralíticos y leprosos 1928). A small army of faithful, called the *brigada roja* (red brigade), encircled, sheltered and protected El Niño from the constant attacks of the press, the medical community, the government, and the church. During the early months of 1928, the Mexican press outside Mexico City varied sharply in its opinions on the Espinazo phenomenon. The provincial dailies in the major northern cities of Monterrey, Saltillo, and Torreón agreed with the need for local government control and concurred with the outrage of the medical community. "Monterrey is threatened with being converted from a mecca of health into one of suffering and death," read one headline (Espinazo he convertido 1928). The article claimed that Monterrey and all of northern Mexico were in danger of a major epidemic. Health authorities in the state of Nuevo León clamored that all manner of persons with every possible disease had congregated, and that it was now time to end this farce. In all probability, such articles were expressing embarrassment about the international attention. It did not help matters that the area had been plagued by a rash of scandalous healers and miracle workers throughout the early part of the century.

A real plague of miracle workers has invaded Coahuila and Nuevo León. The competition between the saviors of mankind intensifies every day, without the caravan of believers knowing who to visit first, since every one of them claims to have derived power from God. (Pretende ser mejor 1928).

The Mexico City press, on the other hand, was largely supportive of El Niño Fidencio, if only in a cynical way. The news generated in the north was an appreciated diversion from the serious problems plaguing the country in the midst of civil war. Dr. Charles Morpeau, a French physician in Mexico, spoke in favor of Fidencio in the Mexico City press. He stated that it would be medical folly to "negate in the name of science the cures of the spiritual forces of the world." He added, "Because all of life is based upon illusion or suggestion, we doctors have not tried to completely understand the nature of our successes. There are many things that happen in medicine that are completely unexplainable. If the truth be known, many have died because of our autosuggestion and inability to treat an illness" (El doctor 1928).

Tales of El Niño's philanthropy were becoming inscribed in lore as his cures and "miracles" were told and retold. The stories of miraculous cures and healings were transformed into lyrics and then into folk songs and religious hymns. These popular songs voiced El Niño's successes and expressed thanks to El Niño Fidencio and to God for their cures. The Mexico City press reported that "the festive songs were sung of the *curandero* in Espinazo and across the country in all of the little towns and public places" (Los poetas campesinos 1928).

Day and night, in the face of adversity, Fidencio continued to console the suffering. He tirelessly attended to his sick; it was his mission. From around the nation, thousands came to Espinazo, accepted his medicine, and listened to his gentle words of spiritual healing. Most returned to their homes without El Niño ever knowing their names. The journalists remarked that the people had been helped by simply looking on the face of El Niño.

Throughout the remainder of 1928 and for several years thereafter, more people bought train tickets to Espinazo than to any other destination in Mexico. This tiny desert village, which formerly had no need for a mail service, was forced to establish a post office that processed the approximately 25,000 to 35,000 letters that had arrived for the throngs in search of a cure (Telégrafo y correo en Espinazo1928). Similarly, *Telégrafos Nacionales* established an office in Espinazo. Fidencio was the first person to utilize the telegraph service, sending a message of thanks to the national office (Telégrafo y correo en Espinazo 1928). Never before had one of Mexico's hundreds of folk healers reached this level of popularity and notoriety. The press followed the story daily. In February 1928, *El Excelcior* printed the following headlines: "Large Caravans of Sick Leave for Espinazo," "Hundreds Of Sick Return to Their Homes Let Down by Fidencio," "Travelers to the City of Pain Die or Are in Worse Condition," "Peregrinations to Espinazo Make Followers of Fidencio Rich," "Contradictory News of El Niño Fidencio's Real Ability," "The Healer of Espinazo Continues Miraculous Cures," "The Cures of El Niño Fidencio Are Amazing and Produce Great Admiration for the Healer," "Everything That Has Been Said About the Celebrated Miracle Worker Pale in the Face of Reality," "The Fanaticism of His Followers Increases," and " 'It's God Who Cures with My Hands,' Says the Miraculous Niño Fidencio."

Within two years, Espinazo began to recover from the frenzy of 1928 and 1929. By 1930, the tens of thousands of insane, deformed, blind, paralytic, and diseased persons searching for a personal miracle were gone. However, a steady stream of the faithful, as well as many newcomers and curiosity seekers, continued to make the difficult trip year after year. During the early 1930s Espinazo began to take on a much more routine way of life. El Niño's popularity in the media continued to decline sharply. He was almost constantly under fire from public health and medical officials, and in later years he was attacked by the church. He was arrested and brought before tribunals in Monterrey on two occasions (Quiros 1991). This period of relentless attack was unquestionably the most important period of his life, because while his celebrity in the media declined, his fame and popularity with the common people continued to soar.

## ESPINAZO: UTOPIA ON THE DESERT

Dr. Francisco Vela, vice president of the state of Nuevo León's committee on public health, secretly visited Espinazo in 1930. The throngs of thousands were gone, the spectacle largely over. Approximately 1,500 sick persons and their families remained, still an enormous number of people compared with the 100 or so permanent residents. Espinazo was once again a place of serenity.

Although Vela attempted to portray the setting as an ineffectual place of healing, he inadvertently provided the first glimpses of Espinazo as an emerging utopian society, a New Jerusalem, built around a central cult figure (Da Cunha 1970). Long, orderly lines of men and women waited patiently for their morning drink of hot herbal medicine or coffee. The dirt streets were perfectly laid out, each with a name; residential sections were named after those in Mexico City.

Fifty children received instruction from a teenage girl in a small building, El Niño Fidencio School. When Vela arrived, Fidencio was seated in a large room called *el foro* (forum), a little theater built for the plays and musical events that were popular with El Niño and his followers. Admirers surrounded him, caressed him, stroked his hair, and kissed his hands and feet as they greeted him and asked his advice. El Niño, always attired in a white tunic and barefoot, was described as looking serene and intelligent. He had a ''rare'' skin color, a mix between brown and white that was almost yellowish; thick lips; large teeth; and light eyes that looked away from the intruding eyes of visitors (''El Doctor Vela González, sin que El Niño Fidencio lo sospechará, estuvo con él,'' in *El Porvenir de Monterrey*, as cited in Quiros 1991: 123–134). Upon arrival, Vela was immediately ushered into the presence of El Niño Fidencio, who extended his hand and asked two of his young helpers to show their guest whatever he wanted to see.

Most interesting to Dr. Vela was a room with a large number of bottles filled with tissue and tumors extracted by El Niño. These may still be seen in Espinazo. El Niño Fidencio performed operations without anesthesia, using only a broken piece of bottle glass as a surgical instrument. Vela claimed to identify many samples as ''obviously'' benign tumors. However, he commented that the most highly trained surgeons of the day would not have dared attempt their removal in their offices, thereby implying the remarkableness of an untrained healer's performing such surgeries.

Vela was escorted to all areas of El Niño's compound—the corral, called *la dicha*, where the demented were kept; the place where the lepers were treated; the maternity ward; the postoperative room; the swing used to treat the mute; the large concrete containers where the fresh herbal medicine was prepared every day; the flower garden; and the famous healing mud pond, *el charquito*. The visitor was stunned by the orderliness of the place and by its simplicity. ''It was like a child was playing hospital in a life-size place'' (El Doctor Vela . . . , as cited in Quiros 1991: 123–134). None of this could possibly work, none of this could possibly be effective, he thought, as the first and then the second, and finally the third funeral procession of the day filed by. The different treatment venues were often hundreds of yards apart, and as Fidencio made his daily treks to see his little sick ones (*infermitos*), he was followed on foot by a parade of the faithful. They sang religious hymns as they walked barefoot through the dusty streets of Espinazo. Later Vela would say:

Fidencio is an innocent, who is not even aware that he suffers from a mental illness which causes him to believe that he has been appointed by God to heal the sick. Those who are not innocent children are those who encircle him and promote his incredible abilities to the masses of suffering people who do not know any better. (Quiros 1991: 123).

The final national media glimpse of Espinazo and El Niño Fidencio came in 1937, one year before his death. The photographic magazine *Hoy*, Mexico's equivalent of *Life* magazine, offered an analysis of the events at Espinazo nine years after the media blitz of 1928. This valuable exposé provides an intimate view of El Niño Fidencio's last year of life. Photographs in the article depict scenes that are familiar even today, because Espinazo has changed little since 1937.

In the late 1930s only a few dozen persons disembarked daily from the trains. Gone were the post office and the telegraph office of eight years earlier. The desperately ill, stripped of hope by their doctors or with no doctor at all, continued to come to Espinazo in search of a personal miracle. Many returned home, disappointed, each day. "I do not even know how to write, sir," Fidencio said to the reporter. "I only use the gifts of healing that God has given me to help these suffering people" (Con Fidencio en Espinazo 1937). One of his young helpers remarked, "Fidencio knows all of the medicinal plants that are used for healing; too bad he never studied medicine" (Con Fidencio en Espinazo 1937).

A photograph's caption in *Hoy* reads, "Behind him, the life-size statue of Christ from whom he claims his power; before him, the suffering, people who have left with cures that defy medical explanation as well as those who will never leave" (Con Fidencio en Espinazo 1937). Some left healed, others left feeling better, some left feeling worse. But all left believing that Fidencio had done for them what no doctor could do. Almost all considered him to be a priest, and they begged for his blessing as he raised his crucifix to the heads of his followers. The article asked, "What sort of man is this, who could have been one of the wealthiest and most powerful in Mexico? What sort of man gives away more than 1 million pesos? What sort of man is this who prefers to live a peasant's life, who shuns even a bed to lie on, and who walks barefoot through the dusty streets of Espinazo to care for the suffering?" (Con Fidencio en Espinazo 1937). The paradox that Fidencio's life presented to the Mexican people further served to support his legitimacy as a beneficiary of supernatural abilities sent to Earth by God to heal the sick, to ease the suffering, and to spread the word of the New Jerusalem.

The *Hoy* article did not speculate about Fidencio's sanity or whether the government should step in to save the region from epidemic. Now aging, tired, and disheveled, he simply and humbly attributed his success to God and reiterated that he had not asked to be chosen for this life. God, having selected him, required him to fulfill his destiny in the service of the poor and suffering.

"I am, in fact, nothing more than a simple peasant following the will of God" (Con Fidencio en Espinazo 1937).

Almost from the beginning of his brief media fame, Fidencio had predicted his early departure from Earth. Daily he emulated and acted out the life of Christ as he understood it. His protectors actively modeled religious symbolism around him, perpetuating the suggestion that El Niño Fidencio was the Messiah, that he was the Christ. El Niño's life in Espinazo so mirrored that of Christ that his followers expected him to die in 1931, at age 33. That he lived until near his fortieth birthday surprised many of his followers. When he did die, the faithful fully expected him to rise from the dead on the third day (Fidencio no quiere salir de Espinazo 1928). Word of his death on October 17, 1938, traveled as quickly as the telegraph and railroad lines could carry the news. From beginning to end, El Niño Fidencio had only ten years of life to treat the ill and serve the poor.

## THE CULT OF EL NIÑO FIDENCIO

As noted previously, cults typically revolve around a charismatic leader. By 1935, an organized cult had developed around El Niño in Espinazo. A central problem confronting most cults is the continuation of the movement after the death of the leader. Rarely does another charismatic step in to replace the original leader.

Charisma, by nature, is unstable. It can exist in its pure form only so long as the charismatic leader is alive. The challenge for followers is to create a situation in which charisma, in some adulterated form, persists after the leader's death. In other words, charisma must be *routinized*, institutionalized in a bureaucratic form. *Bureaucracies* are, by definition, organizational structures that have specialized positions, lines of authority, positions based on merit, and written rules that regulate the behavior of people in the organization.

Vested interests played a part in maintaining the cult of El Niño Fidencio. Espinazo had become one of the most important pilgrimage destinations in Mexico, and it remains so today (Schneider 1995). Legions of faithful, along with those seeking a miracle, journey to Espinazo year after year. Many in and around the small community earn their living by serving these visitors.

The *Fidencista* movement has developed a liturgical calendar based on that of the Catholic Church, integrating with it the centuries-old Native American agrarian calendar that is divided into six-month periods. The *Fidencista* religious cycle also combines traditional Catholic and Native American practices in celebrating the cult of holy persons. Their burial places are revered as sacred sites.

Native American influence in *Fidencista* celebrations is dramatically witnessed as *matachine* dancers, with drums beating and native bows and arrows in hand, travel along the main penitents' route to the tomb of El Niño (Gilles and Trevino 1994).

As El Niño became a prominent folk saint, religious objects bearing his likeness began to be sold in the markets and the pilgrimage sites throughout Mexico. Massive emigration of Mexican workers into the United States between 1938 and the present has spread El Niño's fame. Today, religious artifacts bearing his likeness can be found on an untold number of home altars in Texas and throughout the Mexican communities of the American Midwest (Samora 1971). The widespread representation of El Niño as a saint greatly enhanced the popular belief that he was sent to Earth by God to heal the sick and counsel those in need. This has led to his dual characterization as "divine doctor" and "lawyer" of the poor.

El Niño's physical appearance, simple mannerisms, tunic in the style of biblical times, gentle alto voice, and beardless face further enhanced his growing mythic and cult figure status (Gardner 1992). It is not surprising that followers sometimes refer to him as the "Christ of Espinazo." Before his death, he had begun to act out scriptural events, emulating the life of Christ. Further supporting his cult figure status, El Niño had had an uncanny ability to anticipate questions and provide accurate answers while delivering spontaneous and profound orations on complicated religious topics. Like Jesus Christ, El Niño chose to deliver his spiritual messages by using a combination of parable and allegory, and often staged simple plays to make his point.

### Spiritism

El Niño Fidencio told his followers specifically that he would communicate with them through spirit mediums after his death. He warned them that many would claim to be him; "review them very carefully," he said, "because only a special few will truly deliver my message" (Zapata de Robles 1994). Approximately two years before his death, Damiana Martínez and Victor Zapata, both disciples of El Niño who lived some distance from Espinazo, began to enter trances and channel messages from El Niño. Telepathic messages from El Niño became a defining feature of the *Fidencista* cult. Catholicism provides the basic tenets of *Fidencismo*. Spirit channeling of Fidencio, however, and the resulting shift in focus away from Jesus Christ are the primary reason Fidencismo is not accepted by the Catholic Church (López de la Fuente de González 1993). In addition, Catholicism strictly forbids the celebration of any person before that person has been beatified or canonized. Following El Niño's death, "trance events" created a complex system of spiritual communication between the deceased healer and his followers. The practice continues today, as part of the *routinization of charisma*.

In the waning months of 1938, the organization for the perpetuation of the cult after the death of Fidencio was set in place. El Niño's closest assistants in life became revered as disciples. Damiana was recognized as the principal voice (*vocina principal*) of El Niño Fidencio on Earth and the leader of the movement.

She was the first to occupy the position that came to be called *la directora* (the director). Victor Zapata was charged with denouncing "false voices." His duties evolved into the *el revisador* (inspector general) in later years.

*Fidencista* leadership made a conscious effort to remember and record the messages received from El Niño. Since illiteracy was common in rural Mexico in the 1930s and 1940s, El Niño's spiritual messages or scriptures (*escrituras*) had to be learned by memory and repeated often until an opportunity arose for them to be transcribed.

Approximately 100 "scriptures" have survived, and form a coherent basis for the organization, including the emergent belief system, celebrations and rites, and the nature of the interaction between and among the followers.

### Missionary Efforts

Local neighborhood missions were established outside of the immediate desert towns and villages in northern Mexico. Major *Fidencista* strongholds developed in every major northern city, including Monterrey, Saltillo, Torreón, Guanajuato, and especially the border towns of Nuevo Laredo, Reynosa, and Matamoros. In addition, missions developed in areas where Mexican migratory agricultural workers settled, such as Texas, Indiana, Ohio, Michigan, Colorado, Washington, and Oregon. Each local mission was founded around a trance medium called a *materia* (Zavaleta 1992). The continued success of local missions is also dependent upon the group's ability to identify a member with spiritual gift, or *don*, and to develop new mediums. For this reason, the *Fidencista* experience has always welcomed and encouraged the participation of children, who are viewed as potential mediums. Almost without exception, the founding mediums in the 1940s were female heads of large families. They managed the difficult tasks of raising a family, which were complicated by the growing demands on their time from increased activity in their rapidly growing missions.

At his death, Fidencio was entombed in his hospital building; his followers did not allow his remains to be removed to the cemetery. The establishment of this tomb-shrine propelled Espinazo's status as a pilgrimage site to even greater heights. Miracles are often associated with sacred sites. Today the needy and the faithful come to Espinazo, seeking and receiving miracle cures in the burial room known as *la tumba* (the tomb). Mediums often live great distances from Espinazo but are required to make the trip at least once a year. Many make the pilgrimage more often.

Mediums and their followers sometimes acquire cheap property in Espinazo and build adobe compounds that are used to house them and their followers when they visit for a fiesta (Ovalle de Tamayo 1989). During the fiestas, Espinazo is packed with automobiles and pickup trucks bearing license plates from a dozen U.S. states and an even greater number of Mexican states. Pilgrimages to Espinazo, now referred to as "the Holy Land" or *Tierra Santa*, form the core around which the events of the year revolve. Local missions are always preparing to go to Espinazo or have just returned from there.

Local mediums serve both as advisers and as healers, so that throughout the year, the faithful receive the benefit of healings, concessions, wishes granted, and problems solved. The personal receipt of a miracle creates a spiritual debt (*manda*), that is owed to the granting Catholic saint or spirit. It requires that the recipient perform a penance of gratitude and travel to ''the Holy Land'' to give thanks. Once the recipient has made the promised trip to Espinazo, he or she has fulfilled the obligation and performed the *penitencia*. This process is repeated during the lifetime of a supplicant and guarantees that there will constantly be members of a local mission returning to Espinazo. In addition, those who have received a miracle in their lives serve as a constant marketing device in the Mexican-American community. Their testimonies draw a steady flow of new and needy persons to the medium's healing mission. *Fidencistas* are often devoted to Catholic saints and make regular pilgrimages to Catholic shrines in Mexico.

In the 1940s and 1950s, *la directora* and *el revisador* became the living representatives of El Niño Fidencio on Earth as well as the driving forces behind the cult. Between 1938 and the early 1970s, the *Fidencista* movement continued to grow in strength and numbers with an expanding geographic sphere of influence. The liturgical cycle became fully established, including the semiannual fiestas, and a broad network of functioning local missions were developed.

## THE *FIDENCISTA* MOVEMENT TODAY

During the 59 years since the death of El Niño, skeptics have insisted his memory would fade in time and eventually disappear. In fact, the opposite has happened. Today Fidencio enjoys an unrivaled popularity as a healer and counselor in the pantheon of Mexican and Mexican-American folk saints and Catholic saints. In the United States, the continued popularity of El Niño Fidencio is traced to the fact that the largest part of the Mexican-American community traces its origins to southern Texas and northern Mexico.

Thousands of believers today are loosely organized into a socioreligious community based in healing temples or missions. The *Fidencista* movement is supported at its most basic level by local spirit mediums. Hundreds of missions support hundreds of thousands of regular followers as well as untold numbers of one-time or episodic visitors to the missions.

The growth of *Fidencismo* is enhanced by an informal system of oral communication that operates effectively in the Latino community (Escamilla 1995). The structure and function of *Fidencista* missions in Mexican and Mexican-American communities is based on faith and the unavailability of local medical care. Individuals who seek health care at *Fidencista* missions fall into three broad categories. The first consists of a small inner circle of faithful followers and assistants. A second large group consists of regular attendees. These individuals regularly participate in weekly healing sessions and in special temple activities. The size of the regular group is dependent upon numerous complex factors, including the current popularity of the trance medium. The third group consists of persons seeking treatment on an episodic basis. The size of the third group depends upon the success of the informal, word-of-mouth network established by the regular group. Most of the regular members of a *Fidencista* temple make weekly appearances for simple blessings (*bendiciones*) and positive emotional enforcement. Ritual sweepings, in which the healer uses a sweeping motion with herbs or special sacred objects, are used to rid the patient of "bad vibes." Almost without exception, regular members have received a miracle from El Niño Fidencio. In difficult cases that require continued benefaction, the recipients are expected to remember to whom they owe their good fortune. Offerings are gladly accepted. Loyalty is demonstrated by regular appearances at temple functions and by the general support of temple activities.

First-time visits to a *Fidencista* healer almost always are prompted by a serious physical, emotional, personal, or economic problem in the life of the visitor. Contrary to popular belief, people who seek physical care from a spiritual folk healer (*curandero*) do not do so as a first choice. Almost without exception, physicians have been consulted first. If medical therapy has not been successful, alternative therapies, especially miraculous treatment, are sought. Every *Fidencista* mission has a regular group of persons who give impassioned and convincing testimony concerning impossible and miraculous cures that they have received through the intercession of El Niño Fidencio. These claims are often documented.

Chronic ailments commonly go untreated in the Mexican-American community. Therefore, diabetes, hypertension, arthritis, and similar ailments are common in El Niño Fidencio's patient load.

Physical ailments are treated by Mexican-American folk healers in a variety of ways. They work on the material, the mental, or the spiritual level (Trotter and Chavira 1981). Material-level treatment in *Fidencista* temples is consistent with techniques and remedies found in nonspiritual healing traditions (Kiev 1969). The material and mental levels of treatment are common, but spiritual treatment, directly from the spirit of El Niño Fidencio, is more highly valued.

Healers are said to work spiritually when in a trance state. Individual spiritist healing sessions usually follow a similar pattern. The patient is greeted by the spirit and returns the salutation. The initial greeting is followed by a personal discussion with the spirit of Fidencio about the problem. In physical ailments, El Niño, working through the healer, immediately approaches the problem, using a combination of techniques. These include massage, cleansing and sweeping, and, in serious cases, spiritual surgery. Often El Niño prescribes a remedy that may be a mixture of herbal and religious items, and requests that the patient follow some prescribed process or ritual at home, then pay a return visit to the temple.

The average number of visits to El Niño Fidencio for physical ailments is equaled or surpassed by visits for other personal reasons. Although many of these consultations are of a serious nature, involving major family problems, many are simply routine visits by the faithful for emotional reinforcement. Research has consistently shown that the Mexican-American community is severely underserved in mental health care (Psychiatric Assessment of Mexican-Origin Populations 1995). In the United States, mental health treatment has become commonplace. However, ethnic stereotypes continue to promote myths suggesting Mexican-Americans are poor but happy. They lead well-adjusted, simple lives, free from the common emotional and mental health problems experienced by middle-class Americans. This stereotype supports the contention that Mexican-Americans are not in need of care. Consequently, the fastest-growing population in the country has little or no access to even minimal emotional and mental health care. Because of these high growth rates and the fact that the Mexican-American population is disproportionately poor relative to the general population, we can expect alternative healing systems like the *Fidencista* movement to continue to thrive. In almost every other country in the world, including Mexico, lay practitioners, with limited medical support, care for approximately 80 percent of the population's physical and emotional needs (Velimirovic 1978).

## CONCLUSION

El Niño began by serving the physical and mental health needs of the population. However, an important dimension of the movement that bears his name is its emergence as a folk religion. Throughout Latin America, native belief systems have commingled with Roman Catholicism. The syncretic hybrids that have been produced are thriving alternatives to an often disinterested and unresponsive Catholic Church. *Fidencismo* does not seek to replace Catholicism but simply to be accepted by it. The rejection by the Catholic Church of this movement further alienates huge segments of the Latin American population. Many Latino Catholic parish priests are openly sympathetic to their parishioners' belief in El Niño Fidencio.

The *Fidencista* movement's true charm and charisma, which attracts an ever-growing number of persons to its ranks, is its profound piety. Its strong belief and faith represent an attempt to emulate Christ in their life. *Fidencismo* never ceases to amaze the observer with the beauty of its mystical simplicity. While one feels compelled to explain its mysteries, the more they are explored, the more it is realized that they are not meant to be explained, only lived.

## NOTES

Special thanks for facilitating access to critical original documents in Mexico City to Mtra. Aurora Cano Andaluz, *Coordinadora de la Hemeroteca Nacional de México*, and

Lic. Guillermo Ceron, *Jefe de la Sección de Consulta y Servicios Automatizados de Información, Hemeroteca Nacional de México.*

## BIBLIOGRAPHY

Aspectos de el campo del dolor en Espinazo. (1928, February 18). *El Universal de México*, p. 1.

Boone, E. H. (1989). *Incarnations of the Aztec supernatural: The image of Huitzilopochtli in Mexico and Europe.* Philadelphia: American Philosophical Society.

Brenner, A. (1929). *Idols behind altars.* New York: Payson and Clarke.

Con Fidencio en Espinazo. (1937, October). *Hoy de México*, p. 20.

Condal, P. (1977). Vida y milagros del Niño Fidencio. In E. Harrington (Ed.), *Todo es historia* (pp. 4–35). Mexico City: Grupo Editorial.

Curaciones hechas por El Niño Fidencio: Casos vistos por nuestros enviados en el Espinazo. (1928, February 18). *El Universal de México*, p. 1.

Da Cunha, E. (1970) *Rebellion in the Backlands.* Chicago: University of Chicago Press.

Darley, A. M. (1968). *The passionists of the Southwest.* Glorieta, NM: Rio Grande Press.

Dementes, paralíticos y leprosos, más de mil enfermos esperan que los cura El Niño Fidencico en Espinazo, un verdadero pueblo entorno del él. (1928, February 16). *El Universal de Mexico*, p. 1.

Dos veces por semana habrá caros por Espinazo. (1928, February 19). *El Universal de México*, p. 1.

El campo del dolor en Espinazo. (1928, February 17). *El Universal de México*, sec. 2, p. 1.

El curandero de Espinazo sigue haciendo maravillosas curadas. (1928, February 14). *El Excelcior*, p. 4.

El doctor Char. Moravia Morpeau habla de Niño Fidencio. (1928, March 10). *El Universal de México*, p. 1.

Escamilla, L. A. (1995). *The Fidencista project: A study of collaborative ethnographic videography.* Unpublished Master's thesis, University of Texas, Austin.

Espinazo he convertido en un gran foco de infección. (1928, February 11). *El Excelcior*, p. 10.

Fidencio no quiere salir de Espinazo. (1928, February 20) *El Universal de México*, p. 5.

Gardner, D. (1992). *Niño Fidencio, a heart thrown open.* Santa Fe: Museum of New Mexico Press.

Gilles, B., & Trevino, A. (1994, Spring). A history of the matachine dance. *New Mexico Historical Review.*

Ha traspasado las fronteras del país la fama del prodigioso Niño Fidencio. (1928, February 21). *El Excelcior*, sec. 2, p.1.

Kardec, A. (1986). *The book on mediums.* York Beach, ME: Samuel Weiser.

Kardec, A. (1989). *Spiritualist philosophy: The spirits' Book.* Albuquerque, NM: The Brotherhood of Life.

Kiev, A. (1969). *Curanderismo: Mexican American folk psychiatry.* New York: Free Press.

Krauze, E. (1987). *Plutarco E. Calles.* Mexico City: Fondo de Cultura Económica.

López de la Fuente de González, F. (1993). Personal communication.

Los poetas campesinos cantan El Fidencio. (1928, February 21). *El Universal de México*, p. 1.

Macklin, J. (1973). Three North Mexican folk saint movements. *Comparative Studies in Society and History, 15* (1), pp. 89–105.

Madsen, W. (1967). Religious syncretism. In R. Wauchope, (Ed), *Handbook of Middle American Indians* (Vol. 6). Austin: University of Texas Press.

Morinis, A., & Crumrine, N. R. (1991). *La peregrinación*: The Latin American pilgrimage. In N. R. Crumrine & A. Morinis, (Eds.), *Pilgrimage in Latin America*. (pp. 1–17). New York: Greenwood Press.

Opinión de un médico eminente, Neumayer. (1928, February 20). *El Universal de México*, p. 1.

Ovalle de Tamayo, M. (1989). Personal communication.

Pretende ser mejor que El Niño Fidencio el llamado niño Marcialito también sabe ser político. (1928, January 23) *El Porvenir de Monterrey*, p. 7.

Psychiatric Assessment of Mexican-Origin Population. (1995). *Proceedings of the ninth Robert Lee Sutherland seminar in mental health*. Austin: Hogg Foundation for Mental Health, University of Texas.

Quiros, G. F. (1991). *El Niño Fidencio y el fidencismo* (5th ed.). Monterrey: Editorial Font.

Ricard, R. (1982). *The spiritual conquest of Mexico*. Berkeley: University of California Press.

Samora, J. (1971). *Los mojados: The wetback story*. Notre Dame, IN: University of Notre Dame Press.

Schneider, L. M. (1995). *Cristos, santos y vírgenes*. Mexico City: Grupo Planeta.

Spielberg, J., & Zavaleta, A. (1997). Historic folk sainthood along the Texas-Mexico border. In M. Kearney, A. Knopp, & A. Zavaleta (Eds.), *Studies in Matamoros and Cameron County* (pp. 347–374). Brownsville: University of Texas at Brownsville.

Telégrafo y correo en Espinazo. (1928, February 22). *El Universal de México*, p. 1.

Trotter, R. T., & Chavira, J. A. (1981). *Curanderismo: Mexican American folk healing*. Athens: University of Georgia Press.

Un nuevo panteón por los milagros del Niño Fidencio. (1928, February 10). *El Universal de México*, p. 1.

Velimirovic, B. (Ed.). (1978). *Modern medicine and medical anthropology in the United States–Mexico border population*. WHO Scientific Publication no. 359. Washington, DC: Pan American Health Organization.

The worker of miracles. (1928, February 20). *El Universal de México*, p.1.

Zapata de Robles, C. (1994). Personal communication.

Zavaleta, A. (1992). *El doctor divino: Spiritist healing in the Mexican American community*. Paper presented at VI International Conference on Traditional and Folk Medicine, Texas A&I University, Kingsville, Texas.

# Chapter 6

# Santería

## Mary Ann Clark

Mary Ann Clark, a doctoral candidate at Rice University, is studying the Santería religion for her dissertation. She is particularly interested in how the physical aspects of the religion reflect its philosophical ideas. Her interest in Santería was sparked when she and her husband began drumming lessons taught by a woman who had recently returned from Cuba. After several months of lessons, including instruction in Caribbean culture, her teacher took her to a *tambor*, or dance party, at which her friend was initiated into Santería. At the *tambor*, which included spirit possession, Mary Ann received a personal message and a blessing from a spirit. From this point on, she was intrigued by this religion that uses drumming, dancing, and possession trance.

On Friday, June 11, 1993, the United States Supreme Court overturned a Hialeah, Florida, law forbidding the ritual sacrifice of chickens, lambs, goats, and other animals. The court concluded that the Florida city had unfairly targeted adherents of the Santería religion.

Santería is one of the many syncretic religions created by Africans brought to the Caribbean islands as slaves to work on sugar plantations. These slaves had their own religions, which included possession trance for communicating with ancestors and myriad deities, animal sacrifice, sacred drumming, and ritual dance.

Nominally converted to Catholicism, slaves maintained many of their traditions by fusing Dahomey, baKongo, and Yorùbá beliefs and rituals with the host Catholic culture (Bourguignon 1976: 16, 28). In Cuba one of the fusions evolved into what is known as Santería (Way of the Saints).

Hundreds of thousands of Americans participate in Santería. Some are fully committed priests and priestesses; others are "godchildren" or members of a particular house tradition. Most are of Hispanic-Caribbean descent, but as the religion moves out of the barrios, a growing number of converts are of African-American and Euro-American heritage.

## HISTORY

Assimilation is a process "whereby groups with distinctive identities become culturally and socially fused" (Vander Zanden 1990: 280). However, assimilation is a two-way process. Whenever two cultural or religious systems interact, both are changed. Such interaction transforms old ideas into new ones. A pluralist relationship exists if each system maintains most of its previous identity. The history of Santería is a history of creative responses to an ongoing interaction between and among alien cultures.

The Yorùbá of West Africa were one of the most urban of black African civilizations. Their cities date back to the European Middle Ages. However, in the late eighteenth and early nineteenth centuries, Yorùbá cities were devastated by civil wars and wars with neighboring nations. One of the results of these wars was that many Yorùbás were captured and sold into slavery. By the nineteenth century, 500,000 to 700,000 Africans had been transported to Cuba, most of them of Yorùbá and baKongo descent.

Although life on the sugar plantations numbed the mind and destroyed the body, slaves and freed slaves living in the cities, notably Havana, had opportunities to learn trades and work for wages; this enabled some to buy their freedom and freedom for their families. By the mid-nineteenth century, over one-third of the black population of Cuba were *gente de color*, free people of color; they constituted one-sixth of the total population. (For comparison, in Virginia at the same time, free blacks were one-ninth of the black population and only 1/32 of the total population. Murphy 1994: 21f.).

The *gente de color* created Santería on the basis, for the most part, of old Yorùbá beliefs and practices. During the formative years, it was in the *cabildos* (social clubs), where Afro-Cubans met for mutual support, that nascent religious celebrations were first held. Hidden from the oversight of their Spanish masters, African religious traditions were reinvented and fused with elements of the Spanish culture, an example of assimilation. In the 1880s this syncretism was further embellished by the addition of Kardecian Spiritist traditions brought from France. This enhanced the African-based traditions of speaking with the dead (Perez y Mena 1991: 25).

In 1969 the Cuban Revolution resulted in a large migration of Cubans to Miami, which later resulted in a further dispersion of Cubans to other parts of the country. Like other newcomers to the United States, the Cubans brought with them their culture: music, food, language, religious beliefs and practices. Acceptance of this cultural diversity by the larger society is an example of cultural pluralism. Although the religion is still spreading, the majority of the *santeros*, as practitioners are called, are of Cuban descent.

## BELIEF SYSTEM OF THE SANTERÍA

*Moral integration* is a term used by Durkheim to explain the role that shared beliefs have in binding communities together (Durkheim 1897). This notion is helpful in describing the effects of the belief system of Santería. Although followers often live in urban environments, their beliefs form the glue that holds members together in bonds much like those found in rural communities in Africa.

To understand the Santería belief system, it is first necessary to define *ashe*. For practitioners, *ashe* is the energy of the universe. It is "all mystery, all secret power, all divinity" (Murphy 1994: 130). It is without beginning or end. It is not a particular power but Power itself (Murphy 1994: 147, quoting Pierre Verger). Modern physics teaches us that everything is merely energy moving at different rates of speed. Although the total energy in the universe cannot be changed, one can change portions of the universe by adding and removing energy. In the simplest example, adding energy to water changes it into steam, and removing energy changes it into ice. By understanding these principles, one has the power to control the environment. For the practitioners of Santería, the movement of *ashe*, the energy of the universe, between the visible and invisible worlds influences the environment. Part of Santería religious practice is learning to use *ashe* for the benefit of the individual, the community, and the universe as a whole.

Santería worship involves drumming and dancing as essential rituals. By dancing, the practitioner expresses the *ashe* of the universe and calls into presence the power of the *Òrìshà* (gods).

### Cosmology

There are five different levels of power in the Yorùbá cosmology: *Olódùmaré*, the *Òrìshà*, human beings, human ancestors, and the lowest group (which includes plants, animals, natural entities, and manufactured items). At the highest level, *Olódùmaré* sustains the universe. He is the owner of heaven, the owner of all destinies. He is the chief source of power and is often referred to as the "high god." He is the most remote of beings, and is never approached directly through worship. No shrines are erected in his name, yet he is present in all shrines. No rituals are directed toward him, yet he is invoked in all rituals. No sacrifices are made to him, yet he partakes of all sacrifices. *Olódùmaré* controls the forces of nature, the wind, the lightning, the ocean. In the African traditions, these forces have been humanized and mythologized into a group of beings or demigods called the Òrìshà.

## The Òrìshà

For followers, the Òrìshà function as sacred patrons or guardian angels. They represent approachable power through ritual action. A body of lore surrounds them that is similar to the stories used to describe the ancient Greek and Roman gods. These stories describe the interactions of the Òrìshà with each other and with their human children. Some explain the forces of nature, and others are morality tales designed to instruct and educate. It is on the Òrìshà that most Santería religious activity is focused.

Although the Òrìshà are powerful beings, they are not all powerful. Their existence is dependent upon worship, and their power increases the more they are worshipped. Practitioners provide nourishment through the sacrifice of plants and animals.

In the Yorùbá religion are literally thousands of Òrìshà. Since they represent the forces of the universe and are elements of Olódùmaré, every natural and manufactured thing represents or is associated with an Òrìshà.

## Ancestors

Most people who die become *Egun* (the ancestors). The most elevated of these dead may become Òrìshà. Not all ancestors are accorded special ritual attention. Those who were evil or cruel and those who died young, unable to fulfill their destinies, cannot become *Egun*. However, they may still be the recipients of rituals to "elevate" their spirits.

While it is the Òrìshà who are concerned with the destinies of individual practitioners, it is the ancestors who watch over the moral and social order (Brandon 1993: 15). Reincarnation is considered a positive experience instead of a punishment for past lives. In such a culture the dead are always part of the family, and may be seen in the faces and mannerisms of their descendants.

## The Lowest Group

At the lowest level of power, but still of vital importance, are animals, plants, inanimate objects like rocks, the wind, soil, water, and manufactured items. All of these contain levels of *ashe* that can be used by human beings for the benefit of both the visible and the invisible worlds.

## SPIRITISM

In the Yorùbá cosmology there is no other world but this world, which contains both visible and invisible elements. Visible elements include everything that can be perceived with the senses. Invisible elements include the spirits of these things, the *Òrìshà*, and *Olódùmaré*. It is possible for people to form a channel between the visible and invisible worlds. This channel can be opened by prayer and other types of rituals. Offerings are made to the ancestors on a regular basis. They are often consulted about important family matters. In addition to private rituals, members of a village or town stage regular ceremonies during which ancestors are perceived to visit their descendants.

In the mid-1800s the phenomenon of "table-turning" gained the attention of middle-class Europeans. One practitioner was a young teacher of chemistry, physics, comparative anatomy and astronomy named Léon Dénizarth Hippolyte Rivail (Kardec 1972: 9f.). About 1850 he began research into table-turning. He was soon told by the spirits that he had an important religious mission to fulfill (Kardec 1972:11).

Based on his communication with the spirits, Rivail changed his name to Allan Kardec and wrote a series of books including *The Spirit's Book* and *The Book of Mediums*. Kardec's "scientific" spiritism opened a channel between the visible and invisible worlds for middle-class Europeans. It was different in many ways from spiritualism practiced in the United States. Among other things, the spirits encountered in a Kardecian session were normally highly evolved spirits who had chosen to communicate with the visible world in order to raise the spiritual level of their human companions. Raising the spirits of the recently dead was more common in the United States.

When this form of spiritism was brought to the Caribbean, it developed into a form of séance called a "white-table spiritual Mass." Trained mediums, sitting around a table covered with a white cloth, conveyed messages from the spirit world, performed healing rituals, and provided general aid to those in attendance.

Over time Kardec's form of spiritism was incorporated into the existing African-based traditions of ancestor worship, so that today many *santeros* (followers) are also *espiritistas* (spiritualists). Spiritism provides yet another means of communicating with the dead. However, spiritism and Santería are not combined into a single system; Rather, they are two different religious systems that are practiced by the same people at different times and in different places.

Potential members are sometimes encouraged to set up altars for both ancestors and spirit guides. Many participate in a spiritist ceremony called *misa blanca*, a form of white-table séance. Every person is believed to be surrounded by one or more spirit guides who have chosen to help the person along his or her spiritual journey. No longer is mediumship reserved for trained individuals; there is no performance for an audience. Everyone is considered a potential medium and everyone is encouraged to speak if moved by a spirit. Spirits are believed to have power to help or hinder the actions of humans.

During the séance the group may sing, dance, and pray to invoke the presence of spirits. Participation in spiritual Masses and communication with the dead are often used as an introduction into Santería family and ritual life.

## DESTINY AND DIVINATION

In Santería it is believed that each individual's life path and destiny are associated primarily with a particular *Òrìshà*. It is this *Òrìshà* who "owns one's head." To live in harmony with one's destiny, this *Òrìshà* must become the focus of worship (Fatunmbi 1992: 19).

People make life choices that enhance certain inherent skills and abilities while neglecting others. Divination (foretelling future events), as well as familiarity with a personal guardian deity (*Òrìshà*), is used to determine whether these choices are consistent with a person's destiny and in harmony with his or her inner balance.

Divination also provides a method for communication between the invisible and the visible worlds. Many people come to Santería in a last-ditch effort to solve a personal or family problem. It is common to combine Western-style medical treatment with spiritual treatments associated with divination. The simplest form of divination is the use of coconut pieces to get answers to simple yes/no questions. More complicated problems may be addressed through the use of other methods. For example, questions or problems addressed directly to a particular *Òrìshà* employ a set of brightly colored seashells dedicated to that *Òrìshà*. The most difficult problems and questions provoked by simpler forms of divination must be brought to a *babalawo* (a trained practitioner who specializes in unraveling mysteries).

Often the course of action recommended by these various divination systems requires the client to make a sacrifice or perform a particular type of healing or cleansing ritual. Sometimes sacrifices are simple; a client may be told to toss five pennies into a river to get or keep a lover. However, if the problem is extremely serious, the sacrifice may require the blood of one or more animals.

### Animal Sacrifice

In the early 1990s the city of Hialeah, Florida, passed a series of ordinances that made it illegal "to unnecessarily kill, torment, torture, or mutilate an animal in a public or private ritual or ceremony not for the primary purpose of food consumption" (Greenhouse 1993: 9). The city allowed the killing of animals for a host of other reasons, however, even if the owner was simply tired of taking care of them. About the only exclusion was killing an animal for sacrificial purposes.

The specific purpose of these ordinances appeared to be suppression of the practices of the Church Lukumi Babalu Aye, a Santería congregation. The congregation decided to fight the ordinances as a violation of their First Amendment right to freedom of religion. Ernesto Pichardo, the founder of the church, said, "Animal sacrifice is an integral part of our faith. It is like our holy meal" (Greenhouse 1993: 9). At the hearing before the Supreme Court, Douglas Laycock, a law professor at the University of Texas, said, "The only way to show that sacrifice is 'unnecessary' to the Santería followers is to prove that Santería is a false religion" (Greenhouse 1992: 9). However, the legitimacy of Santería as a religion was never questioned at the hearing.

In the Supreme Court opinion overturning the city's ordinances, Justice Anthony Kennedy, quoting an earlier ruling, said, "Although the practice of animal sacrifice may seem abhorrent to some, religious belief need not be acceptable, logical, consistent, or comprehensible to others in order to merit First Amendment protection" (Kennedy1993).

Animal sacrifice is one of the most controversial aspects of this religion. Sacrifice, the giving of natural and manufactured items to the *Òrìshà* or ancestors, is viewed by practitioners as essential for human well-being. Through sacrifice, it is believed, one restores the positive life processes and acquires general well-being. To fulfill the wants and needs of the *Òrìshà* and the ancestors, practitioners make sacrifices to them. In return, the *Òrìshà* and ancestors are expected to meet the needs of the practitioners. This is not viewed as "bribing" or "buying off" the *Òrìshà*; rather, it is the mutual exchange of *ashe*. "The *Òrìshàs* offer health, children and wisdom; human beings render sacrifice and praise. Each needs the other, for, without the *ashe* of the *Òrìshà*, humans would despair of their God-given destiny and turn on themselves. And without the *ashe* of sacrifice, the *Òrìshà* would wither and die" (Murphy 1994: 15).

When the religion requires the sacrifice of an animal, it is offered to the *Òrìshà* or the ancestor with respect. It is killed quickly and with as little pain as possible. *Santeros* say they understand what the animal has given up for them, and are grateful. Since the *Òrìshà* and ancestors "eat" only the blood of the sacrificed animal, the meat is generally cooked and served to the community as part of the religious feast. Through such meat the devotees share in the *ashe* of the *Òrìshà*.

Sometimes an animal is sacrificed as part of a ritual cleansing. It is believed that such animals absorb the problems and negative vibrations of the person being cleansed. In such cases, the animal carcass is disposed of without being eaten. One of the arguments presented by the city of Hialeah against the Church of Lukumi Babalu Aye was that the discarding of these carcasses was a public health hazard. Indeed, the practice of discarding animals has presented problems to officials not only in Hialeah but also in other cities with a concentration of Santería practitioners. As suggested by Justice Kennedy, cities have to find a way to regulate the "disposal of organic garbage" (Greenhouse 1993: 9) that does not unnecessarily burden the practitioners of the religion.

Another concern is presented by the ASPCA (American Society for the Prevention of Cruelty to Animals). They argue that Santería sacrifice is less humane than methods used in licensed slaughterhouses. They note that animals die slowly and painfully and that they are often kept in filthy conditions before ceremonies. However, *santeros* contend that their methods are no more cruel than other types of legal slaughter, that animals are killed quickly and cleanly, and that they are generally eaten. The animals used are ordinary fowl and four-legged animals commonly available in grocery stores.

## TRANCE POSSESSION

Santería offers the opportunity to talk to God, to be God, and to experience God through the possession of others. It is one of the few religions that call gods into physical presence. Through trance possession, *santeros* can talk to the *Òrìshà* and the *Òrìshà* can talk back.

"Possession" describes physical and psychological changes that affect human consciousness. When a *santero* is talking to the *Òrìshà*, changes in voice tone and speaking patterns are common. There is sometimes a movement from one language to another (for example, from English to Spanish or to a "spiritual" language). Practitioners often assume unusual body postures.

Possession is generally distinguished from "shamanic trance," in which a medium or shaman "travels" to the spirit realm and brings back messages. In Santería, the medium is taken over by a spirit who can bless, lecture to, and dance with the congregation. Individuals can approach the embodied *Òrìshà* with their problems, and the *Òrìshà* can single out individuals or families for particular messages, blessings, or warnings. During the time of the possession event, devotees believe that the gods are truly incarnated and walk with them.

*Òrìshà* are made manifest to the community through the willingness of members to experience possession, to bring to consciousness the special state of mind that indicates that one is "in the spirit." Whoever is empowered and willing thus to "manifest the spirit does so for the benefit of the community to allow others to share in the consciousness . . ." (Murphy 1994: 184–185).

The most common venue for possession is the religious party called a *tambor* or *bembé*. These celebrations are community fiestas in honor of a specific *Òrìshà*. They can be held in a private home or a rented hall, depending on the resources of the sponsor. At one end of the room, a throne or altar is erected. The walls of this area are covered with cloths of various colors, along with other symbols and icons associated with the *Òrìshà* being honored. There is an area set aside for food: fruit, pastries, and cakes. There are flowers and a small basket for offerings.

Music at a *tambor* is provided by a set of sacred drums called *bata* and a type of call-and-response singing. Special drums are considered *Òrìshà* in their own right and are offered sacrifices. There are only a few of these sacred drum sets in the United States, so most drumming events use other types of drums, usually congas. Along with the drum group is a vocalist who leads the singing. Each *Òrìshà* has its own particular set of rhythms, songs, and dance movements. As a particular *Òrìshà*'s rhythm is played, the song leader and congregation sing. *Santeros* who are priests and priestesses of that *Òrìshà* dance in the open space in front of the drums. The songs are designed to call the *Òrìshà* down to take possession of one of those dancing. When a dancer begins to show signs of possession (more intense dance movements, jerky or irregular movements, "spacey" or contorted facial expressions), the energy of the group focuses on him or her until the *Òrìshà* is firmly "seated."

Once the possession process is complete, the dancer no longer exhibits his or her personal mannerisms, reflecting instead the mannerisms of the possessing *Òrìshà*. Because possession involves the complete loss of human consciousness, it appears to be a traumatic experience for the *mount* (sometimes called *horse*, to express the idea that the human is ridden and controlled by the *Òrìshà*). Evidence of the inner battle can be seen in the contortions of the person in the beginning stages of possession. Participants may leave the room at any time. No one is forced into possession, although those who can manifest their *Òrìshà* easily and consistently are valued by the community.

Imminent possession is signaled by changes in the mount, whose actions become less erratic and more controlled. Modern items like glasses and shoes are removed as an ancient being begins to control the mount's body. The newly embodied *Òrìshà* may prostrate himself or herself before the drums that enabled the possession event, and members of the community, particularly those who are priests and priestesses of the embodied *Òrìshà*, prostrate themselves before the mount. Each *Òrìshà* has a typical costume based on interpretations of mythology. As part of the preparations for a drumming ceremony, a new costume is made for the *Òrìshà* who is expected to appear.

The embodied *Òrìshà* will dance, talk to devotees, preach (sometimes in the Yorùbá language, sometimes in the native language of the horse), bless, admonish, and consult with his or her assembled human children. During this time more *Òrìshà* may appear as the drummers and singer continue their music not only for the manifested *Òrìshà* but also for any others who would want to attend the party. Every *Òrìshà* with a priest present will be invoked and given the opportunity to attend. A *tambor* is both a party and a religious celebration. The gods of the religion are brought into bodily presence not just for the blessings they can bestow but also so they can enjoy the festivities.

Although the *Òrìshà* may leave at any time, after several hours the human attendants begin to persuade him or her that it is time to go. The horse is taken to a separate room, where the spirit is dislodged and human consciousness is returned.

The type of possession practiced in Santería is called trance possession because the host has no memory of the presence of the *Òrìshà* or its actions. This means that the presence of a community is extremely important, not only to call down the *Òrìshà* but also, later, to communicate any messages from the *Òrìshà* to its host. If fully possessed, the person entranced is unaware of his or her own actions. Because of the loss of control involved in trance possession, *santeros* are often reluctant to experience possession if they are not well acquainted with the gathered community and confident of their well-being.

## FICTIVE FAMILY

Everyone who is involved in Santería enters the religion under the protection of a *santero* already involved in the religion. In Africa the religion is often passed from parent or grandparent to child, and many of the priestly orders stay within a family lineage. Slavery virtually eliminated the family system. This necessitated fictive families, a new type of family relationship. They were formed not on the basis of blood but of initiation. One was "born" into a religious family through initiations by more senior members of the family. Only those with enough knowledge and *ashe* can give birth to godchildren. Only through an initiation can one become a full adult member of the religion. This means that instead of a church in which people may have only casual relationships with each other, everyone in a Santería family is related through a complex hierarchy of initiations.

When one is initiated into Santería, the priest or priestess becomes the *padrino* (godfather) or *madrina* (godmother). The initiate is instantly related to all the other members of that religious family. He or she instantly acquires brothers, sisters, cousins, aunts, uncles and grandparents in the religion. Just as in a traditional family, the newcomer has certain responsibilities and family obligations.

Those who are newer to the religion—regardless of their chronological age—honor and obey those who have been involved longer. Thus an older man who is newly initiated will defer to a younger woman who has many years in the religion. The most obvious sign of respect is the custom of prostration. Once fully initiated, or crowned, a newcomer is expected to prostrate himself or herself at the feet of all those who are older in the religion. Respect may also be shown in other ways: by listening respectfully, by fetching water or food, or by providing other services to one's elders.

## WARRIORS AND NECKLACES

Many of those associated with Santería are marginal members. Their involvement is often limited to using the *santeros* as spiritual and psychological advisers. They come with a problem and leave with an herbal preparation, a candle, or perhaps instructions for a particular type of offering or prayer.

Sometimes problems are seen as the result of malevolent forces set in motion by enemies, jealous acquaintances, or evil spirits. In such cases it is often suggested that additional "protection" is needed from these forces. Practitioners may recommend the protection of a particular Òrìshà by suggesting that a person wear a bead necklace in the style and color of that Òrìshà.

Sometimes problems are seen as messages from the Òrìshà, signs that one is being called to fulfill a deeper destiny. The first move from petitioner to practitioner is an initiation called "Warriors and Necklaces." The initiation of necklaces implies a deeper involvement in the religion. Normally the initiate receives necklaces associated with the five or seven major Òrìshà.

Godchildren are the basic laborers of the household. They do much of the preparation for various household rituals. One can stay at this level of involvement for years, even a lifetime, participating in many functions but excluded from the most profound parts of the religion. Many, however, choose the deepest commitment and become priests or priestesses dedicated to a particular *Òrìshà* in a ceremony called *asiento* (crowning).

## Crowning

Movement from initiate to priest involves a weeklong initiation ritual followed by a 12-month period of training and taboo. During the ritual the initiate is dedicated to a particular *Òrìshà* and becomes the embodiment of that deity. This ritual is also called *hacer el santo* (making the saint) because it is through this ritual that the religion is continued and the *Òrìshà* become manifest in the visible world.

Marriage is a widely used metaphor for the relationship between an initiate and his or her *Òrìshà*. Murphy, in describing the *asiento* ceremony, tells us that *asiento* is a Spanish word connoting both "seat" and "agreement" or "pact." This ceremony to "make" or "crown" a saint seats the *Òrìshà* in the head of the devotee, but it is also a pact or commitment between the devotee and the *Òrìshà*.

For a year, the initiate is surrounded by white, a symbol of purity and creativity. Immaculate white cloths represent *Obatala*, the *Òrìshà* of purity and creativity, who cools the fires of passion, protects against evil influences, and enhances the character of the practitioner (see Thompson 1984: 11f.). This overwhelming presence of white separates the initiate from the profane community. Like a Catholic nun's habit, a Buddhist monk's yellow robes, or an Islamic woman's veil, the initiate's clothes mark the wearer as a different type of being, one dedicated to a particular way of life.

## RELATIONSHIP TO CATHOLICISM

Many *santeros*, especially those of Hispanic origin, are at least nominally Roman Catholics. The identity is hybrid, dynamic, and contested. Catholic imagery is combined with Santería practice especially at the level of personal devotion. For example, each *Òrìshà* is associated with a Catholic saint, and saints' images often dominate home shrines. In the homes of older or more traditional *santeros*, shrines usually have small statues and other Christian religious paraphernalia. Nevertheless, each of these images stands near symbols of the *Òrìshà* it represents. To knowledgeable observers, Catholic elements are merely another way that Santería is both hidden and displayed.

Santería got its name because of the imaginative use of Catholic elements, belief, ritual, and iconography. As early as the middle of the eighteenth century, the Roman Catholic bishop of Havana attempted to bring Catholicism to the

Afro-Cuban *cabildos* (social clubs) by appointing a clergyman to direct the worship of *cabildos* and directing that a statue of "Our Lady" was to be left for continued worship at each *cabildo*. It was these images that the *cabildo* members carried in processions as part of the festivals associated with specific holy days (Brandon 1993: 70).

It was also the responsibility of each Cuban *cabildo* to stage dances in the style of the African "nation" associated with the *cabildo*. These dances used songs, music, language, and drum rhythms that were distinctive to particular African groups. Brandon suggests that, given the close connection between music, dance, and religion in Africa, these dances often turned into religious ceremonies complete with spirit possession (1993: 71–72). There are indications that the *cabildos'* members carried "fetishes" or "idols" in these processions (Brown 1989: 51). Thus, from within the *cabildo*, African religious practices found their way onto the streets of Havana as both hidden and exposed: hidden behind elements of the dominant religion of Catholicism and exposed through African cultural manifestations.

Many of these African musical elements can still be found within the secular music of the Caribbean. Sacred drums and their rhythms are often heard on the recordings of Cuban artists. In addition, many recordings include songs invoking the *Òrìshà* directly or indirectly.

## CELEBRATIONS

Santería practitioners do not erect church buildings and hold regular services in the style of Christians. However, on any weekend in cities with a sizable population of *santeros*, there are a variety of religious events held in private homes or rented halls. A major event in the lives of all priests is the yearly party celebrating the anniversary of their initiation. The celebration encompasses an entire seven-day period. Because they are personal celebrations, these parties are generally held in the home of the celebrant.

On the first day of the celebration, the *santero* welcomes his religious family to his home. Each guest first greets the *Òrìshà* by prostrating himself on the mat placed in front of the throne area specifically for that purpose. Godchildren of the host generally leave a ritually prescribed gift, such as a plate with coconuts, candles, or money. Entertainment may include live drumming or recorded music, depending on the resources of the host. Each guest is served dinner and encouraged to share desserts that have been prepared for and presented to the *Òrìshà*. At the end of the evening, all guests will take with them a bag of fruit and some of the *Òrìshà*'s sweets, thereby sharing in the *ashe* of the celebration. Members of the family who are unable to attend the main celebration find time during the week to drop in, pay their respects to the *Òrìshà*, and congratulate the *santero* on another year.

## FUTURE OF SANTERÍA

Although attendance at many mainline churches is waning, New Age and alternative religious groups are springing up across the country. Ideas about reincarnation and karma, as well as practices from other religious traditions, have infiltrated mainstream American culture.

In the midst of this religious boom, Santería is beginning to move out of the ghettos and barrios and into the suburbs. More black, white, and Asian professionals are joining the religion. Some have become fully crowned priests, in spite of the language and cultural challenges such initiations pose.

Always an urban religion, Santería continues to have its largest following in the cities of the East and West Coasts. New York and Miami, Los Angeles and Oakland, have Spanish-speaking communities large enough to support the religion on a large scale. However, individual practitioners and religious families can be found in medium and large cities throughout the country. On both coasts, organizations like the Caribbean Cultural Center in Manhattan and the Oni-Ochun Center in Oakland present every aspect of the Santería religion. In addition, groups like the Church Lukumi Babalu Aye, which won the Supreme Court case, have established a public presence in their communities. Slowly the veil of secrecy is being lifted, and the religion has begun to move out of basements and back rooms and into the public eye.

However, greater visibility may spawn a new set of problems for Santería practitioners. The ritual sacrifice of animals continues to be a problem. Although the Supreme Court has said that sacrifice in and of itself is a protected religious practice, cities and *santeros* have yet to work out compromises necessary to protect the welfare of the general public while not overly burdening the practice of the religion. These issues will be worked out on a case-by-case basis as different communities experiment with different solutions to the problems presented.

Perhaps a more worrisome concern is the potential for religious abuse. Religious systems contain weaknesses that open them up to particular types of abuse. Catholics have been plagued by priests who molest young boys. Several well-known Protestant evangelists have been accused of sexual and financial misconduct. Gurus have been accused of requiring sexual favors from their followers. Within Santería, the opportunities for financial abuses abound. Every religious ritual and event requires some type of financial commitment on the part of the participants. Rumors of overcharging for initiations and the selling of sacred goods and services by unscrupulous practitioners are well known. Because there is no central clearinghouse to check the credentials of priests, outsiders often find that they have paid hundreds, even thousands, of dollars for initiations and rituals that were not properly done and thus are not recognized by the larger community.

The veil of secrecy continues to surround many aspects of Santería so separating the legitimate from the fraudulent is difficult—particularly for those who do not speak Spanish. Many popular books on the religion contain "spells" and "rituals" that encourage the uninformed and the uninitiated to attempt work that properly belongs only to the trained clergy. In addition, as in any "magical" religious system, the unscrupulous can prey on the unwary by practicing the dark arts for and against others.

The issues of animal sacrifice, fraud, and sorcery present a challenge to the practitioners of Santería. It appears that these challenges are not insurmountable.

## BIBLIOGRAPHY

Bascom, W. (1980). *Sixteen cowries: Yorùbá divination from Africa to the new world.* Bloomington: Indiana University Press.

Bourguignon, E. (1976). *Possession.* San Francisco: Chandler & Sharp.

Brandon, G. (1993). *Santería from Africa to the new world.* Bloomington: Indiana University Press.

Brown, D. H. (1989). *Garden in the machine: Afro-Cuban sacred art and performance in urban New Jersey and New York.* Ann Arbor, MI: UMI Research Press.

Crapanzano, V. (1976). *Case studies in spirit possession.* New York: John Wiley & Sons.

Durkheim, E. (1897). *Suicide.* (Reprint 1966.) New York: Free Press.

Fatunmbi, F. (1992). *Awo: Ifà and the theology of Òrìshà divination.* New York: Original Publications.

Greenhouse, L. (1992, November 5). High court is cool to sacrifice ban. *New York Times,* sec. A, p. 25.

Greenhouse, L. (1993, June 12). Court, citing religious freedom, voids a ban on animal sacrifice. *New York Times,* sec. A, p. 1.

High court strikes animal sacrifice ban. (1993, June 12). *Houston Chronicle,* p. 2A.

Kardec, A. (1972). *The spirit's book.* São Paulo, Brazil: Lake–Livraria Allan Kardec Editôra.

Kennedy, Anthony. (1993, June 12). Excerpts from Supreme Court opinions on the ritual sacrifice of animals. *New York Times,* sec. A, p. 9.

Lawson, E. T. (1984). *Religions of Africa: Traditions in transformation.* San Francisco: Harper & Row.

Lewis, I. M. (1971). *Ecstatic religion.* Baltimore: Penguin Books.

Murphy, J. M. (1994). *Working the spirit: Ceremonies of the African diaspora.* Boston: Beacon Press.

Perez y Mena, A. I. (1991). *Speaking with the dead.* New York: AMS Press.

Thompson, R. F. (1984). *Flash of the spirit: African and Afro–American art and philosophy.* New York: Random House.

Tweed, T. A. (1997). *Our Lady of the exile: Diasporic religion at a Cuban Catholic shrine in Miami.* New York: Oxford University Press.

Vander Zanden, J. W. (1990). *The Social Experience* (2nd ed.). New York: McGraw-Hill.

# Chapter 7

# Single Women in Amish Society

## Dachang Cong

While a student at the University of Pittsburgh, Dachang Cong learned of the Amish. As a doctoral candidate in cultural anthropology at Yale, he undertook fieldwork on the Amish in northern Indiana, trying to observe and participate in their customs as much as possible. He helped them with farm work and offered free taxi service. Several Amish schools invited him to deliver lectures on China. "It was a blessing to me that the Amish were just as curious about me as I was about them, and this mutual curiosity helped create an agreeable situation for field research." Dachang teaches at the University of Texas, Dallas, and has written several articles on the Chinese and Amish cultures.

The cultural and political climate of North America has encouraged the development of a wide array of social and religious experiments (Berry 1992). Many of these, including the Oneida community and the Rajneeshees, have failed to survive (Carden 1969; FitzGerald 1986: 247–381). In contrast, the Amish are characterized by social vitality, cultural resilience, and economic success (Hostetler 1993; Kephart & Zellner 1994: 5–49; Kraybill 1989).

The Amish, a Christian group with origins in the Anabaptist movement of sixteenth-century Europe, separated from the Swiss Mennonites in 1693 to establish a more conservative sect. In the early eighteenth century, the Amish settled in eastern Pennsylvania. They have since thrived in both the United States and Canada, and now number about 130,000. To the general public, they are best known for wearing "old-fashioned" attire, speaking the Pennsylvania

Dutch dialect, driving buggies, using horses in the fields, and rejecting most modern conveniences, including radios, cameras, and televisions.

The Amish are popular in the United States (Cong 1994). They trigger a nostalgia for rural ideals and offer an alternative lifestyle. They are often regarded as a model minority. Because they are white, Christian, and of European origin, the Amish are more readily accepted by mainstream American society.

Sects are religious groups that emphasize fundamentalism at the expense of intellectualism. Greater levels of commitment are expected of members. Women in sectarian groups often have extraordinary experiences (Foster 1991). This study describes the sometimes extraordinary role of single women in Amish society while exploring their contributions to the success of the sect.

Amish society places a high value on male-dominated family life. For this reason, single women often are treated as marginal. My fieldwork in northern Indiana revealed that there are few single Amish men. Those who are, generally are physically disabled or mentally retarded. By contrast, the number of single Amish women is quite high. In the early 1990s, there were approximately 500 single Amish women in the Amish settlement located in Lagrange and Elkhart counties, Indiana. There were about 20 single women's groups, ranging in size from 15 to 25 members.

From 1980 to 1986, 842 females and 765 males were baptized in this settlement. Sociologists compare the relative numbers of men to women in a group by using a statistic called the *sex ratio*. It represents the number of males in a group for every 100 females in the same group. For the Lagrange and Elkhart Amish, the sex ratio was 90.86. This means only 91 males were baptized for every 100 females baptized during this period. The major reason for this discrepancy is that more girls than boys were born into their communities.

The Amish call single women "leftover blessings." Indeed, single women are blessings in many ways. But are single women blessed? Probably not. The life of singles is not comfortable. This study begins with a general examination of the status and conditions of single women in Amish society. It then describes the lives of Ruby and Martha. Ruby fits the *ideal type* of a single Amish woman, whereas Martha does not. Finally, it discusses the roles and functions of single Amish women within their communities.

## STATUS AND CONDITIONS

*Values* in any society are conceptions of what is good, proper, essential, desirable, worthwhile, and beneficial. They define all types of behavior in society, including *gender roles*. Such roles include the specialized tasks, duties, attitudes, and activities that a society expects each sex to perform. Unlike the broader American society that tolerates a great variety of lifestyles, gender roles in Amish society are clearly stated and strictly fulfilled.

Amish men work in the fields, home shops, or factories. Amish women are homemakers, although they often help with farm work. A typical Amish family is large, with many children. Chores are endless for an Amish woman. In Amish society, favorable status is accorded married males, especially those who are active in church affairs, manage their farms well, and lead wholesome family lives. Their wives are accordingly well regarded. Inevitably, single Amish women have low status. Sociologists often use the term *in-group* to refer to those who share a unique lifestyle and mind-set, and think of themselves as a close-knit unit. Such a definition fits the Amish. The in-group often practices *endogamy*, which requires dating, courtship, and marriage to take place among group members. The Amish do not marry outsiders. If outsiders want to marry with the Amish, they have to join the Amish church first, a demanding procedure.

For the Amish, single life means involuntary celibacy and *stoicism* (the appearance of indifference to pleasure). Amish women are not allowed to date outside their religion. Moreover, lesbianism, premarital affairs, and extramarital affairs are out of the question. Single Amish women become "nuns without a convent."

It is difficult for single Amish women to fit into an overwhelmingly male-dominated, family-centered society. Single women are handicapped in social relations because they do not have a husband or children. They have little in common with married women and may opt to keep their distance. Furthermore, single women must constantly shy away from men to avoid embarrassment and gossip. As a necessary precaution, they tend to dress more conservatively and talk more cautiously.

The overall atmosphere in Amish society is by no means conducive to the comfort of singles. Social events such as weddings, birthday parties, family reunions, work bees, and funerals can be unpleasant occasions for them. The pervasive presence of married couples with children in such situations sometimes makes singles feel lonely and uncomfortable. Even everyday conversations can alienate singles, for marriage, family, and children are major topics.

Single women have to accept the junior status accorded young people, but they cannot enjoy the freedom granted Amish youth. In fact, strained relations exist between youths and single women. Single women are often seen as failures or losers by young people. Their undesirable condition serves to remind young girls of dating age that one must try very hard in the highly competitive "dating game."

The humiliation of these single women often feeds their resentment toward young people. To improve their social status, single women distance themselves from youth groups and constantly maintain their moral image. Often, they are disdainful of what they perceive to be the loosened moral standards of youth.

Single Amish women have to wage a lifelong struggle with a difficult question: Why are they single? Some conclude that they are not attractive or bold enough to attract men. Indeed, the fact that many bolder and more attractive girls have found spouses makes it impossible for them to dismiss such a conclusion. During my study, a single Amish schoolteacher opined that some parents shared this unflattering image with their single daughters. Unfortunately, single Amish women can only partially be comforted by the argument that they are victims of a societal emphasis on physical beauty. Beauty, though to a more limited extent than in larger society, appears important even to the "plain people." Inevitably, many single Amish women painstakingly search for biblical answers to questions about the necessity and virtues of single life. But there are few direct biblical references to the issue. And the all-male clergy have done little to provide theological explanations.

Some single Amish women assert that God must have some noble reasons for having them remain single. Despite their disadvantaged position, single Amish women have made conscientious efforts to prevent their single life from becoming too unpleasant. Many of them still hope to marry. And most believe their afterlife experiences will be just as rewarding as those of their married counterparts.

In northern Indiana, single Amish women have formed friendship and support groups. Such groups generally consist of 15 to 25 members. These larger groups tend to break down into three or four subgroups, usually consisting of three to seven members. The subgroups generally meet on a biweekly or monthly basis. They may have a singing party, go to a restaurant, or take a short trip. Gatherings of the larger group are held two to four times a year, so that singles from different subgroups have a chance to know each other and to share fellowship. In addition, single women often form "circle letter groups" to exchange ideas and to share feelings.

There are certain advantages to the single life. Compared with married women, constantly burdened with daily duties, single women have more time and money to spend on themselves. Many singles enjoy reading and travel, which are effective ways to combat loneliness. Although church elders and married people sometimes criticize singles for reading too many love stories and taking too many trips, they rarely resort to disciplinary measures to coerce singles into submission.

Single women can devote more time to the care of their parents than their married siblings. In this sense, they are truly "leftover blessings." Reciprocally, many Amish parents have made genuine efforts to help their single daughters. For example, an old Amish man helped his two single daughters start a fabric store and a quilt-making business. Equally significant, he made necessary arrangements so that the two single daughters, rather than his married children, would inherit his farmhouse. Single women also maintain close relationships with their siblings, especially married sisters. They tend to form strong ties with their nephews and nieces. In many cases, nephews and nieces take care of their single aunts when the latter become old and sick.

Amish society, though not geared to a single lifestyle, does indeed provide protection for single women. Sexual harassment of a single woman by a married man has rarely occurred, according to my Amish informants. Indeed, the nunlike status of single women serves to prevent them from being forced into unpleasant situations.

## RUBY'S STORY

Ruby is a typical single woman in Amish society. Besides taking care of her father, she makes quilts to sell, cleans houses for non-Amish people, and does odd jobs such as baby-sitting for busy Amish mothers. Ruby used to belong to a youth group that she joined because some of her cousins and friends were members. Ruby was more conservative than the average girl in the group. She started to date at the age of 18 and had dated four boys by the time she turned 23. She never went steady with a boy. During these dating rites, physical beauty often counted for more than character. Ruby recalled that several beautiful girls in the group were really popular. Boys in the group were competing with each other to win the heart of one of these beautiful girls. Ruby was largely ignored— she was shy and was not trying hard to get a boy.

Ruby's twenty-third birthday seemed to be a transition point in her life. At that time, she realized that she would have little chance to marry. Most of the 23-year-olds she knew were either married or soon to be married. Ruby was scared by the harshness and loneliness associated with single life, but she gradually faced reality.

She continued to attend Sunday singings until she turned 25. She then felt increasingly uncomfortable, however, and dropped out. Moreover, younger members of the youth group apparently expected her to leave. Fortunately, Ruby was well received at home. Her father and siblings were sympathetic. They tried to convince Ruby that it was not her fault she was single, and that God must have a good reason for it. Some older singles in the community lent further help. Ruby was invited to several singles meetings at which she learned a great deal about how others coped with the difficulty of a single life, made a good living, and offered various services to the community.

The initial adjustment to a permanent single life often is difficult. Ruby's adjustment was no exception. As it became clear to her that she would be her father's "leftover blessing," she realized it would be primarily her responsibility to take care of him in his old age. Second, she decided to make a livelihood by making quilts and cleaning houses. Third, she started to wear longer dresses in more subdued colors, which were regarded as appropriate for a single woman. Fourth, she began to talk less and to take extra precautions in dealing with others, especially married men. She understood very well that others expected a single woman to be chaste, quiet, and well-behaved.

In addition, Ruby had to be very responsive to the needs of relatives and neighbors. The Amish believe a single woman should never be too busy to help a new mother or to take care of a sick relative. The pay for such odd jobs is usually small. Yet, at the same time, single women are often envied by their married counterparts for having some money.

Through hard work and thrift, Ruby managed to save a good sum of money. She often made small loans to siblings, relatives, friends, and neighbors at no interest or at low interest. She lost money by doing so, but it was almost compulsory for her to act generously. Ruby estimated that between 1980 and 1991, she loaned over $50,000 to others.

Lack of emotional support and loneliness are the major problems that many single women have to face, but they are not supposed to complain. If they do, they are regarded as strange or discontented. Ruby tries very hard to hide her loneliness and never complains, except to her single friends.

Ruby belongs to a singles group of 20 members divided into three subgroups. Her subgroup has seven members and meets every two weeks. They usually have a meal together, sing hymns, and talk about single life. Occasionally they take a trip. In addition, her group holds a gathering twice a year. Ruby also belongs to three circle letter groups. Writing and reading letters have been positive and enjoyable pastimes for her. To further lessen loneliness, Ruby reads novels, keeps a diary, and writes poems.

Many years have passed since Ruby joined the ranks of single women. To her, single life is no longer as hard as before. She still hopes to be married one day, most likely to a widower. If not, she plans to live with one of her nieces when she becomes old and to let the niece inherit her property. Ruby holds an unwavering faith in the Amish religion. She states that she will fare worse and have less chance to go to heaven if she decides to drift into the outside world.

## MARTHA'S STORY

Most single Amish women bear their daily hardship and loneliness with courage and forbearance. They are devoted to the Amish religion and strive to attune themselves to the Amish community. Nevertheless, over the years, a number of them have chosen to join a Mennonite church in which women have more freedom and a greater role to play. Martha is one of those who chose to leave the Amish religion.

Martha admitted that she was already quite different from other Amish girls by the time she was in her early teens. She liked to study and dreamed of traveling all over the world. Also, Martha wanted to become a career woman instead of a typical farmer's wife, dominated by her husband and overburdened with housework and children. In school, she was a top student and did well in mathematics, which proved to be very useful to her career. In 1975, Martha started to work as an accountant in an egg-packing plant and remained there until the summer of 1987. The job paid well, and she managed to save a good sum of money.

Martha was independent-minded and did not belong to any youth group. She dated two Amish boys in her late teens, but neither of them appreciated her ambition. They obviously were more interested in looking for a typical Amish girl, meek and unambitious. Martha's independent thinking scared them. Moreover, Martha was regarded as too proud and too smart. Consequently, she remained single.

In 1979, Martha moved away from home and rented an apartment. Her roommate was Laura, a like-minded Amish woman. They both disliked being dominated by men, and they both wanted to have independent careers and to see the world. It was fortunate that the district they moved to was one of the most liberal in the settlement. If they had moved to a conservative district, they would have encountered strong disapproval.

Martha and Laura like to travel. They have visited almost every state of the United States and every province of Canada. In 1978, Martha and Laura traveled to Israel. In 1980, they visited seven western European countries. Soon after they returned from Europe, they signed on for a Caribbean cruise. Before they left for the cruise, there was a big stir in their church district. Quite a few church elders tried to discourage them, for fear there would be drinking, gambling, dancing, and romance on the ship. Martha and Laura promised that under no circumstances would they participate in those activities. The young bishop of the district was open-minded and did not threaten disciplinary measures. The cruise, according to Martha, was not as wild as she expected. The crew and passengers were curious about Martha and Laura, but kept a respectful distance from them. Many mistook them for nuns.

For a number of years, Martha and Laura, sponsored by a local Mennonite church, hosted foreign students at Christmas. In 1987, they visited Japan and stayed with some of the girls they had hosted. The women were overwhelmed by Japanese hospitality, and found that the Japanese work as hard as the Amish. After their return, many Amish came to them with searching questions about Japan.

Martha enjoys learning. She finished high school through G.E.D. (general equivalency diploma) courses. More impressive, she took German, French, and Spanish courses at a Mennonite college. She also took correspondence courses in business accounting from a college in Chicago.

Laura joined a conservative Mennonite church in 1984. She was then allowed to own a car, a telephone, and a radio. Martha benefited from these modern conveniences by sharing an apartment with Laura. Laura was happier and felt more useful as a Mennonite. She especially enjoyed volunteer service opportunities offered by the Mennonites. In 1985–1986, she served as the director of an international student hostel in Washington, D.C.

Laura's change of church affiliation had a tremendous effect on Martha. As early as the middle 1970s, Martha wondered whether the Amish way of life would be the best choice for a single woman like herself. She did not feel comfortable as an Amish church member, especially during the social hours after Sunday services. She had little to talk about with the married women or young girls. Often, she ended up talking with men about the local economy and national politics. In addition, she felt strongly that by remaining Amish, she would never have a chance to do the mission work that she had always dreamed of doing.

In 1987, Martha was ready to make the change. With support from Laura and a number of Mennonite friends, she came to feel certain that God would approve of her plan. Martha talked with her father about her intention, then with her bishop. Both encouraged her to stay in the Amish church, but neither threatened to punish her. Martha joined a conservative Mennonite sect that allows cars and conducts mission work.

Martha was not shunned by her family or by the Amish community—a very rare case, indeed. According to Martha, her family and church had been sympathetic with her conditions and fully prepared for her departure. She was thankful. In the summer of 1987, she quit her job at the egg-packing plant and joined a Mennonite mission in West Germany. This relieved her of the great anxiety usually associated with a change of church affiliation. Martha has been a devoted mission worker since 1987.

## ROLES AND FUNCTIONS

Amish society values male dominance, marriage, family, and children. As a result, the status of single Amish women is both marginal and ambiguous. Nevertheless, single Amish women have many important roles and functions in the general well-being of the Amish community.

First and most noticeably, single Amish women play an intellectual role. As a group, they are the best-educated in Amish society. Single women have more time to think, read, and write. Quite a few of them are poets, writers, and artists. Although the Amish do not display a great deal of interest in art, some women are well known for their artistic talents, especially in quilting and doll-making.

Teaching in an Amish school is generally regarded as a perfect occupation for a single Amish woman. Teaching requires time and devotion, which a married woman does not have because her time is needed elsewhere. Low salaries discourage Amish men from becoming teachers. Although the Amish allow their children to complete only the eighth grade, teachers are required to pass a high school equivalency test or a standardized twelfth grade achievement test.

Amish teachers usually live in a small cottage near the schoolhouse. The families of pupils take turns furnishing her with milk, eggs, fresh vegetables, and canned food so that she does not have to do much grocery shopping. The yearly salary ranges between $4,000 and $6,000. Since her expenses are low, she earns a good living. Perhaps more important, an Amish school provides a comfortable niche for her. To a large extent, she is separated from the rest of the Amish community. Teaching and being with children reduce her loneliness. In addition, she enjoys fellowship and support from her colleagues, who are mostly single women. There are frequent visits between schools, and teachers hold monthly meetings.

Traditionally, single Amish women take care of their aged parents and relatives. They are hired at low wages to attend to the old and sick in the community. They also help new mothers and busy mothers. Since the Amish do not operate nursing homes and nursery schools, single women are indispensable.

In recent years, more and more single Amish women have chosen to work in factories, shops, and restaurants. Many take up sewing, hat-making, quilt-making, baking, gardening, cleaning, and some other occupations that are much needed by the Amish community. Some single women operate small dry goods stores or fabric stores to serve their neighborhoods.

Amish men depend heavily on their wives for help with farm chores and for emotional support. Consequently, it is a great blessing, albeit a leftover one, to Amish widowers that they can remarry easily.

## SUMMARY

In Amish society, there are significant numbers of single women. Because Amish society is male-dominated and family-centered, single women have low social status. Nevertheless, single Amish women have many important functions in their communities. They tend to be the most educated, and often play essential intellectual roles. They fill important occupational slots, such as teachers, health care providers, and business managers. Many act as financiers for family and friends. Also, some serve the important function of second wife. Indeed, single Amish women are blessings to their communities.

## BIBLIOGRAPHY

Berry, B. (1992). *America's utopian experiments: Communal havens from long-wave crises.* Hanover, NH: University Press of New England.

Carden, M. L. (1969). *Oneida: Utopian community to modern corporation.* Baltimore: Johns Hopkins University Press.

Cong, D. (1994). The roots of Amish popularity in contemporary U.S.A. *Journal of American Culture, 17*(1), 59–66.

Foster, L. (1991). *Women, family, and utopia: Communal experiments of the Shakers, the Oneida community, and the Mormons.* Syracuse, NY: Syracuse University Press.

FitzGerald, F. (1986). *Cities on a hill.* New York: Simon & Schuster.

Hostetler, J. A. (1993). *Amish society* (4th ed.). Baltimore: Johns Hopkins University Press.

Kephart, W. M., & Zellner, W. W. (1994). *Extraordinary groups: An examination of unconventional lifestyles* (5th ed.). New York: St. Martin's Press.

Kraybill, D. B. (1989). *The riddle of Amish culture.* Baltimore: Johns Hopkins University Press.

Newman, C. (1989, September). The Shakers' brief eternity. *National Geographic, 176*, 302–325.

# Chapter 8

# The Church of Scientology: A Quasi-Religion

## David G. Bromley and Mitchell L. Bracey, Jr.

David G. Bromley, professor of sociology and religious studies at Virginia Commonwealth University, is editor of *Journal for the Scientific Study of Religion* and founding editor of the annual series Religion and the Social Order. He has written or edited 12 books in the area of sociology of religion. His most recent book, published in 1998, is entitled *Prophetic Religion in a Secular Age* (written with Anson Shupe). Scientology is a featured religion in that book.

Mitchell Bracey completed his master's degree in sociology at Virginia Commonwealth under Bromley's direction. He is enrolled in the doctoral program at the University of Kentucky.

Religion fills a basic human need. Consequently, all societies have some form of religion. Societies vary greatly, however, in terms of the scope and importance of religion in the day-to-day activities of its members. Sacred societies, for example, weave religion into the fabric of their institutional structures. In such societies, religion is often inseparable from other institutions, such as education and government. Secular societies, on the other hand, set religion apart from other institutions.

Within secular societies, religion may assume different forms. Most are traditional, some are less so. A traditional view of religion includes beliefs and practices related to the supernatural and the meaning of life that are shared by most members of society (Stark 1996). *Quasi-religions*, on the other hand, are unconventional "organizations which either see themselves or are seen by others as 'sort-of' religious" (Greil and Rudy 1990: 221).

Quasi-religions straddle the boundary between sacred and secular groups within a society, and have a nonreligious as well as a religious character. Examples include the *New Age* movement and *transcendental meditation*. Quasi-religious therapies are sometimes offered by quasi-religious groups. The therapeutic aspect of these therapies invariably involves self-help and self-actualization. A common belief among members is that individuals possess a true self that is the full and natural expression of human potential. The goal of therapy, then, is the development of this potential.

Mental well-being can best be achieved by realizing that the barriers to full self-actualization are artificial. It is within the power of each individual to eliminate such artificial restraints and their negative effects. The process becomes a spiritual mission. The Church of Scientology, with its myriad self-help programs, provides excellent examples of quasi-religious therapy (Atack 1990; Bainbridge 1987; Corydon and DeWolf 1987; Miller 1987; Wallis 1976; Whitehead 1987; Zellner 1995).

In some ways Scientology fits a standard sociological definition of religion. Based on revelations by its founder, L. Ron Hubbard, Scientology states that there is a logic and order in the world that defines a larger purpose for humankind. The supernatural is seen as a force in human history, and humans must establish a relationship with it.

Scientologists are convinced that spiritual knowledge is the key to human purpose and salvation. A community of believers gathers at significant times to affirm these beliefs and engage in rituals. These prescribed rituals enhance understanding of, and provide contact with, the supernatural. Religious functionaries are authorized by the church to provide spiritual leadership. Both leaders and adherents possess a solemnity of purpose and devotion to the stated beliefs and rituals.

At the same time, Scientology is at odds with conventional conceptions of religion. Whereas its adherents believe in the supernatural, they do not focus their beliefs or practices on a supreme being. In fact, Scientologists believe that each member possesses godlike potential. Many of the trappings of conventional religious bodies are conspicuous by their absence or are relegated to unimportant roles in Scientology. This is because the Church was not a church at its inception. Scientology was a chain of self-help therapy groups before Hubbard announced that it was a religion.

Today, Scientology has as much of a therapeutic look as a religious look. For example, clergy and traditional church ceremonies are not central to the religious lives of Scientologists. There are no traditional church buildings at which the faithful regularly gather. Scientology operates on a fee-for-service basis, providing services to clients. The Church is not financed through gifts and offerings from members. From the perspective of an outsider, members more closely resemble consumers than parishioners. Finally, Scientology uses scientific research to measure its benefits. It urges practitioners to evaluate any results they experience. Conventional churches, on the other hand, are based on faith and results are not examined critically.

Scientology is a mixture of religion and therapy that evolved from a popular self-help therapy, *Dianetics*. Its quasi-religious character becomes evident when one examines the history, leadership, belief system, rituals, organizational structure, and membership of the movement. Also important are the sociocultural conditions that gave rise to Scientology.

## SCIENTOLOGY: ORIGINS AND BELIEF SYSTEM

The Church of Scientology is the brainchild of its talented, charismatic founder, Lafayette Ronald Hubbard. Known affectionately as Ron to his followers, Hubbard was born in Tilden, Nebraska, in 1911. The life histories of religious founders are often shrouded in mystery. Hubbard's life story is no exception.

Scientology produced a biography to enhance the founder's personal qualities. According to church-sponsored publications, Hubbard was a very precocious child, perhaps a child prodigy. Through an Indian shaman, his lifelong quest for spiritual knowledge began when he became blood brother to the Blackfoot Indians. By the age of 12, Hubbard began studying under Commander Joseph C. Thompson, the first U.S. military officer to study under Freud in Vienna. As a young man, Hubbard became a world traveler. He explored Guam, Java, India, the Philippines, Japan, and China. He is said to have gained further insight into the mysteries of the universe from his investigation of their ancient cultures.

In 1930, Hubbard entered George Washington University, where he studied mathematics, engineering, and nuclear physics but did not earn a degree. He began a career as a writer in several genres but became best known for his science fiction.

Hubbard's spiritual discoveries began in 1945, while he was recovering from injuries suffered while serving as a naval officer that left him crippled and blind. Hubbard immersed himself in Freudian psychoanalytic theory and Eastern philosophy. Combining these with his own knowledge of nuclear physics, he developed basic principles governing the workings of the human mind. These later became the central elements of his religious doctrines. He applied his theories to his own physical condition, healing himself in the process.

After returning to civilian life, Hubbard formed a strong friendship with John Campbell, Jr., the editor of the popular magazine *Astounding Science Fiction*. Campbell credited Hubbard with curing his chronic sinusitis. Impressed with Hubbard's theories and his own cure, he featured an article on the practice Hubbard had named Dianetics. The article, which gave Hubbard his first mass audience, appeared in the May 1950 issue. Publication of the magazine and of Hubbard's book, *Dianetics: The Modern Science of Mental Health*, triggered a wave of popular interest in Dianetics (Hubbard 1976). It became the common person's alternative to expensive, extended psychotherapy. Within a year after the publication of *Dianetics*, Hubbard had attracted a sizable but unorganized grassroots following. The book was a national best-seller, and Hubbard became a much sought-after lecturer. In late 1950 he founded the Hubbard Dianetic Research Foundation to service public demand for his new therapy. Hubbard's prophetic revelations are the core of Scientology's belief system.

Hubbard continued to expand upon these initial revelations throughout his life. His theology includes a belief in past lives. He believed that he had been Buddha, as well as Rhodesia's founder, Cecil Rhodes, in previous lifetimes. In 1967 Hubbard moved the leadership of Scientology to a flotilla of oceangoing ships that sailed for several years outside the national territorial waters of many countries.

When he returned to the United States, Hubbard remained reclusive and deeply involved in extending the applications of his early revelations. In 1980 he withdrew from public life and remained in seclusion until his death in 1986. Church leaders announced that Hubbard's body had become an impediment to his work. He had, therefore, "dropped his body" and was continuing his research on another planet.

## FROM DIANETICS TO SCIENTOLOGY

Hubbard's prophetic revelations center on the human mind. He believed the mind consists of three parts: the somatic, the reactive, and the analytical. The somatic mind functions to regulate all the basic mechanisms that sustain an organism's life. The reactive mind "works on a stimulus-response basis which is not under a person's volitional control and which exerts force and power over a person's awareness, purposes, thoughts, body and actions" (Hubbard 1988: 159).

The analytical mind is "the conscious, aware mind which thinks, observes data, remembers it and resolves problems" (Hubbard 1988: 145). During periods of stress, the analytic mind shuts down and the reactive mind comes into play. The reactive mind forms a detailed memory of experiences that occur while the analytic mind is inoperative. The memory records are remarkably complete, even those formed during periods of unconsciousness. Specific sensory details of the traumatic sounds, sights, smells, and tactile sensations are remembered as a series of mental images. "Mental image pictures are actually composed of energy. They have mass, they exist in space, and they follow some very, very definite routines of behavior, the most interesting of which is the fact that they appear when somebody thinks of something. If you think of a certain dog, you get a picture of that dog" (Church of Scientology 1992: 143). These mental images are accumulated on what is known as the "time track." It is analogous to a motion picture reel.

The memory records of traumatic events are called *engrams*. Stored in the reactive mind, they cause the individual to respond in an emotional and irrational fashion to anything that produces an association with the original traumatic experiences. They inhibit the full expression of adult potential and are analogous to Sigmund Freud's repressed desires or Carl Jung's complexes.

## CLEARS AND THETANS

The goal of Dianetics therapy, referred to as *auditing*, is for an individual to reach the level of *Clear*. This name comes from the button on a calculator that erases previous calculations. Clears are *optimal individuals*. They have been cleared of false information and memories of traumatic experiences that prevent them from adapting to the world around them in a natural and appropriate fashion. Clears, therefore, will be more successful in everyday life. Indeed, they are particularly well suited for lives as managers. They will be healthier, experience less stress, and possess better communication skills than non-Scientologists.

Beyond these more mundane abilities, reaching a state of Clear permits individuals to achieve identities separate from their bodies. As one of Scientology's advertisements puts it, "Go Clear—For the first time in your life you will be truly yourself" (Stark and Bainbridge 1985: 266). Hubbard conveyed the extraordinary capacities that Clears possess by comparing them to Buddha and Christ—who, he claimed, achieved a status only slightly above that of Clear. As Dianetics developed, auditors began reporting new and puzzling findings. Clients were identifying traumatic memories that had occurred before they were born.

Soon after the publication of *Dianetics*, Hubbard announced that individuals had lived previous lives. The reports of past life memories took Dianetics beyond mental health into the realm of the spiritual. It led Hubbard to postulate the existence of immortal essences called *thetans*. Thetans, he believed, possess virtually infinite powers. They are not part of the physical universe made up of matter, energy, space, and time but have the ability to control that universe. In the primordial past, thetans were celestial beings who experimented with human form as a cosmic game for entertainment.

Thetans choose to be humans, the highest position within the natural order. They can enter a human body in many different ways. Some choose to enter the fetus of a pregnant woman, and others enter newborn infants. In the process of experimentation, however, thetans lost contact with their higher origins and became trapped in the bodies of mortal persons.

Thetans move from body to body through successive lifetimes. Their previous identities and activities are obscured at each new reincarnation. As a result of this amnesia, thetans come to accept the illusion that they are nothing more than physical bodies. The great spiritual discovery of Scientology is that all humans actually are immortal thetans. A thetan is the person himself or herself, not the body or name or mind. It is that which is aware of being aware, the identity that **IS** the individual. One does not have a thetan, something one keeps somewhere apart from oneself. One is a thetan. In Scientology the loftier goal of the auditing process is to help individuals restore themselves to their original, natural, spiritual condition. The person is "(and discovers himself to be) a **BEING** (spiritual agent) of infinite creative potential who acts in, but is not part of, the physical universe" (Thomas 1970: 8). As Operating Thetans, Scientologists can assume total control of, and responsibility for, all their personal actions, as well as external physical phenomena—a condition called "at cause."

The Church of Scientology remains noncommittal about the existence of God or a Supreme Being. They believe that humans are not spiritually advanced enough to comprehend the deity concept. Hubbard concluded that years of auditing had failed to produce any evidence of a Supreme Being. Still, the theology does allow for the possibility of such a Being. The belief in the immortality of each individual's spirit means that death, "dropping the body," is not a pressing concern. The spirit simply secures another body in which it can survive and grow. The important goal, therefore, is achieving one's true identity.

In Scientology, "vastly more emphasis is given to the godlike nature of the person and to the workings of the human mind than to the nature of God" (Whitehead 1987: 34). This emphasis on the transcendent quality of each person is revealed in the eight dynamics of the universe. These dynamics, a ranking of levels of survival, begin with individual survival. They continue through sexual reproduction and family survival, followed by survival of groups and nations, then species survival, survival of all life forms, survival of the physical universe, survival of the individual as a spiritual entity, and, finally, survival through infinity/oneness ("the allness of all"). This highest level is survival of a spiritual entity united with the universe. This hints that God can be viewed simply as "infinite potential" (Church of Scientology 1992: 33).

There are significant impediments to the goal of achieving one's ultimate potential by becoming "at cause" in the universe as an Operating Thetan. These obstacles, which must be confronted, include communication problems and malevolent individuals or their organizations.

Communication has a preeminent status within Scientology. Indeed, misinformation or miscommunication is analogous to original sin, inhibiting individual growth and relationships with others. Distorted information and breakdowns in information flow and processing are the root causes of most problems. The concept of the misunderstood word (referred to as "a misunderstood") has a central position within Scientology's teachings. For example, reading failures of comprehension and retention can be the result of not clearly understanding a word.

Scientologists believe that the majority of human beings are essentially good. About 20 percent of the population, however, are "suppressive persons." Of these, only about 2.5 percent are hopelessly antisocial. A person, even though not suppressive, is called a "potential trouble source" if he or she shows signs of antisocial behavior. A potential trouble source is believed to be under the influence of a suppressive person. To solve existing problems, the potential trouble source must sever ties with the suppressive person. Scientologists also believe a hidden "third party" precipitates any conflict between two parties. "While it is commonly believed to take two to make a fight, a third party must exist and must develop it for actual conflict to occur" (The Church of Scientology 1994: 307). Scientology has created "third party law," a Church procedure for conflict resolution, that locates the source of turmoil between two disputants in the motives and actions of a third party.

Larger conspiratorial forces are at work as well. True spiritual awareness in the Western world has been undermined because the study of the spirit has not progressed as it should. This crime has been perpetrated primarily by the humanities. Psychology and psychiatry have been the most destructive. The Church professes that the study of the mind and the treatment of mental and emotional disorders should be the exclusive purview of religion.

Suppressive persons are disruptive. Engrams, stored in the reactive mind, and breakdowns in communication are primarily responsible for societal ills. Elimination of all reactive minds would remove impediments to communication, thus elevating the condition of all humanity. For this reason, Scientology's ultimate goal is to "clear the planet." This would eliminate the chronic human problems of war, pollution, insanity, drugs, and crime. Scientologists believe that their personal spiritual salvation depends upon achieving this larger goal.

## THE RITUALS OF SCIENTOLOGY: CLEARING THE REACTIVE MIND

The central ritual in Scientology is "auditing." It is a word-association technique by which auditors identify engrams (memories of traumatic events) through observing a respondent's subtle reaction to key words. Before the auditing process can begin, trainees must develop skills in unobstructed communication. A variety of training exercises or "training routines" teach them to focus undivided attention on another person.

One exercise involves a student's maintaining eye contact with another for as long as two hours. The objective is to "be there," and "any flinching or evasion of the other person's face, dropping off, yawning, or fidgeting is grounds for a 'flunk.' " Another training exercise is called "bullbaiting." Students are subjected to "words or behavior designed to provoke laughter, anger, or other reactions" (Whitehead 1987: 136).

Memories of past events may cause psychic distress; therefore, bullbaiting is designed to keep the auditing practice on track by teaching students to focus attention on the task at hand. The immediate objective of auditing is to eliminate engrams. Exposing an engram will clear up its negative impact on behavior. Once cleared of engrams, individuals can relate to experiences directly rather than through the distorting filter of the reactive mind. One practitioner observed, "It's as if an unwanted, vaguely perceived radio program had been turned off. The background chattering of the Reactive Mind, as coming from a far place, has ceased to grind out its naggings, urgings and inhibitions in my ear. And against the sudden calm, the chirping of little birds can be heard and I breathe freely and focus clearly . . ." (Whitehead 1987: 236).

For Scientologists, eliminating engrams improves their capacity for self-direction. As one practitioner put it, "I saw my old life as one big reactive mind. My moods had been affected by everything around me: weather, places, people. A person with a reactive mind was like a piece of lint blown about on a windowsill" (Wallis 1976: 178).

At higher levels of auditing, individuals learn to communicate with, and gain knowledge of, their past lives as thetans. They also develop the capacity to transcend the physical universe and develop self-determination. Individuals are not responsible for their own engrams; those are the result of external traumatic events. However, once they are aware of Scientology, individuals become responsible for their liberation.

"Misunderstoods" (misunderstood words) are cognitive errors made by the individual. Through Scientology, individuals can liberate themselves from problem social relationships by addressing problems of miscommunication. A phase of the auditing process involves monitoring an individual with an *e-meter*. This device, developed by Hubbard, is a skin galvanometer like a crude lie detector. It records electrical impulses transmitted through the skin. The auditor asks questions and observes fluctuations in the e-meter's needle. Scientologists believe that the e-meter records the electrical charges contained in the engrams of the reactive mind. When a stored emotional charge (engram) is identified and discussed sufficiently (audited), it will no longer produce an emotional response. The charge it contains will be released, and the e-meter's needle will register no reaction because it has been cleared.

There are several "grades" that must be completed sequentially in order to attain the level of Clear. In addition, there are a number of "Operating Thetan levels" beyond Clear. Progression through these stages provides training as an auditor as well as individual spiritual development. Auditing, according to practitioners, expands mental and physical powers, promotes physical and mental healing, and provides greater confidence and serenity. For example, one Scientologist reported being healed of a chronic condition that had afflicted him across lifetimes. "Is my chronic illness handled? It is indeed. I've had it going more aeons than I can easily remember. And now it's gone. No more, finished, handled. And it feels great. Thanks to my Auditor for the application. Thanks to the Commodore for the Tech" (Church of Scientology 1992:162).

Another Scientologist reported gaining startling mental abilities, such as "always knowing who's calling on the phone before it rings, and being able to check the progress of my cooking hamburger without walking into the kitchen" (Church of Scientology 1992: 206–207). In many cases Scientologists report using these newfound powers and abilities to help others rather than themselves.

Advanced practitioners claim to exercise extraordinary powers that override the physical laws of nature. Consider this account from an Operating Thetan:

Today was fantastic. I walked downstairs to get some coffee and the coffee machine was buzzing. So I put my hands out and moved them around the machine, putting out beams to bounce back and thereby I could tell by watching the particles flow exactly where the error in the machine was. I found it and corrected the molecular structure of that area in the machine and the buzzing stopped. Then I heard my air conditioner rattling so I looked at why it was rattling and it stopped. (Harris 1981: 148)

The benefits of auditing go beyond individual liberation. Auditing empowers the individual by first eliminating the effects of the reactive mind. Finally, the reactive mind is completely eliminated. As this process proceeds, the individual is able to move from a concern with personal survival toward goals that transcend the individual. For example, many social problems develop from misunderstandings. Accurate communication becomes necessary to resolve these problems. One Scientologist concluded that even war could be eliminated if honest, accurate communication and broadly based affinity could be established.

I was on the one side, see. And I'd been captured, or rather, let myself be captured, and executed—along with several others—by the firing squad. But the night before I was shot, the leader of the other side came to visit me in my cell. We had a long discussion and it turned out that we both had the same ideals, the same feelings about things. We were in agreement! What were we fighting about? It was absurd. Here I and thousands of people were dying because the two sides were in a big MISUNDERSTOOD about each other's purposes. . . . And all wars are like that. (Whitehead 1987: 259)

For Scientologists, individual liberation and empowerment are necessary to form meaningful relationships and achieve larger humanitarian goals.

## THE ORGANIZATION AND OPERATION OF SCIENTOLOGY

Scientology has organizational branches, each of which performs specialized tasks. The educational division provides a series of courses and exercises that members must take. There are several hundred "missions" and "churches" that offer this introductory training at the grassroots level. Organized as franchises, they pay a percentage of their receipts to the central organization. They can sell Church services so long as they meet standards established and monitored by special divisions of the Church. Advanced training beyond what is provided by the local churches and missions is offered at Scientology's management center and "mother church" in Los Angeles.

Another organizational branch delivers Hubbard's technologies in areas such as moral revitalization, education, and drug-use and criminal rehabilitation. Narconon International provides drug education and rehabilitation services, and Criminon seeks to rehabilitate criminals. They teach study and communication skills as well as personal values, including individual responsibility. Applied Scholastics teaches students how to learn and eliminate barriers to effective study. The World Institute of Scientology Enterprises (WISE) provides business-related services. WISE offers training in business skills such as hiring, decision-making, plan implementation, and organizational streamlining. The services provided by these nonprofit organizations are used by many organizations, including public school systems and many major corporations. Corporate clients include Elizabeth Arden, Perrier, Bank of America, Chevron, General Motors, Mobil Oil, and Allstate Insurance (Rupert 1992). All these Scientology programs claim success rates substantially above those of their competitors.

A third organizational branch within Scientology attempts to expose and eliminate organizations thought to impede the progress of society and humanity. An example is the Citizens Commission on Human Rights which devotes considerable effort opposing what Scientology considers psychiatric abuses.

Hubbard expressed unremitting hostility toward psychiatrists, branding them "outright murderers." He contended that they planned to become "confessors" and counselors to heads of state around the globe (Kent 1991). He asserted that psychiatrists have had negative effects on the past lives of individuals and "are the sole cause of decline in this universe" (Kent 1991:10). Scientology publications continue the campaign against psychiatry.

The book *What Is Scientology?*, for example, asserts that psychiatry is a "conglomeration of half-baked theories" espoused by a "priesthood." Psychiatry has not produced any results "except an ability to make the unmanageable and mutinous more docile and quiet, and turn the troubled into apathetic souls beyond the point of caring" (Church of Scientology 1992: 526). Psychiatry's mission is not "healing" but "control." The Citizens Commission on Human Rights has waged a national campaign against the use of the prescription drugs Prozac and Ritalin. It has not, however, succeeded in gaining a ban on the drugs (Karel 1991). It continues to oppose the use of electroshock and "mind-altering" drug treatments in psychiatric facilities.

The Committee on Human and Public Safety fights against Interpol, the international police organization. Scientologists contend it has collected and disseminated false information on their organization. They also charge Interpol has abused the rights and privacy of citizens in various nations. They further suggest it has organizational links to the KGB as well as historical connections to Nazism. Federal agencies that Scientology has criticized include the Internal Revenue Service, the Federal Bureau of Investigation, and the Central Intelligence Agency. The Church opposes computerized data banks containing information on private citizens. It encourages the use of the Freedom of Information Act to access public documents. Finally, it condemns government cover-ups of discrimination and abuse.

A fourth organizational branch within Scientology includes a number of control organizations, among them the Ethics System, the Justice System, and the Religious Technology Center. The Church systematically gathers and evaluates statistical measures used to monitor all Church "products." Statistics are compiled to ensure that a "valuable final product" is produced—one that meets

Church specifications. These statistics also measure how well an individual measures up to Church standards.

Hubbard established the Ethics System to ensure that Scientology technology is administered precisely as he developed it. The Justice System plays a central role by evaluating ethical standards. It sanctions deviance, rewards productivity, and strengthens organizational strategy and individual commitment. Any action that is not in compliance with Scientology's policies or that reduces its profitability is an ethics violation. Ethics and productivity are intimately connected because of the Church's utilitarian philosophy.

A detailed offense code defines various acts as errors, misdemeanors, crimes, or suppressive acts. The most serious offenses are suppressive acts. These limit the operation or development of Scientology and thus, in the Church's judgment, hinder the betterment of humankind.

The Religious Technology Center is a critical part of the control system. It is dedicated to protecting the Church's doctrinal integrity. Because many of the religious materials are licensed products, their use is restricted to those authorized by the Church. As a corporate entity, the Religious Technology Center holds the legal rights to all Church materials. The Church has tried to keep its theology secret, but copyrighted materials must be available to the public.

## MEMBERSHIP

The Church of Scientology recruits members in a variety of ways. Most of the converts come through outreach organizations. For example, one convert connected through the drug treatment program:

By the time I was 17 years old, I was doing a lot of drugs and was going downhill fast. I had dropped out of high school and left my chances of a good education and successful life behind. . . . I did L. Ron Hubbard's Purification Program and my life was literally saved. . . . If not for Scientology technology I am certain I would not be alive today. (Church of Scientology 1992: 261)

Family and friends are also important sources of converts. Over half of practicing Scientologists report that they were introduced to the Church by a friend or family member. Half of these family introductions were by parents. Scientology has a youthful membership. Over two-thirds of the current members are between 20 and 40. Approximately 56 percent of all current members were introduced to the Church between the ages of 21 and 30. Scientology reports that the vast majority of its members are white-collar workers, and among these, managers predominate. Nearly 15 percent of the members report owning their own business (Church of Scientology 1992: 199).

Converts report that they apply Scientology to their lives and receive a sense of confidence, control, direction, and purpose. For example:

It seems I've been searching for eons for what I know now. I feel at peace. I am calm and certain. Things that never made sense now make sense. It's so hard sometimes to say enough to really acknowledge the magnitude of what processing is and does. OT levels are the most precious thing in the universe. (Church of Scientology 1992: 309)

Those who pay for services are called ordinary members. Scientology training can be very expensive, particularly at the higher levels. List price for courses may be as much as $1,000 per hour. However, at the lower levels, members may audit one another free of charge.

A second type of membership includes persons who join the staff and work for the Church. They normally sign contracts for five years or less, and receive services and training at a reduced price.

The third membership category is known as Sea Org. Staffing for all the organizations above the mission and church levels comes from Sea Org. It is analogous to religious orders within more traditional churches. The Church reports about 5,000 Sea Org members. They constitute "the dedicated core of the religion, each of whom has signed a pledge of eternal service to Scientology and its goals . . . and work long hours for little pay and live a communal existence" (The "Sea Org" 1992: 6).

## SCIENTOLOGY IN SOCIOCULTURAL PERSPECTIVE

The Church of Scientology is one of the clearest examples of a quasi-religious therapy system. There are other movements, of course, that have similar organizational characteristics. The best-known of these include transcendental meditation, Silva Mind Control, EST (Erhard Seminar Training), Life Spring, and Synanon.

All contain religious elements, implicitly or explicitly, in their beliefs and practices. Such groups can be understood in terms of the social and cultural environment that gave birth to them.

Many changes have taken place in our society since World War II. These developments have affected public and private life differently. In public life, the growth of government and corporations has been astounding. It is easy for the individual to get lost in the magnitude of these organizations and to feel insignificant. This feeling is compounded by the rapid changes taking place within these organizations. An important part of this change is the increase in the degree of specialization in public life. As our society becomes more specialized, individuals are required to perform a greater variety of roles. Often there are conflicting expectations among these roles, so that people experience role conflict. They feel scattered, without a sense of an integrated social life. They are little cogs in big machines. They are merely functionaries, temporary incumbents of permanent positions. The organization is more important than the individuals that comprise it. As Randall Collins observes:

The crucial encounters in this form of organization, then, are those which constantly reinforce the notion that men are only occupants of positions who are subject to records and formal rules; ritual deference is to the rules themselves and to the organization in the abstract, not to any particular individuals. (Collins 1975: 294)

A final change is the increasing separation of the public and private spheres. As individuals face greater difficulty in finding personal meaning on the job, they increasingly turn to private sphere relationships. However, there have been major changes in the private sphere.

In the case of the family, for example, there is greater emphasis on personal freedom and self-fulfillment. Personal freedom has come about because of a loosening of formal obligations to family, ethnic, religious, and community groups. Consequently, there has been a decrease in support from these groups. As individuals seek greater personal freedom, long-term commitment to traditional moorings in family and community becomes increasingly less viable. It is not surprising that serial relationships have come to characterize both marriage and occupational careers.

The result of these developments in the public and private spheres is that individuals find themselves more regimented in the former and more liberated in the latter. At the same time, performance expectations have heightened in both spheres. As psychologist Martin Seligman wryly commented, "We blindly accept soaring expectations for the self. . . . It's as if some idiot raised the ante on what it takes to be a normal human being (1988: 52).

In both spheres the individual is the basic building block of the social order. In the public sphere, individuals must perform their segmented tasks in the impersonal bureaucratic machine. Seeking identity in the private sphere, individuals pursue fulfillment and personal growth. In describing the changing nature of individualism in American society, one social scientist summed up the change between the 1940s and the 1970s as a shift from identity grounded in institutions to a more fluid and personally constructed identity:

A self that can gain happiness by accepting its identity and circumstances, that must be unified, committed to some larger purposes, and judged on the basis of ideals is replaced by a self that must change its identity and situations, take risks in order to grow, and define and pursue its own personal goals. (Veroff et al. 1981: 529)

If individuals' accomplishments do not measure up to these elevated expectations for self-fulfillment, the potential is created for a novel form of alienation. It is "a divorcement of the individual from himself or the failure of the individual to find his real self, which he must employ as the base for organizing his life" (Turner 1969: 396). In this quest for true selfhood, individuals constantly evaluate their behavior to be sure that it is natural and not simply conformity to social expectations. Too many institutional attachments thus become not simply undesirable but actually pathological. It was in this context that Americans began looking for ways to protect, nurture, and develop selfhood.

## THE EMERGENCE OF QUASI-RELIGIOUS THERAPIES

The enormous popularity of the various quasi-religious therapies beginning in the 1960s, can be traced directly to the Esalen Institute in Big Sur, California. From its founding in 1962, as many as 6 million people participated in various encounter sessions and workshops over the next decade. There followed a variety of encounter groups that used many methods, including biofeedback, meditation, isolation tanks, fasting, martial arts and calisthenics, sexual release, dance, art, breathing, massage, special diets, hypnotic regression to past lives, and even ESP. They redefined and expanded the concept of therapy. A common theme linking these diverse groups is that human nature is innately good, but its expression has been limited by conditions of social life that individuals have come to accept as natural and inevitable. Because these limitations inhibit the expression of essential humanness, everyone can benefit from the new therapies.

Therapy is not limited to a small group of emotionally damaged individuals. All persons can explore their own potential and nurture such qualities as autonomy, self-awareness, aliveness, and spontaneity. These "user-friendly" therapies are accessible, affordable, and acceptable to a broad spectrum of the population. In addition, the consumer is in control of the therapy. Veroff and his colleagues emphasize that "younger cohorts thus seem to have been most easily socialized to the new norm for turning to mental-health specialists. While we see a large general change in formal help-seeking, we should remember that the change affected younger people in particular" (Veroff et al. 1981: 532, 540). Scientology is populated by younger persons.

In many respects Scientology has been very successful. In 1992 the Church reported that its materials were available in 74 countries around the world. It is projected that its teachings will be available in every nation by the beginning of the twenty-first century. Scientology counts over 1,000 churches, missions, and related organizations, and has over 10,000 staff. Literally millions of people worldwide have participated in its courses, read its publications, and/or attended Church-sponsored lectures. The Church reports that about 17,000 practitioners had reached a state of Clear by 1980, and that number had grown to nearly 50,000 by 1995.

Scientology is popular because it addresses feelings of alienation from government and business life. It also meets expectations for personal fulfillment. Scientology offers an explanation for alienating conditions and a means for transforming the circumstances of living. The expansion of therapy as an industry that offers solutions to personal and interpersonal problems is extraordinary.

As it becomes commonplace for individuals to experience periodic feelings of self-doubt, anxiety, alienation, dissatisfaction with social relationships, and inability to realize personal aspirations, therapeutic services become a normal feature of social life.

Scientology is different from traditional therapies because it seeks a higher level of personal empowerment. It does not assume that the individual must conform to societal expectations. The ultimate reality, Scientology asserts, is "I-ness." Human beings are like machines. They need to be programmed correctly or their spiritual essence will be suppressed. For Scientologists this involves eliminating the incorrect programming. Sources of these errors include incorrect learning (misunderstoods), traumatic experiences (engrams), and incorrect programming (prenatal engrams). The goal of this process is to teach individuals to communicate accurately so that they can form effective relationships.

In addition, individuals must be taught that they are in control of themselves and their environment. Finally, evil in the form of forces that obstruct personal growth and accurate communication, and oppose Scientology itself must be conquered. Once individuals have the capacity to exercise cognitive control, they can express their true essence. The potential for growth becomes virtually limitless. Scientologists symbolize this limitless potential as a transcendent entity, the thetan. It has the capacity to contravene even physical laws of the universe, including mortality.

Although the Church has created a bureaucracy to liberate the individual, its bureaucracy is not constrictive because it is under control of practitioners who protect the Church against social intrusion. However, the significance of Scientology probably is not found in either its clashes with conventional society or its long-term survivability. Rather, Scientology is better understood as one of a number of groups that emerged in a very specific sociocultural context. It offers a vision of how a social world that has created a range of debilitating consequences for ordinary individuals might be understood, transformed, and set right. From a sociological perspective, Scientology and other quasi-religious therapies provide a valuable lens through which to view the promise and travails of contemporary society.

## BIBLIOGRAPHY

Atack, J. (1990). *A piece of blue sky: Scientology and L. Ron Hubbard exposed.* New York: Carol Publishing.

Bainbridge, W. (1987). Science and religion: The case of Scientology. In D. Bromley & P. Hammond (Eds.), *The future of new religious movements* (pp. 59–79). Macon, GA: Mercer University Press.

Church of Scientology. (1992). *What Is Scientology?* Los Angeles: Bridge Publications.

Church of Scientology. (1994). *The Church of Scientology: 40th anniversary.* Los Angeles: Bridge Publications.

Collins, R. (1975). *Conflict sociology.* New York: Academic Press.

Corydon, B., & DeWolf, R. (1987). *L. Ron Hubbard: Messiah or madman.* Secaucus, NJ: Lyle Stuart.

Greil, A., & Rudy, D. (1990). On the margins of the sacred. In T. Robbins & D. Anthony (Eds.), *In gods we trust*. New Brunswick, NJ: Transaction.

Harris, M. (1981). *America now: The anthropology of a changing culture*. New York: Simon & Schuster.

Hubbard, L. R. (1976). *Dianetics: The modern science of mental health*. Los Angeles: Church of Scientology of Los Angeles.

Hubbard, L. R. (1988). *Science of survival*. Los Angeles: Bridge Publications.

Karel, R. (1991, September 6). FDA refuses Scientologists' request to ban Prozac. *Psychiatric News*.

Kent, S. (1991, November). *International social control by the Church of Scientology*. Paper presented at the meeting of the Society for the Scientific Study of Religion, Pittsburgh, PA.

Miller, R. (1987). *Bare-faced messiah: The true story of L. Ron Hubbard*. New York: Henry Holt.

Rupert, G. (1992). Employing the new age: Training seminars. In J. Lewis & G. Melton (Eds.), *New age* (pp. 127–135). Albany, NY: SUNY Press.

The "Sea Org"—power behind Scientology. (1992, October). *Cult Observer, 9–10*, 6.

Seligman, M. (1988, October) Boomer blues: With too great expectations, the baby-boomers are sliding into individualistic melancholy. *Psychology Today*, 52.

Stark, R. (1996) *Sociology* (6th ed.). Belmont, CA: Wadsworth Publishing Company.

Stark, R., & Bainbridge, W. (1985). *The future of religion: Secularization, revival and cult formation*. Berkeley: University of California Press.

Thomas, R. (1970). *Scientology and Dianetics*. Los Angeles: Church of Scientology.

Turner, R. (1969). The theme of contemporary social movements. *Journal of Sociology, 20*, 390–405.

Veroff, J., Douvan, E., & Kulka, R. (1981). *The inner American: A self-portrait from 1957 to 1976*. New York: Basic Books.

Wallis, R. (1976). *The road to total freedom: A sociological analysis of Scientology*. London: Heinemann.

Whitehead, H. (1987). *Renunciation and reformulation: A study of conversion in an American sect*. Ithaca, NY: Cornell University Press.

Zellner, W. (1995). *Countercultures: A sociological analysis*. New York: St. Martin's Press.

# *Freedom Park*

## *William Zellner and Marc Petrowsky*

William Zellner has long had an interest in sects and cults, both
secular and religious. He is especially interested in groups with de-
valued perspectives. Freedom Park attracted his interest because it
typifies what, sociologically, a cult is. Through long association, he
and cult leader Ron Morris have become fast friends, though they
share no commonality of thought.

Marc Petrowsky received his Ph.D. from the University of Florida
and is an associate professor of sociology at East Central University.
He is coauthor of an introductory text and has a research interest in
beliefs and their effects on behavior.

What is a cult? There are almost as many definitions of the term as there are
books addressing the topic. For example, many ministers tend to define any
religious organization professing a belief system radically different from theirs
as a cult. Some even refer to the Mormon Church (9.5 million members) and
the Society of Jehovah's Witnesses (5.1 million members) as cults. Many of
these same pastors label the Roman Catholic Church, the largest Christian denomination in the world, a cult.

Journalists and law enforcement officers tend to apply the label ''cult'' to any
group deemed to have committed a deviant act. For example, a headline in a
major magazine following the mass suicides at Jonestown, Guyana, read ''Religious Sect Becomes Cult.'' Almost without exception, news reporters and police use the term as a synonym for ''evil'' religion.

For sociologists, the best working definition of a cult is the residual product of the more easily defined terms *ecclesia, denomination, sect,* and *established sect.*

An *ecclesia* is a church without competition, sometimes by fiat, that is accepted by most members of a society. Examples are Islam in Iran, the Anglican Church in England, and the Lutheran Church in Norway. There is usually little conflict between church and state, and each is supportive of the other. There are, of course, exceptions, such as the veto power over governmental decisions maintained by Islamic leaders in Iran.

*Denominations*, like the ecclesia, are large and structured. They are not supported by the state, and there is some competition with other denominations for members. Children born into the group generally accept the faith without question, and a continuing constituency is assured. Because of our immigrant heritage, the United States has more denominations than any other country in the world. Examples are the American Lutheran, United Methodist, Roman Catholic, Episcopal, and Presbyterian churches.

A *sect* is a relatively small religious group, usually a more conservative splinter from a larger religious organization. Membership consists of converts—those who have found the "truth." Intensive commitments and demonstrations of faith are expected of the believers. Lay leadership is the norm. Church business is usually conducted by a "society of brethren" who refer to each other as brothers. Women generally have their own societies, in the form of auxiliaries, within such groups, and are rarely allowed to serve in the ministry.

Sects tend to be fundamentally at odds with society. Ecumenical relations with other religious groups rarely exist. If a sect endures, it generally becomes less antagonistic toward society, and it begins to resemble a denomination.

Occasionally sects will survive and grow, yet still maintain distance from the larger society. Sociologist J. Milton Yinger calls such groups *established sects.* Examples are the Latter-Day Saints (Mormons), Jehovah's Witnesses, Amish, Hutterites, and Seventh-Day Adventists.

*Cults* tend to be quite small and very secretive, whereas sects usually exist more openly in society. Often members lay claim to a body of knowledge they believe only a select number in society are capable of understanding. Most feel they are persecuted by a world incapable of "fathoming the truth." In spite of that perceived difficulty, most zealously seek converts.

Perhaps the most striking difference between a cult and other religious organizations is the cult's lack of organization. A cult is usually headed by a powerful, charismatic leader. There is no hierarchy, and what the leader says is law on all matters, from philosophy to financial dealings, to relationships with a doubting world.

A cult is the only type of religious organization that depends on *charismatic authority.* The life of a cult relies in great measure on the health of its leader, for when the charismatic dies, or loses his or her appeal, the cult usually dies as well.

Cults usually reject and withdraw from the rest of society. Followers tend to be poor and often have given up on society's institutions as a means to achieve success. The early followers of Christ were such people. Christianity appealed to the poorest classes of Israelites, subjugated and enslaved by the Romans. It is important to remember, however, that not only Christianity but all major religions, Islam and Buddhism included, began as cults considered deviant by the larger religious organizations of the time.

Are cults common? Sources vary dramatically as to numbers. Ronald Johnstone notes that "there are between 500 and 600 known cults operating in the United States" (Johnstone 1988: 286). Leonard Broom estimates that "between the mid-1960s and the mid-1970s, over 300 new religious movements appeared in the San Francisco Bay area alone" (Broom et al. 1990: 191).

There is no such thing as a cult registry. Cults form and dissolve very quickly. Most disappear before the general public is aware that they ever existed. Only a few get into trouble with the law (the groups publicized by the media), so police blotters are a poor place to begin a census. Unfortunately, no one really counts cults. Nevertheless, the number of cults in the United States at any given time is probably in the thousands. They are found from New York to California, and even in the religiously conservative South.

The Freedom Park movement, headquartered in Latta, Oklahoma (population 900), in an area commonly called "Little Dixie," typifies sociologists' definition of a cult. To understand Freedom Park, its structure (or lack of it), its members, and its founder, is to understand what a cult is. We begin with Freedom Park's founder, Ron Morris.

## RON MORRIS

Ron Morris is founder and charismatic leader of the Freedom Park movement. When he was six years old, a pigeon he later named Homer landed on his shoulder during a tornado that destroyed part of Roff, Oklahoma. "There was a clear, nonverbal communication between myself and that bird." The pigeon told him that God had chosen him for an important mission. The bird left without saying what the mission was or why he was chosen. From that time forward, however, Ron knew he was going to hear directly from God during his lifetime.

In 1978 God spoke directly to Ron, telling him that he was going to have to save the world from nuclear destruction. God didn't tell him how to do it, only that it was his responsibility.

### Ron's Childhood

Born on Christmas Day, 1941, the same month and year the Japanese attacked Pearl Harbor, Ron laughingly lays claim to messiahship. His father worked in an Ada, Oklahoma, cement mill; his mother was a housewife. Ron says his father was abusive, beat him all the time, but his mother was just the opposite. Her nature was so loving that it more than made up for his father's ill temper.

Ron says that his father had problems and took them out on him. As a child he couldn't understand that, but he never doubted that his father loved him.

Ron says he did well in school, right from the start. He graduated in 1959 from a rural Oklahoma high school, a straight "A" student and a star athlete; he ran the mile and was a starter on the basketball team. He further claims that he was a troublemaker from time to time: "I never went with the crowd on anything."

For example, by the time he was 12 years old, Ron had a job at an Ada theater. Always tall for his age, at 13 he used his money to buy a chopped 1945 Harley Davidson motorcycle with a suicide clutch and gooseneck handlebars. He hid the machine in an abandoned barn, and at night he would put on his dark-colored glasses and black leather jacket and cruise. More often than not, he went to Okarche, Oklahoma (90 miles distant), rather than stay in Ada. "In Okarche, if you were big enough to put your money on the bar, you could buy dinner, a beer, and play the slot machines. I guess I led two lives as a teenager."

Ron was raised in the Church of Christ, in which his grandfather was a preacher. He attended church with his mother almost every Sunday until he was 13 or so. When she made going to church an option, he quit for a time. Now he will go to church for a month or two, find it intellectually unchallenging, and quit for a while. Church, he believes, is a place where one can't change the minds of others, and he doesn't like arguing with people.

Ron believes that originally the Christian message was one of love, that Christ wanted us to be one big family. "I have always believed that. But I don't believe in the set rules churches establish. Like you have to go to church every Sunday. Christ gave us a message of love, and that is what we should remember." He still believes in Christ, but not in everything that the churches attribute to Christ after his crucifixion. He claims to think in terms of Christ wandering around with his disciples, teaching people. He believes the Bible was written for people living 2,000 years ago, and that trying to interpret it literally brings about conflict.

After high school, Ron took courses at a business college. Upon completion he worked in the oil fields for a few years, until he crushed his foot while working on a rig. Eventually the foot healed enough that he was able to join the army.

### Military Service

In the service, Ron was assigned to the United States Security Agency. He was in the service nearly three years and achieved the rank of specialist fourth class (the rank immediately above private first class). He was rarely assigned to a base, but traveled and did his own thing. He says it was easy: "The army is a gigantic, bureaucratic mess and nobody knows what anyone else is doing. I learned how to cut my own orders, and I got to see most of the world that way."

Nobody believes what I did in the army. Why should they? It sounds ridiculous. But the army is a giant, chaotic bureaucracy, a blind, mindless entity. I was smart enough to do anything I wanted to do. I was caught once with orders I had cut myself, and all I did to get out of trouble was cry, and claim they made a mistake. It was such a big lie that everyone believed I was telling the truth. The next day I cut myself new orders and went far away from where I was caught.

When asked what the United States Security Agency does, Ron laughs and says he doesn't know what they do, only what he did. He moved around so much that he got lost in the shuffle. He assigned himself to the Pentagon and learned that often trouble was ''invented'' in order to maintain a need for the military and its covert services.

When John F. Kennedy was killed in 1963, Ron thought that all was lost, and for a time he was despondent. He does not subscribe to a conspiracy theory. He believes Oswald killed Kennedy; but if he had not, someone else would have. It was a time of chaos, and there were many waiting in the wings to kill the president had Oswald failed. Ron remained despondent until he came to the realization ''I had survived, 'micorisea' [one of Ron's central ideas that will be explained later] exists, and I am responsible for the destiny of America.'' So he cut his discharge papers and left the army.

## Higher Education

In 1968 Ron graduated from East Central University in Ada, Oklahoma, with a bachelor's degree in education. He claims his earlier successes in the classroom continued. He made top grades. On the negative side, he says that he was once physically removed from a psychology class by sheriff's deputies on suspicion of selling beer to minors. He was later found innocent of the charge. In describing this incident, he says the episode was similar to what happened to the Branch Davidians in Waco, Texas. He believes the government used unnecessary strong-arm tactics in arresting him just as it used unnecessary force on the Davidians. In 1971 he earned a master's degree in education administration from the University of Central Oklahoma at Edmond. He claims to have done additional advanced work in math and science.

## Making a Living

Ron began teaching in 1968 and ended his career in 1978, when he decided that his mandate to save the world could not be accomplished by working as an educator. It would be through the ''order of chaos'' and an effective manipulation of the ''hundredth monkey syndrome'' (two of Ron's concepts).

When he returned to Ada in 1978, Ron was determined to test his theories. In order to do that, he had to understand how people thought and acted. Going into the pest control business, which he successfully operates to this day, was his answer. It was a way to get into homes that he would not otherwise have access to. Ron claims to be a speed-reader without peer. He says he went into the homes of the elite, killed their pests, and read their diaries, correspondence, and what they had on their bookshelves. In that way he learned how government was manipulated and controlled by the elite.

### Ron Arrested

In the summer of 1993, Ron was arrested for growing marijuana. Following are excerpts from a letter he wrote to the court prior to his sentencing.

August 18, 1993 two men rushing through the woods in camouflage uniforms with high-powered rifles arrested me for cultivating an illegal weed in my back yard. Now I know how Koresh must have felt when he saw his attackers coming. I thought I was to be killed. I was trembling for my life when Ronald, my pot-bellied pig, charged the sheriff. I pleaded with the sheriff not to shoot him and he didn't. I was handcuffed behind my back and taken to jail. . . .

Later that night in jail, as I lay on the cell cot and listened to the sheriff on television (surrounded by my son's guns and some of my plants) I heard the sheriff say "We have had him under surveillance since 1991 . . . and he doesn't seem to realize that he could get life in prison for this." At that moment I had to go to the bathroom. Life for growing a weed? They know and I can prove that I have never sold or bought any drug or weed. . . . Now I was scared. [I thought] keep quiet, don't talk, be good and you will get off with a fine and suspended sentence. You won't get the death sentence that jail would bring. And so I kept quiet. I have said nothing to the press, but I have thoughts and I have written down these thoughts. And now I am more afraid of *not* speaking for my beliefs, because all beliefs are at stake.

. . . Your honor, I made someone mad. For this . . . I have been branded a criminal on the radio, television, and in the newspaper, and yet, I can't convince myself [that I am a criminal].

. . . Your honor, the wrong was not my doing, but the state's. I ask that you dismiss these charges against me and return my property, then file a restraining order to keep the state off Freedom Park One.

Until his arrest, Ron had led something of a dual life in Ada. He frequently wrote letters to the editor of the *Ada Evening News*, addressing issues important to Freedom Park One. His letters were usually read with some measure of amusement. Most people did not realize that the successful businessman was also the infamous cult leader from Latta, Oklahoma. His picture in the newspaper and on TV changed that.

I really didn't want to change my lifestyle, so I decided to defuse the situation. So instead of staying away from my next Kiwanis meeting, I showed up in handcuffs. Everybody laughed and that was the end of it. I'm on probation, but I still do the same things I always did, except grow marijuana.

But not everything was the same. I found the following note in one of his many journals, dated a month after his arrest: "Church day at the church [his house]. No members present since the arrest. My studies indicate that tolerance of others is a survival tactic. I will tolerate their absence."

## ZELLNER MEETS RON

In the fall of 1985, I moved from Nebraska to accept a teaching position in the sociology department at East Central University in Ada. My area of specialization is social movements, religious and secular. At the end of my first semester, a student turned in a paper devoted to a Freedom Park meeting he had attended earlier in the year. He described Ron, and said he wasn't sure Ron believed in God, but he talked of a "strange attractor" that seemed something like God. Ron also said that modern humans are descended from "dog people," and that the "Mediterranean people," before the great flood filled the Mediterranean basin, used a soundless, mental language to communicate. The meeting was held in Ron's yard, and there were about twenty people there. The student said Ron and Ron's ideas scared him somewhat.

I called Ron, and as we spoke, I found his ideas novel. His beliefs, his followers, and the structure of his organization (Ron funds Freedom Park out of his own pocket), were typical of a cult. I asked him if he would speak to my "Sects and Cults" class. He was not reluctant.

Ron has been speaking to my classes since the spring of 1986. Students seem to like him, even though most don't understand much of what he has to say. On closing his first lecture, he invited the class to a Friday night Freedom Park meeting at his house. Six of Ron's followers were at the meeting. I remember one in particular, who was wearing parts of a Nazi uniform, including helmet. Ron accepts anyone willing to listen to him. When I asked him later how he felt about the man dressed as a soldier, he said, "I can work with him if he is here. I can't if he is out on the street."

We squeezed together on the furniture and floor in Ron's living room. Incense was burning on every lightbulb in the house. The odor was overwhelming. I had no idea why Ron would burn incense; it seemed uncharacteristic. When I asked students later what they thought, many smiled at my naïveté. Ron's meeting with his followers had been in session about an hour before our arrival. Most guessed that the incense was used to cover the odor of marijuana. Some years later, after Ron was arrested for growing marijuana, he admitted that, indeed, the marijuana odor was the reason the incense was used. He said he had not supplied the marijuana, but he didn't object to the use of it in his house.

Perhaps the most unusual part of the meeting was its abrupt ending. At 7:45 Ron smiled broadly, thanked us for coming, said he enjoyed our visit, and invited us to come back. When I asked him later why the meeting was closed so abruptly, he said, "*Dallas* comes on at 8:00, and me and my group watch the show and discuss it. J. R. Ewing [played by Larry Hagman] represents all that is evil in the world . . .''

Ron has always attracted unusual people to Freedom Park. Indeed, many of his former followers have been societal outcasts. In whatever other ways some may view Ron, few would deny that he is a compassionate man. He has given some of his followers jobs when no one else would hire them. Still others, when they were homeless, moved in with him and his family. Some of these people now hold responsible positions in the community. I have spoken with some ex-members, and all say they never thought of Ron as a messiah, though they believe he is a genuinely decent individual.

The term *charisma* is used very broadly. Laypeople and media alike are quick to use it when describing a politician, rock musician, or movie star. By this they mean that the person in question is endowed with special abilities setting him or her apart from ordinary mortals.

Max Weber, the giant of German sociology, had an altogether different understanding of the concept ''charisma.'' Although he did not deny that charismatic leaders could possess unique abilities, he also recognized that such persons could be quite ordinary. The criterion that sets such people apart from the bulk of humanity is that followers attribute superhuman characteristics to them.

Most of Ron's followers were and are from working-class backgrounds, and more than a few are attracted to him for only a very short time. Ron seems to lose one convert for every two he gains. And during times of crisis, such as following his marijuana arrest, there was mass desertion.

Following are some of Ron's concepts introduced to me and my students over the period of 1986–1997.

## MICORISEA

High on Ron's priority list when I first met him was ''*micorisea*,'' defined as growing things in a new way, new kinds of farming techniques and the like. Specifically, Ron says it is a process of regeneration and detoxification, using natural materials and waste products. He points out that if a new system develops out of chaos (explanation later), we are going to have to find new ways of feeding people. In the development of micorisea, Ron says he did a lot of work with microbes, creating symbiotic systems that purify the earth and atmosphere in the process of growing food. Ron does not believe in chemical fertilizers. He says the principle of micorisea is like the automobile, currently in the developmental stage, that will clean the air while it is running.

The purpose behind building Freedom Park was to develop a place where Ron could live and get healthy, and so his family could do the same thing. ''I didn't get a lot of help from my family, so I built it as best as I could by myself. And I feel real good about it. If a chaotic event happened and I couldn't go to town, I could take care of my medical and food needs and survive without much deprivation.''

Ron believes the world is going to be a very different place after the passing of the industrial age. Associated with micorisea is Ron's vision of "Project Ocean City." Cities will be built in the ocean, mostly from the pollution products of today's world. Ron's vision is quite detailed, far too lengthy to describe here. In sum, however, ocean cities will provide food and other survival needs in his vision of the new age. Ron also believes that interplanetary travel is a necessary survival tactic for humankind.

## THE DOG PEOPLE

Ron has had several visions of man's early history. The first human developed suddenly from a species that was close to his own. In determining how he should live, the new species investigated other primate cultures. He rejected them in favor of dog culture, because it was more family-oriented.

Ron believes that there has always been a "way." The way to go at that time was the primate way. There has always been a different way, but only man has had the choice to take another path. Ron thinks the biblical Adam's offspring killed off the Neanderthals and a variety of other primates.

Killing the other primates was a survival tactic. It allowed our ancestors to compete for food without interference from similar species. Ron believes that early man was not an efficient predator. He followed dogs, eating their leftovers. By the end of the "dog culture" age, the dogs were our slaves. Humankind then moved to the Mediterranean basin.

## THE MEDITERRANEAN PEOPLE

The Mediterranean basin was a Garden of Eden that, Ron says, was much as it is today. People could produce and do what they wanted to do because they didn't have to worry about survival.

The land was so rich that humans had nothing better to do than start different races. "Some people thought black was beautiful, so they stayed out in the sun until they got blacker and blacker and blacker. Others thought that white was more beautiful, so they stayed out of the sun." Ron believes races developed as a matter of choice rather than as a product of evolution. Communication was not verbal, and people got along. Ron likens the situation to the time in the Bible before the construction of the Tower of Babel (Genesis 11:1–8), when all humankind shared a common language.

Life in the Mediterranean basin was wonderful until it was disrupted by chaos, the flood that put Noah to sea. Those who escaped the flood were dispersed all over the planet. The family of man, in separate groups, became diverse, developed different languages and cultures.

## HUNDREDTH MONKEY SYNDROME

Central to an understanding of Ron Morris's belief system and the order of chaos is the hundredth monkey syndrome. Small islands near Japan are inhabited by macaque monkeys. As part of an effort to feed the monkeys, ships unloaded sweet potatoes for them. The freshly dug yams were covered with dirt and grit. For this reason, the monkeys didn't find them palatable. On one of the islands a sort of monkey genius named Imo began taking her yams to a stream to wash them. One by one, monkeys that watched her do this began washing their yams. After about 100 monkeys knew how to clean yams, a critical mass was reached, and suddenly it appeared that all the monkeys on the island knew how to clean yams. Then, miraculously, the yam-washing jumped from Imo's island to all the other islands in the area.

The monkeys had no direct communication with each other. Ron believes this kind of spontaneous learning is a survival tactic, and is the result of pheromone communication. Pheromones are substances that act as molecular messengers, transmitting information from one member of a species to another member of the same species. For example, female silkworm moths secrete a substance that attracts male silkworms from a great distance for mating purposes. And a male pig carries in his saliva a steroid that, when sprayed on the face of a sow, induces a rigid stance that facilitates mating.

Ron believes that pheromone communication goes well beyond sexual enticement. He believes the monkeys, after a critical mass was reached, communicated the news about yam-washing to the other islands through the use of pheromones.

A similar concept exists in sociology. Sociologists use the concept "parallel evolution" to explain a process by which humans in different places applied the same solutions to survival problems at about the same time in the course of evolution. For example, the development of aqueducts by the Chinese and Incas occurred at about the same time. Communication of any kind between these groups is not deemed possible. Sociologists generally view such developments as coincidental.

## THE ORDER OF CHAOS

For most of us the "order of chaos" is an oxymoron, words that cannot be used together, like "trained spontaneity," "thunderous silence," or "jumbo shrimp." Ron admits that it is hard to explain, but chaotic events occur in an orderly fashion. And if you know when chaotic events are going to occur, you can exert influence to control them. On an individual basis, if you know you are going to get cancer, which would be a chaotic event in anyone's life, you can begin to work to control outcomes before you are afflicted. On a grander scale, Ron believes history can be altered through his theories.

Ron has no formula for predicting chaotic events. He believes, however, that he has developed a prescience for seeing the onset of "chaosity" (Ron's word). In 1978 he believed that a nuclear war (chaotic event) was inevitable between the Soviet Union and the United States. It would happen in 1989 or 1990. Through pheromone communication he planned to implant a consciousness in world leaders that peace, above all else, was of the utmost importance to human survival. If he could convince enough leaders on each side that war would destroy humankind, a critical mass would develop (hundredth monkey syndrome) and nuclear war would be avoided.

## FALL OF THE BERLIN WALL

Ron has visions, but at times "I have trouble interpreting my visions." One vision triggered the belief that he would have to find nine followers who believed pheromone communication could avert nuclear disaster. He, along with his nine, would then work to influence world leaders in the direction of peaceful solutions to world problems.

For years he tried to find nine believers but failed. Yes, people showed up at his house every Friday night and listened to him. But he was never able to get more than three or four adherents, at any given time, who fully believed that they could change the destiny of humankind.

Nevertheless, in the early spring of 1989, he came to one of my classes and told the students that he was going to bring down the Berlin wall the following fall. "I know you all think I'm nuts, but I'm going to do it. I've never been able to find the nine followers I thought I needed, but I think I can do it with my daughter's help. We have to do it because nobody else will. And if the wall doesn't fall, there is going to be a nuclear war. And if most of humankind is destroyed, we will not be able to enter the information age."

Ron told us he was working on the weaknesses of the people he was communicating with, which included President Bush in the United States and Gorbachev and Yeltsin in the Soviet Union. For example, the United States had to be powerful and let the Soviet Union know that it wouldn't back away from an arms race that the Soviet Union could no longer afford. He focused on the image of President Bush as a "wimp," transmitting pheromone messages to him that he had to be strong, so people would not think he was weak. (Ron finds it particularly amusing that a nobody in Latta, Oklahoma, was "pushing the president's buttons without him knowing it.")

When the wall fell the following November, about half that class of 50 visited my office one by one, to remind me of Ron's prediction.

## NEURAL INTEGRATED COMMUNICATION

"Neural integrated communication" (NIC) is one of Ron's futuristic projects. Computer specialists tell us that silicon chips will soon allow us to carry around small pocket devices that will include a computer, fax machine, and telephone— in essence, a universal communicator. Ron believes that this device will be the ultimate in artificial intelligence, but that he has discovered an even better method of communication.

His communication system is based on microbes and an ectoparasite similar to the mites found in human eyebrows. Ron's device, far more powerful than any in IBM's world, would replace the silicon chip with programmed microbes.

Ron believes that ectoparasites, which use genetic material as a food source, can be attracted to the human brain. Once embedded and feeding on gray matter, these ectoparasites would release pheromonally charged microbes. Ron says that this "sounds much more gruesome than it is in actuality." The microbes would interact between human brains, which are nothing more than chemical processors. He calls it "real intelligence" because microbes and ectoparasites, unlike a computer chip, have an actual life. In essence, Ron views his living chip as software between brains. It would not send word messages that could be misinterpreted, but pictures. In other words, if you were thinking of a blue bird, NIC would send a picture image of a blue bird to the receiver that could not be confused with a red bird.

## CHAOTIC NATIONS LAND ACQUISITION FOUNDATION

Ron defines the Chaotic Nations Land Acquisition Foundation as Freedom Park's organization to fund the digital world that will come into existence in the information age. "It has the power to break Orange County [California], the Bank of Japan, or Bank of America." It is intended to support digital citizens, members of the Freedom Park family, by allowing them to disappear from the government.

Ron admits that this concept is difficult to explain. Early in the information age, not everyone is going to be able to accept the changes brought on by chaos. Many, if not most, people are going to attempt to maintain the current system, which has no vision and is doomed to repeat history.

For a time, the digital world will be hidden from the world as we know it. Digital people will live on this planet along with everyone else, but they will be invisible because they will erase themselves from the simplistic computers used by those who refuse to join the information age—no Social Security numbers, bank accounts, driver's license numbers. Ron says, "Everything is based on cryptography, and only digital people will know the codes."

Chaos will not destroy everything in the existing world, because digital people will bring the good things with them from the current system into the new order. Ron notes that capitalism will survive; bad things such as welfare will not.

With the real producers in society escaping en masse into the digital world, the tax base will begin to disappear. Politicians will continue to have to raise taxes to replace what has been lost to the invisible world. This will alienate those who are the last to escape.

Ron believes that the only people who will not ultimately flee to the digital world will be government workers and their children, and those who are not very intelligent.

If you want to be free and you want to be capitalistic, you are going to want to live in the digital world. This is a new survival tactic over a pseudo survival tactic, statism. I say "pseudo" because statism has never succeeded. No state has ever lasted more than a few hundred years.

Just as the Adam I recognize chose dog culture over primate culture, I made a choice. I chose entry into the information age instead of nuclear holocaust by causing the Berlin Wall to fall.

Ron says that at one time it bothered him not to be recognized for this feat, but it no longer does.

## THE INTERVIEW

In 1995, Kaleb Bennett, a student research assistant, and Zellner, visited Freedom Park One. Several afternoons were spent on Ron's 100 acres in an effort to better understand the Freedom Park movement. It was a nice time of year, just before the onset of the oppressive, unrelenting heat that defines Oklahoma summers.

Ron invited us into his den. Atop a TV cabinet is a birdcage with an open door. The cage belongs to Pippen, a green conure. Pippen looks like a sailor's parrot but is smaller, about the size of a parakeet. She bobs about on Ron's head while he talks. Inevitably, Pippen tires of this and descends his forehead toward his nose. Ron bridges the middle of his nose with his forefinger, waiting for Pippen to perch on it. When she does, he swings her away from his body; she usually stays on his finger for a few minutes before flitting back to the top of his head. The cycle is repeated until Ron leaves the room. I found the bird's antics humorous but disconcerting. I was glad when Ron asked if we would like to walk and talk.

There are several outbuildings on Ron's acreage, including an aviary that was once a large mobile home. A small outbuilding that served as command headquarters for Ron's militia also has been converted to an aviary. (I had been there before the conversion. His weaponry consisted of a .22 rifle, a shotgun, and two or three other light arms.)

Ron told us he has 900 birds, 60 varieties. He says he has been experimenting with them, and he now has some that can only be found only in his aviaries. He calls them the birds of chaos. Kaleb and I agreed that some of these birds were having offspring without Ron's knowledge, despite the fact that he seems to know each of them personally. Birds are everywhere, and 900 is an obvious undercount.

Recently, Ron has been wholesaling some of his birds to pet shops. For the most part, however, he considers his aviaries a hobby. Ron rarely works at the pest control business in the afternoons. He says he goes in most mornings and makes whatever critical decisions have to be made. He adds that his wife is a better bureaucrat and manages the business better than he does after he decides what is to be done.

The interview began at a spring-fed pond, one of the prettiest spots on Ron's acreage. Tapes from the meeting are punctuated with bird sounds; especially talkative were peacocks, guinea fowl, and geese. The interview is not presented in its entirety.

*Zellner*: Why did you agree to this interview, Ron? You know people are not going to accept what you say. They are going to view you as crazy or worse.

*Ron*: I'm well aware of that. It doesn't make any difference what people think of me now. I want this interview published, so when the last copy of your book is found hundreds of years from now, people will know that the way they communicate and solve problems is nothing new. A guy named Ron started it all, by taking a different "way" many years ago.

*Zellner*: You understand those guineas, Ron? (I jokingly asked about the chattering birds.)

*Ron*: I'm learning their language.

*Zellner*: Pheromones?

*Ron*: Nah, a language just like we're speaking, only guinea language. They . . . use it within the species as a survival tactic. Just like we use our language. By the way, it's a heck of a lot easier to learn guinea than to learn to control pheromones.

*Zellner*: What are they saying?

*Ron*: They are mostly talking about you. I usually come out here alone. They are afraid that you might cause a chaotic event. (chuckling)

*Zellner*: Well, just tell them that there is order in chaos.

*Ron*: It is difficult to recognize the order of chaos. Most of us live orderly lives most of the time. We know that what we did yesterday and what we do today will make tomorrow. Then something will happen to throw our lives into chaos. I believe that such chaotic events can be predicted and to some extent controlled.

*Zellner*: How can you control chaos?

*Ron*: If you tie the order of chaos to the hundredth monkey syndrome, you can communicate with others on the level of survival. That's where the pheromones come in. You can do remarkable things, make great changes. You can, for example, cause people to work together to move from the industrial age to the information age. I know, because I did it.

*Zellner*: How have you tested your theories?

*Ron*: To test my theories, I had to increase my knowledge manyfold about many things to find out how everything operates. I couldn't do that in education. I was finding education stifling, because everything was based on an order of statism. I didn't know what was wrong with that. I just knew it was wrong. At the time, I didn't know what the truth was.

I stopped and said to myself, "We're fixin' to have a nuclear war by 1990."

At the time I wasn't sure if it was by God's direction or I took it on myself to intervene, to stop what seemed inevitable. I didn't believe that some group, some organization, some other individual was going to do it. So I had to.

I wasn't in good health. Doctors had told me that. And I thought I was going to die in about four years. So I set out to accomplish what I had to do in that period of time. I studied chemistry and looked into the pest control business. I needed a business that would get me into people's homes so I could see what they were thinking and doing. I had to understand people.

Also, I wanted to be in a business that made money, because I am selfish, and because you can't help anyone else unless you help yourself.

While I was studying the pest control business, I was in training with an insurance company, paying $1,000 a month, good money at the time. Nevertheless, I decided to go into pest control. I knew by the order of chaos that the business would take care of me, and I could do my experiments. When I first went to work in the business, I worked hard. Now I own controlling interest, 51 percent. Another of my goals was to be worth a quarter of a million. I have accomplished that, too. Another goal was to be in control of my own time. I have accomplished that as well. I was able to do these things because I understand the order of chaos. And that has nothing at all to do with religion, which you seem to be interested in.

*Zellner*: You say that Freedom Park is a religious movement. Where does religion come into this?

*Ron*: In my study of the order of things, I learned that there has always been chaotic events leading from a past age to a new age, such as the fall of the Berlin Wall leading to a new harmony between nuclear powers. The way that new systems are created from the ashes of the old have always fascinated me. There is a religious experience associated with it.

I believe that God did create us in his image. Therefore, since he was a creator, we are creators. In the same way that our creator created us, we create. For example, we create software for humanlike robots. We give them brains, a skeleton, and to some degree a self-sustaining system. We continue to seek our purpose and place in this world, and this is a religious experience for me.

Also, religion works well as a survival tactic for humans. We can intellectualize God as good, and try to lead good lives as He would want us to do. Intelligence works for humans, but not for all species.

*Zellner*: What do you mean?

*Ron*: It's not a proven survival tactic for chickens.

*Zellner*: (Laughs) Why not?

*Ron*: It's bad for chickens to be real intelligent. The more intelligent you are, the slower you are to react, because you think. And a slow chicken is a dead chicken. So that's what I mean, a survival tactic that is fitting for you and me would not work for some other species. If used right, love of God will work for us as a survival tactic. Love of state fails every time.

*Zellner*: Let me change the subject. Why don't you think you were ever able to find nine believers?

*Ron*: You tell me.

*Zellner*: I've told you a hundred times; you should have had a powerful bird like an eagle or maybe a bird of peace like a dove land on your shoulder. Who's going to follow a cult leader who can't do better than a common pigeon? (Ron ignored me.)

*Ron*: Most people are just concerned with the right now. How they can make the most money and consume as much as they can. Groups are concerned with how much money they can get or how they can position themselves to get more money. It is an ongoing power struggle between those who have and those who don't. Most people, though, are like sheep. I call them the "species of Earth." They don't realize that they have a soul to lose, or that they have any control over their lives whatsoever. They are not active participants in life, so to say. I have a real problem with communication; I have never had the ability to convince people that they could participate with me in exerting control over chaotic events.

Ten years after the birth of Freedom Park One, I was still under the delusion that I was going to find nine followers, and that I would become famous. It didn't happen. (Laughing) God eventually had to tell me that I had misinterpreted a vision.

You know, there was even a time when I actually thought I was God. That wasn't right, either. (an even heartier laugh followed)

You lose people when you talk about religion, and then turn around and talk about science and genetics and all that. What I know doesn't fit with the general understandings of today. Because of that, I cannot develop public acceptance. My work is so unique that I can only test it through results. For example, when I told your class that I was going to bring down the Berlin Wall, I don't think any of them believed me. Do you think any of them would have been willing to help me? No! Even my church members didn't believe me. Only my daughter.

Even after the fact, I don't think your students believed that my daughter and I were responsible for the fall of the Wall. And you don't either. (chuckling)

*Zellner*: Right on both counts. But I'm real glad we can still be friends.

*Ron*: Nevertheless, the fall of the Wall, which was my doing, was the beginning of the transition period, a short stretch of time, which must precede the information age.

With the fall of the Wall, the Soviet Union fell. One thing I really regret is having had to put the Russian people in such desperate economic circumstances. But it had to be done. Russia will become stable again, and then the information age will truly begin. Until she regains her economic strength, we will remain in the period of transition.

***Zellner***: When will the transition age be over?

***Ron***: I know exactly when it will end, if I haven't misinterpreted a vision— 2007. It is the anniversary of man. I have no idea which anniversary, two-thousandth, six-thousandth, six-millionth, or any other number. Nevertheless, by then, the digital people will be in control. The industrial age will be over, and the information age will no longer be challenged.

***Zellner***: Is there a time limit on the information age? Will there be a new age after that?

***Ron***: The information age coincides with the thousand years of peace talked about in the Bible. The Bible says there is going to be a short war after the thousand years. One of my followers says the war will be between humankind and genetic robots we have created, demanding equality. He could be right. I don't really know what is going to happen after the war.

***Zellner***: Over the years I have met a number of your followers. Who are they? Why do they leave?

***Ron***: "Followers" is really not the word for them. They are "individual sovereigns." If you as an individual can make a difference today that will make real differences tomorrow, you are a sovereign. That's one of the reasons I could never find nine who would make a difference.

I could never find nine individuals who would listen to me about the order of chaos, because most individual sovereigns don't listen to anyone. The rewards in society come to those who never buck the status quo. Most people are so brainwashed by the state that they have no chance of ever becoming an individual sovereign. The pool I can draw from is very limited.

***Zellner***: Amen, to the rewards part.

***Ron***: And most people will seek to punish those who seek knowledge beyond which they possess. I know that from being a boss. All you have to do to be a boss is be willing to take blame and be disliked. We talk about self-motivation, but there isn't a lot of it. Most people want someone they can blame for their failures. And most of us fail from time to time.

We aren't even taught self-motivation in the schools. We are taught to act in accordance with the greatest good for the greatest numbers. This perpetuates the state. And you know what I think about that.

***Zellner***: What about the man in the German uniform that came to your meetings?

***Ron***: There is no doubt that he was an individual sovereign. We argued all the time. But as long as he agreed not to hurt anyone, I was glad to have him around.

Another one that came around all the time was my brother-in-law. He was a

Christian. He was confused all the time. He liked attending the meetings, but he just didn't understand what was going on. I hate to say it, but he isn't very smart.

The two closest to me, who still show up, are certainly not sheep. They know what is going on. They are both Christians like I am, so we get along better than I did with the one you call the Nazi.

***Zellner***: What are you doing now that your God-given mission has been completed?

***Ron***: I'm studying chaos with my zebra finches. Zebra finches and man are not a lot different, at least as far as understanding chaotic events, catastrophe, and chaosity. I control their environment, the temperature in their buildings, their food supply. They are well taken care of, and they prosper. After a while, their society becomes more complex, and they build different castles and everything. Soon they are thieving and stealing from each other. If I let things run their course, they would become diseased, and ultimately they would be wiped out. It's fun to watch them operate in chaos. But I don't let it go on too long. I know how destructive chaos can be, so I step in and stop what would be the ordinary path of events.

I guess I'm a born meddler. (Laughing) I meddle in the lives of my finches, and they don't know it. They don't know what control I have. And I meddle in the lives of humankind, and they don't know the control I have.

***Zellner***: Are you doing anything else?

***Ron***: I use my understanding of chaos to invest in the stock market. Understanding chaos gives me all the financial rewards I could want. It's just like having a key to the bank, and nobody knows that you have it. In other words, if the market is chaotic, which I say it is, and chaos has order, which I say it does, then I can profit from knowing that. I follow about 100 stocks, and when I see that a chaotic event is going to affect the stock, I buy it or sell it.

Do you remember the time that I told your class that it is right to have everything, but that it isn't right to take it? Remember, I am a Christian. What I take is what I can go to bed with at night, without feeling guilty.

You have to remember that the only limitations [sic] on what I do is my conscience. I can control my destiny. Laws don't bother me; there are always ways around them. The laws of man, as far as I am concerned, are completely corrupt. They are not enforced fairly. Laws are made to enrich some at the expense of others. If the laws of man were truly for justice, intended to protect the family from fraud and trespass, then I would support them. All our laws do now is perpetuate the state and those with vested interests in statism.

***Zellner***: Your drug arrest certainly must have been a chaotic event in your life. Why couldn't you predict it?

***Ron***: It was chaotic, and I could have predicted it. All the signs were there. I stupidly chose to ignore them. I really don't want to get into that.

*Zellner*: Who's to say you weren't lucky on your prediction that the Berlin Wall would fall?

*Ron*: (Laughs) I don't expect you to believe I did it. Nobody does. I told you I was going to do it months before it happened, before anyone else even thought it was possible. I not only told you, I told 50 of your students I was going to do it. I did it. God told me to do it, and I did it. It doesn't make a bit of difference to me whether you believe me or not.

*Zellner*: What about the war in Iraq? I'll admit you predicted war in the Middle East, but that's not a difficult prediction. There is always a war in the Middle East. Why didn't you work on Bush and Saddam Hussein to stop the war with Iraq, just as you worked on Bush, Gorbachev, and Yeltsin to bring down the Wall?

*Ron*: We get back to the nine sovereigns. I still think I could control world events with nine true believers. I tried using my pheromones to influence Hussein, but it just wasn't enough. It was impossible to communicate with him. But I really believe that I have done all that God intended me to do.

## IN SUMMATION

Ron Morris is one of my favorite people; there is nothing evil about him or Freedom Park. He is a good person, always willing to lend a helping hand. He has provided for those in his inner circle in various ways—food, clothing, housing. And he is a valuable member of the community in many other ways.

For example, one of my university colleagues noticed suspicious insects under his house. He called an exterminator. An agent for the company crawled under his house, was there for a few minutes, and returned with the bad news that it would cost $1,400 to rid his dwelling of the pests.

A second company was called. Again an agent crawled under the house and stayed a few minutes before resurfacing. Indeed, it was termites. The agent asked how much the other company had bid to eliminate the house eaters. When my friend said $1,400, the second bidder said he would do it for $1,100.

Ron was called. He, too, crawled under the house. Emerging 20 minutes later with a puzzled look, he said, "You don't have termites." Because most of us don't understand the pest control business, we tend to be at the mercy of those in the business who are unscrupulous. Ron has a reputation for honesty in business. And I think he is honest in all aspects of life. I don't believe Ron brought down the Berlin Wall, but I am fairly confident that he believes he brought it down.

I doubt that Ron will ever find nine individual sovereigns to help him with his work. However, he is satisfied that his goals in life have been accomplished. Indeed, he thinks it would be appropriate if he had a leadership role in the information age, but he doesn't believe that will happen.

Like most of the thousands of cults that have existed in this country, Freedom

Park will, in all probability, silently disappear. It will not become a Waco. Ron will not become an L. Ron Hubbard (Scientology) or Sun Myung Moon (Moonies). And, like most other cults formed in our culture, Freedom Park will not have had a negative impact on the larger society.

## BIBLIOGRAPHY

Broom, L., Bonjean, C. M., & Broom, D. (1990). *Sociology: A core text with adapted readings*. Belmont, CA: Wadsworth.

Johnstone, R. L. (1988). *Religion in society: A sociology of religion* (3rd ed.). Englewood Cliffs, NJ: Prentice-Hall.

# Index

# About the Editors and Contributors

## EDITORS

MARC PETROWSKY, Ph.D., associate professor of sociology, East Central University, Ada, Oklahoma, is a coauthor of *Introduction to Sociology: Order and Change in Society* (6th ed.).

WILLIAM ZELLNER, Ph.D., is professor of sociology at East Central University in Ada, Oklahoma. He is author of numerous articles, essays, and books, including *Extraordinary Groups* (6th ed.) and *Countercultures: A Sociological Analysis*. Among works in progress is *Southern Comfort: An Analysis of Southern Religious Institutions*.

## CONTRIBUTORS

ROBERT W. BALCH, Ph.D., professor of sociology at the University of Montana, Missoula, has published extensively in the area of unconventional religions. He is currently on leave, collecting additional data for a book on Heaven's Gate.

MITCHELL L. BRACEY, JR., is enrolled in the doctoral program at the University of Kentucky.

DAVID G. BROMLEY, Ph.D., professor of sociology and religious studies at Virginia Commonwealth University, is editor of the *Journal for the Scientific Study of Religion*. He has written or edited 12 books in the area of sociology of religion. His most recent book is *Prophetic Religion in a Secular Age* (with Anson Shupe).

MARY ANN CLARK is a doctoral candidate in religious studies at Rice University. Her research interests center on the physical objects of the Santería religion and how they embody philosophical and religious concepts.

DACHANG CONG, Ph.D., assistant professor of sociology at the University of Texas, Dallas, has written several articles on the Chinese and Amish cultures. Most recently he published *When Heroes Pass Away: The Invention of a Chinese Communist Pantheon.*

ANSON SHUPE, Ph.D., professor of sociology at Indiana University–Purdue University, Fort Wayne, is author, coauthor, or coeditor of 24 scholarly and trade books and numerous journal articles. His most recent book is *In the Name of All That's Holy: A Theory of Clergy Malfeasance.*

MICHAEL TRAUGOT was a leader of Students for a Democratic Society while a student at Harvard. After graduation in 1967, he moved to San Francisco and became involved in the youth movement. He has written *A Short History of The Farm.*

ANTONIO N. ZAVALETA, Ph.D., dean of the College of Liberal Arts, University of Texas, Brownsville, has research interests in how culture affects health care. As both an elected and an appointed public official in south Texas, he has been actively involved in health care delivery, research, and policy implementation for the U.S.–Mexico border region.

ISBN 0-275-95860-4

9 780275 958602

HARDCOVER BAR CODE